BARBARIC TRAFFIC

PHILIP GOULD

Barbaric Traffic

Commerce and Antislavery in the
Eighteenth-Century Atlantic World

HARVARD UNIVERSITY PRESS

Cambridge, Massachusetts, and London, England   2003

Library of Congress Cataloging-in-Publication Data

Gould, Philip, 1960–
    Barbaric traffic : commerce and antislavery in the eighteenth-century Atlantic world /
Philip Gould.
      p. cm.
    Includes index.
    ISBN 0-674-01166-X (alk. paper)
    1. Antislavery movements—United States—History—18th century. 2. Antislavery
movements—Great Britain—History—18th century.   3. Slave trade in literature.
4. Antislavery movements in literature.   5. Slave trade—United States—History—
18th century.   6. Slave trade—Great Britain—History—18th century.   7. Slave trade—
Africa—History—18th century.   8. Capitalism—Social aspects—History—18th century.
9. United States—Commerce—History—18th century.   10. Great Britain—Commerce—
History—18th century.   I. Title.

E446.G68 2003
306.3'62'097309033—dc21   2003042325

For my parents, Stan and Joan Gould—
and for Alex

Acknowledgments

Over the last six years, during the research and writing of this book, I have enjoyed the scholarly resources and professional environment of Brown University. The reference librarians at the John Hay Library were particularly helpful. I also benefited from doing research at the John Carter Brown Library. Many of my colleagues here in the English Department also have been very supportive. This project grew significantly from the guidance I received from both Jim Egan and Leonard Tennenhouse—two brilliant critics and wonderful friends. I want to thank other colleagues as well: Nancy Armstrong, Mutlu Blasing, Mari Jo Buhle, and Ellen Rooney. My experience of teaching with William Keach has been crucial. Bill introduced me to important texts and contexts in eighteenth-century British literature. Finally, I'd like to thank many of my graduate students whose comments, both in and out of seminar, challenged my thinking in innumerable ways.

I am grateful for the fellowships I received from the American Antiquarian Society and the John Nicholas Brown Center for the Study of American Civilization. Their administrative staffs and research librarians were most helpful. In particular, I thank John Hench and Caroline Sloat at the AAS. My research also benefited from trips to the Boston Athenaeum, the Boston Public Library, the Historical Society of Pennsylvania, the Library Company of Philadelphia, and the Newberry Library in Chicago. Like most scholars, I also benefited from informal conversations and the exchange of work. This field of inspiration, so to speak, includes Lawrence Buell, Vincent Carretta, Rhys Isaac, Mason Lowance, John Saillant, David Shields, Frank Shuffelton, Eric Slauter, Zabelle Stodola, Fredrika Teute, and Roxann Wheeler. Certain sections of this book have appeared in different versions in journals and anthologies. Part of Chapter 4 appeared as "Free Carpenter, Venture Capitalist: Reading the Lives of the Early Black Atlantic" in *American Literary History*

12 (2000), pp. 659–684, and in *Genius in Bondage: The Literature of the Early Black Atlantic* (University of Kentucky Press, 2001). An earlier version of Chapter 5 appeared as "Race, Commerce, and the Literature of Yellow Fever in Early National Philadelphia," *Early American Literature* 35 (2000), pp. 157–186.

My family is my lifeblood. Nick, Sophie, and Alex require innumerable duties and provide profound joys. Athena and I gain both ballast and motion from our children. They create the daily rhythm in which we move.

Contents

Illustrations

BARBARIC TRAFFIC

Introduction

> But the evils attending the Slave Trade are of a nature very different,
> and of a far greater magnitude than those which necessarily result
> from the mere condition of slavery.
>
> —William Belsham, *An Essay on the African Slave Trade* (1790)

In "Paradise of Negro-Slaves—A Dream," the noted American physician and antislavery writer Benjamin Rush (leading member of the Pennsylvania Abolition Society yet owner of a slave) imagines an ideal place for the African dead. Far removed from the fallen world, the "paradise" of this dream vision unsurprisingly occasions the opportunity to recount the horrors of slavery, but it accomplishes another goal as well.[1] The dream vision is as much the story of Rush's place in the Anglo-American antislavery movements that were gaining support in this era as it is the story of the abuse of Africans themselves. Indeed, these political movements were in large part self-reflexive.

In Rush's paradise African slaves piously await their glorification in heaven. They tell him their sad and sentimental tales and show Christian forbearance toward their former masters. All the slaves were "'once dragged by the men of your colour from their native country, and consigned by them to labour—punishment—and death."[2] Their stories of heartless transactions crystallize the barbarity of slave trading as an illicit form of exchange. But then "a little white man" enters the dream; in one hand he carries "a subscription paper and a petition" and in the other "a small pamphlet on the unlawfulness of the African slave-trade." "While I was employed in contemplating this venerable figure—suddenly I beheld the whole assembly running to meet him—the air resounded with the clapping of hands—and I

1

awoke from my *dream,* by the noise of a general acclamation of—ANTHONY BENEZET!"[3]

The sketch serves to illustrate, among other things, the transatlantic scope of antislavery writing. Rush claims that his dream was inspired by the English abolitionist Thomas Clarkson, whose *Essay on the Slavery and Commerce of the Human Species* (1786) was perhaps the single most influential antislavery work in the years preceding the formation of the English Society for Effecting the Abolition of the Slave Trade in 1787. Clarkson's footnotes, for their part, acknowledge that he had read Benezet's seminal antislavery writings. (In addition to Clarkson, Benezet influenced a wide array of antislavery writers across the Atlantic world, including Olaudah Equiano, the Abbé Raynal, Granville Sharp, and John Wesley.) Rush's self-insertion into this transatlantic milieu supports his antislavery credentials, and his invocation of Benezet shifts the focus of sympathy.

This book covers the historical period between the rise of antislavery movements in the 1770s in Britain and America, and the abolition of the slave trade there in 1807–08. I intend to analyze late eighteenth-century literature against the slave trade in part as an expression of the changing commercial culture in the Atlantic world. It is not a formal history of antislavery but a study of its literary and cultural importance, for antislavery writing engaged in the ongoing meditation on the relations among trade, culture, and civilized manners. Its branding the African slave trade as "barbaric" commerce made other forms of commerce seem civilized and legitimate.

Many modern historical studies of early antislavery politics have accounted in unique ways for the incompatibility between chattel slavery and the rise of liberal capitalism. Originating in Eric Williams's highly controversial *Capitalism and Slavery* (1944), this perspective generally has challenged the older, more idealized historical image of antislavery reform. Williams, a West Indian scholar heavily influenced by Marxist thinking, questioned the motives of antislavery reform and argued that the eighteenth-century Atlantic slave trade provided the economic foundation for the later triumph of English commercial and industrial capitalism. When the protective tariffs and commercial regulations, which had protected the West Indian slave and sugar economies for more than a century, eventually became obsolete, bourgeois "reformers" assailed the outmoded imperial system as a way of promoting their own capitalist interests. "The rise and fall of mercantilism is the rise and fall of slavery."[4]

Modern antislavery scholarship has undermined the historical accuracy of the Williams thesis, but it also has left in place its essential premise. "Few historians today discount the possibility of some connection between capitalism and antislavery."[5] In the last three decades, the historiography of eighteenth-century antislavery movements has articulated, in varying ways, the ideological dissonance between liberal capitalism and chattel slavery. David Brion Davis, for example, argued that early antislavery writing lent legitimacy to the emergence of an industrial capitalist order in Great Britain that was concerned with balancing freedom with labor discipline: "Abolitionists could contemplate a revolutionary change in status precisely because they were not considering the upward mobility of workers, but rather the rise of distant Negroes to the level of humanity. . . . British antislavery provided a bridge between preindustrial and industrial values; by combining the ideal of emancipation with an insistence on duty and subordination, it helped smooth the way to the future."[6] While Davis has refined and clarified the argument that antislavery represented a form of bourgeois cultural hegemony,[7] others have revised his understanding of the historical and ideological role of capitalism in facilitating the growth of antislavery movements.[8] Yet they maintain the fundamental assumption about the historical importance of liberalism. As the historian Ira Berlin recently has put it, "The destruction of slavery and its corporate ethos—as a means of organizing society as well as a means of extracting labor—was a central event in the rise of capitalism and the triumph of liberalism, certainly in the West and in other parts of the world as well."[9]

My study of literary antislavery is about what gets lost in the story of the triumph of liberalism. Whereas the liberal argument assumes that sentiment was merely symptomatic of commercial and industrial capitalism, I emphasize the mutually constitutive relation of sentiment and capitalism. I argue that the "free" trade advocated by antislavery reform was different from the laissez-faire ideologies of modern liberal capitalism.[10] Consider, for example, the "Remarks on the Slave Trade," which appeared in 1789 in the Philadelphia publisher Mathew Carey's periodical *American Museum*. "Where is the human being," the author asks, "that can picture to himself this scene of woe, without at the same time execrating a trade which spreads misery and desolation wherever it appears? Where is the man of real benevolence, who will not join heart and hand, in opposing this barbarous, this iniquitous traffic?"[11] Such language demonstrates that the discourse of feeling included the subject of commerce itself. Put another way: for the slave trade to be

considered "barbarous," commerce itself had to be understood as a moral
and cultural form of exchange.

Sentiment saturates this era's literature against slave trading. English
Quakers petitioning Parliament in the 1780s to abolish the trade referred to
it as "unrighteous traffick."[12] Across the Atlantic, African American ministers celebrating the abolition of the trade in 1807 similarly referred to the
"abominable traffic" and "the unnatural monster."[13] Between the 1760s
and 1810s British and American reformers engaged in the same rhetorical
tactics, calling the African slave trade an "inhuman Commerce"; a "base
and inhuman Trade"; "this inhuman commerce"; "a complete system of
Robbery and Murder"; an "unrighteous bloody commerce" and "iniquitous
business;" "that unhappy and disgraceful branch of commerce"; "the cruel
and barbarous Slave Trade"; "this iniquitous traffick" and "this infamous
traffick"; a nefarious commerce" and "vile commerce"; an "iniquitous commerce" conducted by "men-stealers, though far worse than high-way robbers"; "this abominable trade"; "A TRADE, conceived in iniquity, carried on
in the most base and barbarous manner, productive of the worst effects, and
big with the most horrid and dangerous consequences."[14]

Even this small sample suggests that the debate about the slave trade itself
was much more than a political strategy to deflect contemporary anxieties
about the immediate emancipation of African slaves. Instead, the language
cited above clearly challenged the compatibility of commercial society—
slave-trading society—with enlightened civilization.[15]

Such a relation was represented through the historical discourse of manners.[16] This term, as J. G. A. Pocock pointed out long ago, was central to the
rise of "commercial humanism" in early modern European societies and
emphasized the civilizing effects of the trade, exchange, and consumption of
commercial goods:[17]

> This keyword [manners or *moeurs*] denoted a complex of shared practices
> and values, which secured the individual as social being and furnished the
> society surrounding him with an indefinitely complex and flexible texture;
> more powerfully even than laws, manners rendered civil society capable of
> absorbing and controlling human action and belief. . . . Commercial society,
> characterized by the incessant exchange of goods and services, moral and
> material, between its members, was that in which "manners" and "polite-
> ness" could reign undisturbed, and philosophy was perceived as the socia-
> ble conversation which Enlightenment sought to make it.[18]

Emphasis on manners helps to unlock the ideological complexity with which antislavery writing characterizes trade as either "civilized" or "barbaric."[19] The category of manners allows us to think about the rise of commercial capitalism outside of the tired binary between "republicanism" and "liberalism" that once dominated eighteenth-century American studies.[20]

Yet during the eighteenth century the category was itself highly fluid and chronically contested. "Manners" were intimately connected with such discursive formations as politeness, sociability, wit, humor, sentimental feeling, enlightened Christianity, and trade.[21] The historian Lawrence Klein has noted the pressure in British culture to distinguish between "true" and "false" manners. Philosophers like Anthony Ashley Cooper, the Third Earl of Shaftesbury, imbued politeness—which derived from the French *politesse*, or the superficial art of pleasing—with moral and sentimental feeling to distinguish it from false appearances, linguistic duplicity, and seduction.[22] Moreover, the very association of enlightened manners with commercial sophistication was itself highly unstable. According to the historical theory prevalent in the eighteenth century, each society naturally progressed from nomadic/hunting to agriculture to commerce, and eventually fell into cultural decline. Within this schema, commerce initially socialized human behavior by refining the passions.[23] Thus in an early number of *The Tatler* Richard Steele describes the "man of conversation" who "acts with great ease and dispatch among men of business. All which he performs with so much success that, with as much discretion in life as any man ever had, he neither is, nor appears, cunning."[24] However, this formula for civilized society was neither static nor foolproof. Consider a piece on trade that was reprinted in an American periodical in 1803:

> Trade is a fluctuating thing; it passed from Tyre to Alexandria, from Alexandria to Venice, from Venice to Antwerp, from Antwerp to Amsterdam and London—the English rivaling the Dutch, as the French are now rivaling both. All nations almost are wisely applying themselves to trade; and it behooves those who are in possession of it to take care that they do not lose it. It is a plant of tender growth, and requires sun, and soil, and fine seasons to make it thrive and flourish; it will not grow like the palm tree, which, with the weight and pressure, rises the more. Liberty is a friend to that, as that is to liberty: but nothing will support and promote it more than virtue, and what virtue teacheth—sobriety, industry, frugality, modesty, honesty, punctuality, humanity, charity, the love of country, and the fear of God.[25]

The passage grapples with the elusive issue of whether trade civilizes or debases society. Lady Commerce is mobile, capacious, and capricious; she is simultaneously the subject and object of refinement distinguishing civilized from barbaric peoples. Yet she also engenders the "weight and pressure" of avaricious passions. Commerce, the source of forms of cultural refinement, has the destructive ability to produce barbaric behavior in otherwise polite society.

The subject of the African slave trade marked off the boundaries between civilized and savage, or free and enslaving, forms of trade. It thereby legitimated multiple and diverse forms of commercial capitalism, specifically by deploying the discourses of enlightened, or "Christian," manners. To condemn the slave trade was to uphold the precarious state of civilized commercial identity. As one writer for the *American Magazine* put it in 1787, "It was not till Christianity influenced the manners of men, and introduced a spirit of mildness and justice in our dealings with others, that slavery received its first check. Civilization, or rather the reflection of Christianity upon the human mind, shewed slavery in its true colors, and taught us to pay a proper respect to our species."[26] Literary antislavery utilized with great effectiveness cultural fears of aristocratic vice and degeneracy, which pervaded British-American societies for much of the eighteenth century.[27]

It is not my purpose here to unmask the "false" consciousness or self-serving ideologies of abolitionist reform.[28] My study aims rather at interrogating the meaning of "liberalism." This involves a direct challenge to the C. B. Macpherson cultural model of "possessive individualism." As T. H. Breen has argued, we should resist pinning "the excesses of modern industrial capitalism on early modern Lockeans" and thereby projecting a "rapacious, materialistic, self-absorbed individualism back onto [this eighteenth-century] world."[29] In this same vein, the political scientist Thomas Horne maintains that "bourgeois virtue" in eighteenth-century America "was not based on an individual psychology, it did not justify unlimited accumulation, and it did not deny (and in fact asserted) that social responsibilities accompanied rights."[30] A similar reconsideration has revisited the foundational writers and treatises of liberalism. Case in point: Locke and Adam Smith. "Just as Locke's enterprise is misunderstood," writes James T. Kloppenberg, "when his liberalism serves as the midwife of possessive individualism, so Smith's purpose is distorted when the market mechanism he envisioned as a means to a moral end is presented as itself the goal of political economy."[31]

*   *   *

This book interprets the categories of "literature" and "American" expansively. I analyze the development of literary antislavery in the historical terms in which Anglo-American eighteenth-century writers and readers understood the category of "literature"—that is, as the "world of letters." This includes antislavery sermons, orations, political tracts, petitions, public and private epistles, autobiographies, and of course belletristic genres such as fiction, poetry, and drama.

I place early American antislavery writing in a transatlantic context, while recent scholarship on early antislavery literature tends to focus on Britain. The excellent work of Srinivas Avaramuden, Laura Brown, Markman Ellis, Suvir Kaul, Charlotte Sussman, Helen Thomas, and Roxann Wheeler does recognize the transatlantic reach of eighteenth-century antislavery, but these studies generally emphasize the cultural relations and exchanges between metropolitan London and the West Indies.[32] The circulation of antislavery ideology and language during the period between the 1750s and 1810s certainly includes British North America as well. Since the 1980s, social historians like Breen, Jack P. Greene, and J. R. Pole have emphasized the importance of colonial "British" America as well as the enduring relevance of British culture in the post-Revolutionary United States.[33] Literary critics and historians have begun to read colonial and early national American culture in comparative, transatlantic, and even multilingual contexts.[34]

Postcolonial studies add another dimension to the transatlantic scope and method of this book. Homi K. Bhabha, Stuart Hall, and others emphasize the importance of such concepts as hybridity, exchange, and mimicry in order to conceptualize the fundamental connections between imperial and colonial discourses. In the words of Edward Said, "Once we accept the actual configuration of literary experiences overlapping with one another and interdependent, despite national boundaries and coercively legislated national autonomies, history and geography are transfigured in new maps, in new and far less stable entities, in new types of connections."[35] Such a transfiguration questions the distinction between metropolitan and colonial—or British and British-American—cultures. While the political emergence of the United States out of colonial America during the 1780s certainly was different from twentieth-century colonial political movements, postcolonial theory goes far in describing the position of the United States between the 1770s and 1810s. Indeed, as Peter Hulme has argued, some critics have undervalued the critical importance of postcoloniality for the post-Revolutionary United States.[36] Political independence did not translate immediately into cultural independence: both Britain and the United States continued to participate in the slave trade; both exploited West African societies, and their respective—and connected—antislavery movements opposed such exploitation in largely the same cultural terms.

Writing about the slave trade took place throughout the British Empire, the colonies of British America, the Caribbean, and West Africa. British and American antislavery reformers corresponded widely. Both ideas and people crossed and recrossed the Atlantic. The famous Somerset decision, for example, whereby Lord Mansfield reluctantly ruled in 1772 on the incompatibility between slavery and English law, sparked the antislavery correspondence between Anthony Benezet and Granville Sharp (who actually argued the case). Later editions of Benezet's *Some Historical Account of Guinea*, first published in 1771, included part of Sharp's *Representation of the Injustice and Dangerous Tendency of Tolerating Slavery* in its appended material. Both men, moreover, were similarly influenced by the Abbé Raynal's *Philosophical and Political History of the Settlements and Trade of the Europeans in the East and West Indies* (1770). The antislavery sections in the Scottish philosopher John Millar's *The Origins of the Distinctions of Ranks* (1781, 3rd ed.) showed an awareness of Benezet's writings, as did the exchange over slavery between Benjamin Rush and Richard Nisbet in Philadelphia. Benezet's work also influenced the antislavery poetry that the young Robert Southey and Samuel Taylor Coleridge wrote as they became friends at Oxford.

British and American Quakers had been corresponding throughout much of the eighteenth century over the troubling issue of slavery.[37] Benezet's student, William Dillwyn, traveled to England where he met Thomas Clarkson and other English activists. Similarly, the Huntingdonian Methodists in England patronized Phillis Wheatley during her short visit, and later sent the African American immigrant John Marrant to preach the gospel in Nova Scotia. James Swan emigrated to New England and wrote against slavery from the colonial periphery but with a British audience primarily in mind. The Virginian Arthur Lee's antislavery tract responded to the 1764 edition of Adam Smith's *Theory of Moral Sentiments*. Antislavery autobiographies by figures like Olaudah Equiano and Venture Smith epitomize Black Atlantic writing and the hybrid identities that such diasporic movement produced. And if the representation of Ibo life in *The Interesting Narrative of Olaudah Equiano* significantly served as proof of African humanity, it derived largely from the English translation (from the French) of Michel Adanson's *A Voyage to Senegal, the Isle of Goree and the River Gambia* (1759), a text that early, influential Quakers like Anthony Benezet and John Woolman cited in their own antislavery writings.[38]

In addition to religious groups, the antislavery movement included new constituencies not immediately identifiable by religion, in Britain and America alike. It gave rise to works by poets like Anna Barbauld, Hannah More, and William Cowper. Olaudah Equiano, who framed his work as a plea for Parliament to abolish the African slave trade, also wrote within this political-commercial context. An obviously political—and politicized—genre, eighteenth-century antislavery writing reveals variations upon a commercial aesthetic that shaped such writing according to the categories of trade and manners, civilization and savagery.

These categories challenge the meaning of "race" in this period. Recent works by Nicholas Hudson and Roxann Wheeler emphasize the relative instability of this term during the eighteenth century, particularly its flexible relation to the cultural categories of civilization and barbarity.[39] The language of antislavery supports this view of the contested and protean nature of racial ideology. My argument throughout emphasizes how the slave trade collapsed the opposition between civilized and savage—or European and African—societies. I seek to avoid historical presentism and reject the belief that racism historically produced African slavery in the western hemisphere. In her famous challenge to Winthrop D. Jordan's *White Over Black* (1968), Barbara Fields wrote: "To assume, by intention or default, that race is a phenomenon outside history is to take up a position within the terrain of racialist ideology and to become its unknowing—and therefore uncontesting—victim."[40]

Much of the scholarly discussion of race in the eighteenth century understandably recognizes the influence of natural philosophy's determination of the very terms of humanity. Philosophical debates about the meaning of race and humanity divided chiefly between "monogenism" and "polygenism." The former clung to biblical authority and posited the singular creation of mankind found in Genesis; the latter was perhaps more self-consciously "enlightened" and "scientific" in breaking from such authority and theorizing different and unequal human species. Involving a wide array of such notable European, British, and American thinkers as David Hume, Thomas Jefferson, the Abbé Gregoire, Lord Kames, Immanuel Kant, and Samuel Stanhope Smith, these arguments over racial difference did not neatly align with proslavery and antislavery positions.[41]

Although my own discussion takes account of this philosophical debate, I envision the culture of antislavery in more expansive terms. Late eighteenth-century antislavery literature was by its nature "popular" so far as it aimed to reach and persuade the wider metropolitan and colonial reading publics. Hence discussions of race entered the less erudite and more popular discourses (such as those disseminated by periodicals) that dealt with subjects like commerce, feeling, manners, and the many other enlightened *topoi* of bourgeois culture.[42]

The subject of Chapter 1, the "commercial jeremiad," itself registers the legacy of Protestant ideology and rhetoric upon the commercial arguments against slave trading. I compare the language of earlier and religiously driven antislavery writing—particularly among Quakers—with later writings that appeal more to the cultural ramifications of commerce, marking the movement from theology to ethics, specifically commercial ethics. Over time antislavery culture preoccupied itself less with sin and more with manners, and "Christian" behavior came to signify the values of benevolence, feeling, and refinement.

Chapter 2 begins by questioning traditional critical paradigms that present Anglo-American antislavery poetry as either cheap sentimentalism or condescending racism—or sometimes both. By first establishing the ideological elasticity of "race" in this era, it shifts the terms for critical analysis to cultural categories of "civilization" and "barbarity." The problem of identification is paramount in this poetic genre that asks readers to see themselves as suffering African families torn asunder by the slave trade, or to consider their own relations with the slave traders they tacitly support. These confusing and problematic identifications go a long way in explaining, for example, the poetic convention of the African speaker. The paradox of Christian and civilized yet cruel and barbaric does not lend itself neatly to Christian-African identification and brings a deep anxiety to antislavery poetry, an anxiety that is often resolved by the sentimental motif of the African slave's suicide. This chapter explores the relations between British and American poets like William Cowper and Phillis Wheatley as well as Anna Barbauld and Philip Freneau.

Chapter 3 continues the argument about the inadequacy of racial categories by turning to the antislavery literature written during the American wars with Algiers and Tripoli between 1785 and 1815. Compounding American captivity among Moslems, the British impressment of American mariners and British seizure of American shipping brought confusion to the racial dichotomies in American literatures of captivity and slavery. American propaganda held the British to be as "barbaric" as the Moslem world—indeed it culturally merged the two. The question of the place of British culture in America underlies much of the Barbary slavery and captivity literatures of this period. No better instance of it than the transatlantic literary figure Susanna Rowson, whose drama *Slaves in Algiers* (1794) is the subject of the main discussion, as are Royall Tyler's *The Algerine Captive* (1797) and Washington Irving's *Salmagundi* papers (1807–8).

Chapter 4 examines the early autobiographical literature of what Paul Gilroy has called the "Black Atlantic." Its focus is primarily upon the oral autobiographies of John Marrant and Venture Smith that were written down by white editors. I situate these works rhetorically within eighteenth-century discourses about "liberty" and "rights." Both Marrant and Smith pushed at the semantic boundaries of individual rights—boundaries that were in this historical period unsteady enough to be easily and even safely redrawn.

The cultural limit for black participation in discourses of liberty and rights is the focus of Chapter 5. I discuss the public exchanges that took place in print during Philadelphia's yellow fever epidemic of 1793–94 between publisher Mathew Carey and African American leaders Richard Allen and Absalom Jones. They responded vigorously to Carey's claims that the city's blacks had intentionally driven up wages for carting the sick and burying the dead during this social and medical crisis. This historical episode reveals the extent to which white and black writers were struggling over such crucial ideas as labor, equity, value, the market, and republican community. The role of sentiment, its relation to capitalism, and the formation of racial and cultural boundaries forged by this relation all come to a head in this final chapter.

CHAPTER 1

The Commercial Jeremiad

> But we, in an enlightened age, have greatly surpassed, in brutality
> and injustice, the most ignorant and barbarous ages: and while we
> are pretending to the finest feelings of humanity, are exercising un-
> precedented cruelty.
>
> —William Fox, *An Address to the People of Great Britain, on the Propriety of
> Abstaining from West India Sugar and Rum* (1792)

> I know of no method of getting money, not even that of robbing for
> it upon the highway, which has so direct a tendency to efface the
> moral sense, to rob the heart of every gentle and humane disposi-
> tion, and to harden it, like steel, against all impressions of sensibility.
>
> —John Newton, *Thoughts Upon the Slave Trade* (1788)

Why did eighteenth-century antislavery writers associate the
slave trade specifically with "ignorance and barbarity"? How did such an association affect literary representations of the slave trade? I propose to answer these two questions by directly connecting them—by reading antislavery aesthetics, in other words, in the context of eighteenth-century
ideologies of trade, manners, and civilization. Anglo-American antislavery
writings of this period represent African slaves as the subject of both sentimental and commercial identification. Consider, for example, the initial version of Jefferson's *Declaration of Independence*, which calls the slave trade an
"execrable commerce" foisted upon colonial Americans: "This piratical warfare, the opprobrium of INFIDEL powers, is the warfare of the CHRISTIAN
king of Great Britain." If the language here was inflated for political gain,
Jefferson had made much the same argument two years earlier in *A Summary View of the Rights of British America* (1774). In it he claimed that Americans in effect were enslaved to two kinds of "goods" circulating in the British imperial economy:

12

An act of parliament had been passed imposing duties on teas, to be paid in America, against which act the Americans had protested as inauthoritative. The East India company, who till that time had never sent a pound of tea to America on their own account, step forth on that occasion the assertors of parliamentary right, and send hither many ship loads of that obnoxious commodity.

But previous to the enfranchisement of the slaves we have, it is necessary to exclude all further importations from Africa: yet our repeated attempts to effect this by prohibitions, and by imposing duties which might amount to a prohibition, have been hitherto defeated by his majesty's negative: Thus preferring the immediate advantages of a few African corsairs to the lasting interests of the American states, and to the rights of human nature, deeply wounded by this infamous practice.[1]

Although Jefferson's attitudes toward African Americans have been the subject of ongoing critical and historical controversy, in this instance he significantly represents them as toxic commodities. Indeed, both British tea and African slaves are goods, of sorts, that lay at the center of the present imperial-colonial crisis. Both do harm to colonial American consumers. Yet each has a distinctive relation to imperial regulation. To free the tea trade means disentangling it from mercantilist regulation, but to free the African slave trade means imposing such regulation (in the form of "duties") as to eradicate it. This slippage suggests the complexity of the meaning of "free" trade in this era—a complexity informing my evaluation of the political literature against slave trading in Britain and America that was produced between the 1770s and 1810s.[2] Certainly, the language Jefferson uses to characterize the slave trade suggests a much broader range of cultural meanings for commerce than merely the accounting of profit and loss. It resembles, for example, that of his friend James Madison in the *Federalist* #42. While advocating the right of the newly conceived federal government to regulate foreign commerce, Madison condemns "a traffic which has so long and so loudly upbraided the barbarism of modern policy."[3] Jefferson's condemnation is similarly premised on the understanding of trade commensurate with the "candid world" to which the *Declaration* appeals.

I call this cultural narrative against slave trading the "commercial jeremiad."[4] It arose in context of the long-standing use by antislavery writers of Protestant discourses about human sin, Christian morality, and divine judgment. The commercial jeremiad represents the gradual process of secularization of these Protestant discourses in antislavery writing—the use of traditional languages and rhetorical conventions in formulating modern commercial ideologies. During the eighteenth century the meaning of "Christian" morality in antislavery writing increasingly accorded with modern values of enlightened behavior, which were themselves imbricated in larger questions about the nature of trade, manners, and consumption.[5] As T. H. Breen has argued, in Revolutionary America,

> [i]ncreasing opportunities to consume triggered intense print controversies about the character and limits of luxury, the moral implications of credit, the role of personal choice in a liberal society, and the relevance of traditional status hierarchies in a commercial world that encouraged people to fashion protean public identities. Heated debates on these issues represented an initial effort by large numbers of Americans throughout the colonies to gain intellectual control over the marketplace, to make sense of their new experiences, and to bring ideology into line with a commercial system that they found inviting as well as intimidating.[6]

The slave trade equally highlighted cultural questions about the nature of consumption, credit, and social stability.[7] Put in Breen's terms, it comprised part of "the semiotics of everyday life" whereby Anglo-Americans "communicated perceptions of status and politics to other people through items of everyday material culture, through a symbolic universe of commonplace 'things'."[8] Here the metaphor for late eighteenth-century antislavery writing is that of an important and densely layered discursive arena in which Anglo-Americans simultaneously lamented the plight of captive Africans and confronted nagging commercial and cultural dilemmas. How did one distinguish between moral and illicit forms of prosperity? What were the social consequences of commercial capitalism—cultural refinement or licentious corruption?

Christian Commerce

The answers to such questions turn on the changing meaning of "free" trade in this era. Eighteenth-century antislavery writing registers this discursive change. I will focus on a couple of prominent examples of early antislavery writing as a way of showing the polemical movement from biblical precept to enlightened manners. Largely the work of early Quaker humanitarians, this writing cites such scriptural passages as Exodus 21.16 aggressively ("He who kidnaps a man and sells him, or if he is found in his hand, shall surely be put to death"), and holds up biblical law as the standard by which contemporary readers were to measure their sins. For example, in 1693 the Quaker reformer George Keith, who emigrated to Pennsylvania and was later disowned by Quakers there for his unconventional piety, argued that the slave trade "is contrary to the Principles and Practice of the *Christian Quakers* to buy Prize or stollen Goods . . . and therefore it is our Duty to come forth in a testimony against stollen Slaves, it being accounted a far greater Crime under *Moses*'s Law than the stealing of Goods."[9] Notwithstanding the disturbing association of Africans with stolen "goods," Keith understands the slave trade as the violation of divine law, the sinful transgression that surely incurs "God's Judgments upon them." Early influential Quaker writings in British America, like John Hepburn's *The American Defense of the Christian Golden Rule* (1715) or Ralph Sandiford's *A Brief Examination of the Practice of the Times* (1729), make much the same argument. Though certainly not devoid of feeling, these writings place that virtue almost exclusively in the context of biblical precept. Hepburn, for example, insists that "[t]he parting the Husband from the Wife, and the Wife from the Husband; and the Children from them both, to make up their Masters Gains, they force them thus to break the seventh Command, and commit Adultery with other strangers, or other mens Wives or Husbands."[10]

Such premises similarly inform the most famous antislavery debate in Puritan New England, that between Samuel Sewall and John Saffin. The transatlantic context for this debate was the Royal African Company's loss in 1698 of its monopoly of the slave trade, which immediately increased the number of African slaves imported into British American ports such as Boston. An eminent jurist in the Bay colony, Sewall penned *The Selling of Joseph* (1700) in response to this development, returning to the biblical scene of slave trading in Genesis 37, where Joseph's brothers sell him to the Ishmaelites for twenty pieces of silver. Like his Quaker counterparts, Sewall cited scriptural evidence for African humanity (in Acts 17.26 and Psalms 115.16) and for the illegality of slave trading (Exodus 21.16). He also significantly assailed the trade so as to link immoral consumption to apocalyptic retribution, an argument that again likened Africans to dirty goods: "If *Arabian* Gold be imported in any quantities, most are afraid to meddle with it, though they might have it at easy rates; lest if it should have been wrongfully taken from the Owners, it should kindle a fire to the Consumption of their whole Estate."[11] The slave merchant John Saffin's rebuttal, however, just as rigorously invoked those parts of Genesis and Leviticus establishing precedents for Hebrew slavery, and criticized Sewall's implied denial of a divinely organized social hierarchy that slavery helped to maintain.[12] A few years later, the debate culminated with the publication in London of another antislavery essay in John Dunton's *Athenian Oracle*. Sewall later had part of it reprinted in New England. Calling the slave trade a "disgrace to Christianity," it questioned New English civilization in terms of religious principle: "For I am very persuaded, that if a fair and honest Trade and Commerce had been carry'd on amongst [the Africans], and no violence had been done to their Persons; Christianity must have gotten as great footing by this time amongst them, as it has amongst the poor *Infidels of New England*."[13]

The trope of infidelity begins to suggest the cultural (and not merely theological) meaning of "Christian" identity. Certainly, late eighteenth-century antislavery writing continued to invoke biblical evidence for moral leverage. Specific passages from Exodus, Matthew, Acts, and Paul's epistles facilitated the antislavery moral critique and, to a lesser extent, the argument for African humanity. During the Revolution and its aftermath, American antislavery writing often used Protestant rhetorical conventions to make slavery part of the problem of national sin.[14] Samuel Hopkins, for example, privately complained in 1787 to the Quaker Moses Brown that the Constitutional provision extending the slave trade for twenty years endangered the survival of the nation, and cited the typological precedent of Israel's punishment in Joshua 7: "I fear that is an *Achan,* which will bring a curse, so that we cannot prosper."[15] Warner Mifflin's antislavery address to Congress similarly concluded "that this extensive and rising republic may be exalted by righteousness, and not overturned by pride, oppression, and forgetfulness of the rightful Ruler and Dread of Nations."[16] Nearing the end of the era in which the trade was constitutionally protected, the ex-Caribbean planter Thomas Branagan warned: "It is equally as easy to judge, of the approaching downfall of a nation; when degeneracy of manners; a contempt for God and his worship; accumulated debauchery; seduction and oppression not only prevail, but become fashionable. . . . [that] God cannot, without the greatest partiality, suffer the sinful nations of modern times to escape with impunity will not admit of a doubt."[17]

The phrase "degeneracy of manners" suggest the ideological changes that were gradually displacing biblical precept with cultural norms of Enlightenment. These were in large part founded upon widespread cultural beliefs that trade socialized humanity. In George Bickham's *The Universal Penman,* for example, the entry for "Commerce," with an engraving of a group of British merchants gathered around a bill of lading, is glossed in prose and verse celebrating a "well regulated Commerce" dispersing British goods "in all the Markets of the World" (see Figure 1). The poem reads:

> Then, pregnant Commerce! Art y' source of Peace,
> Parent of Arts, and Parent of Increase;
> By thy diffusive Stores all Nations smile,
> Thou art to every Clime a Second Nile.

The poem imaginatively brings Africa "home" to Britain through the trope of a "Second Nile." The visual representations in the background of importing and exporting goods reinforce the ideal of the commercial unification of the civilized world ("all Nations"), while imperialist overtones resound in the prose summary's depiction of British commerce as "so many Squadrons of Floating Shops."

Late eighteenth-century antislavery writing utilized this sort of model of civilized trade chiefly by manipulating traditional Protestant languages against slavery. Biblical rhetoric was newly absorbed and re-deployed to make modern arguments against the slave trade. For example, Branagan teased out the cultural implications of the apocalyptic argument: "But why do I say barbarism? What Oriental nation, what Savage people ever encouraged and supported such a cruel commerce in human flesh or kept so many of their fellow men in ignoble bondage as the Americans as well as the other refined nations of Christendom now support and keep?"[18] During the Revolutionary era the American pulpit recast the jeremiad against slave trading in terms of cultural degeneracy. As the title of the Baptist minister Elhanan Winchester's *The Reigning Abominations, Especially the Slave Trade* suggests, the catalogue of contemporary vices the author attributed to colonial Virginians in 1774 actually culminated with the slave trade. This antislavery sermon is so interesting not only because it was later printed in London, probably to bolster the newly formed English Society for Effecting the Abolition of the Slave Trade (henceforth English Abolition Society) while Winchester was living there, but also because, in both its colonial American and British publications, it puts scripture in the service of promoting cultural enlightenment. Winchester cited Paul, Solomon, and the apocalyptic gospels as evidence against "a most infamous commerce" that deadened benevolence: "Avarice tends to harden the heart, to render the mind callous to the feelings of humanity, indisposes the soul to every virtue, and renders it an easy

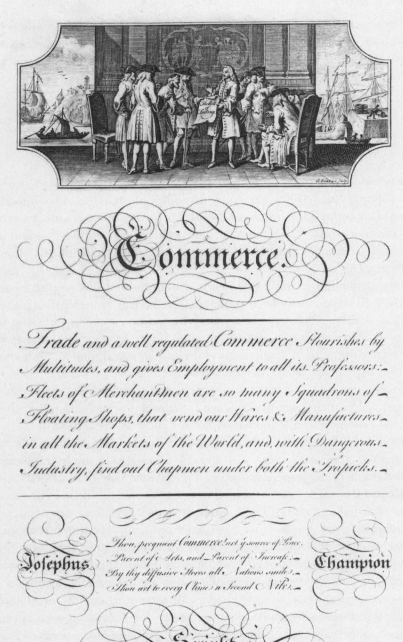

Commerce.

Trade and a well regulated Commerce Flourishes by Multitudes, and gives Employment to all its Professors: Fleets of Merchant-men are so many Squadrons of Floating Shops, that vend our Wares & Manufactures in all the Markets of the World, and, with Dangerous Industry, find out Chapmen under both the Tropicks.

Josephus

Thou, pregnant Commerce! art ÿ source of Peace,
Parent of ÿ Arts, and Parent of Increase:
By thy diffusive Stores all Nations smile,
Thou art to every Clime a Second Nile.

Champion

Scripsit.

Figure 1. "Commerce." From George Bickham, *The Universal Penman* (London, 1741).

prey to every vice."[19] Several years earlier, the minister Samuel Cooke similarly warned his audience ("When God ariseth, and when he visiteth, what shall we answer!"[20]), but he also notably situated the specter of divine vengeance within the context of a particularly cultural form of declension. As "patrons of liberty, [we] have dishonoured the christian name,—and degraded human nature, nearly to the level with the beasts that perish."[21]

The antislavery rhetoric of Christianity was founded upon the opposition between civilization and savagery. But the African slave trade directly challenged these categories by suggesting that Europeans and Americans involved in the trade were effectively made "beasts." By the 1770s and 1780s, Quaker opponents to the trade, for example, were referring to it "as the scene of violence and barbarities, perpetrated in order to procure [Africans], by men professing the Christian religion."[22] Indeed, the comparison between early and late eighteenth-century Quaker antislavery writing demonstrates the overall movement from biblical precept to ethical imperative.[23] Compare Hepburn's *American Defense of the Christian Golden Rule* (1715) with William Dillwyn's *Brief Considerations on Slavery* (1773):

> Now the buying and selling of the *Bodies* and *Souls* of Men, was and is the Merchandize of the Babylonish Merchants spoken of in the *Revelations*. . . . For how will ye answer when ye are brought before Gods Tribunal, and there appear naked and bear [sic] before the Son of Man, if ye have lived and died in Opposition to his Everlasting Gospel?[24]

> The practice of ages cannot sanctify error; but the progress of reformation has, in all, been gradual. . . . Having thus briefly considered the slave trade as contradictory to the divine and social law, it is needless to urge the impropriety of any, and especially a free people, being in anywise concerned in it.[25]

The earlier emphasis upon biblical law gives way to the contemporary standards of enlightened civilization. The change reveals a new kind of historical self-consciousness. Whereas Hepburn's comment on the "Babylonish Merchants" affirms the relevance of scriptural authority, the second passage inverts this model by carefully distinguishing the barbaric past from the enlightened present. Here slave trading violates the ideological *equivalence* of biblical injunction and enlightened mores, the convergence of letter and spirit captured by the phrase "the divine and social law."[26]

The correlation between commercial and enlightened society was, however, highly problematic in this era. Antislavery writing reveals the extent to which late eighteenth-century Anglo-Americans uncertainly considered the long-term effects of commercial development upon civilized society. Montesquieu had argued in *The Spirit of the Laws* (1748) that "Commerce cures destructive prejudices, and it is an almost general rule that everywhere there are gentle mores, there is commerce and that everywhere there is commerce, there are gentle mores,"[27] but he also cited examples of the morally debilitating effects of advanced forms of capitalism.[28] Influenced by Montesquieu, the Scottish Enlightenment generally upheld a four-stage theory of progressive history, which believed that "barbarism was not a stage that had been left behind, but was a state that could be imminent and recurrent."[29] In these kinds of writings, throughout much of the eighteenth century, the social and historical volatility of trade figuratively expressed itself in the feminization of commerce. Consider, for example, a well-known passage from *Cato's Letters,* written in the aftermath of the infamous South Sea Bubble episode, where John Trenchard summarizes the effects of "Dame Commerce":

> Nothing is more certain, than that trade cannot be forced; she is a coy and humorous dame, who must be won by flattery and allurements, and always flies force and power: she is not confined to nations, sects, or climates, but travels and wanders about the earth, till she fixes her residence where she finds the best welcome and kindest reception; her contexture is so nice and delicate that she cannot breathe in a tyrannical air; will and pleasure are so opposite to her nature that but touch her with the sword, and she dies. But if you give her gentle and kind entertainment, she is a grateful and beneficent mistress: she will turn deserts into fruitful fields, villages into great cities, cottages into palaces, beggars into princes.[30]

Terry Mulcaire has argued that the passage is evidence of "the quasi-magical value-making power of Credit" that appeals directly to the "radically unstable creative power of the aesthetic imagination": "Credit's symbolic femininity represents this instability not merely as a frightening volatility but also a potentially infinite resource. . . . Credit's power is an artifact of polite civilization."[31] The volatility of such power requires regulation—regulation of trade as well as of the passions of the aesthetic imagination stimulating that trade. For, as *Cato* attests, the "delicate" cultural refinement spawned by commercial exchange may actually go too far. The distinction between re-

finement and seduction may blur as this "beneficent mistress" produces luxuriant decadence associated with "palaces" and "princes."

In this context, the literature against African slave trading tries to demarcate the boundary between virtuous and vicious commerce. Perhaps the
most single influential authority opposing the slave trade during the era before widespread antislavery political organization was the British political
economist Malachy Postlethwayt, who actually had served in the Royal African Company before turning against the slave trade and the mercantilist
apparatus supporting it.[32] The "leading contemporary theorist in the years of
imperial expansion"[33] directly influenced such antislavery writers as Anthony Benezet, James Dana, James Swan, and Arthur Lee, among others.
His *Universal Dictionary of Trade and Commerce* (1767) provided not only statistical evidence against slave trading, but also a rich source of commercial language. Indeed, the monstrous tome's epigraph from John Gay's "To His Native Country" frames commercial nationalism in just these terms:

> O Britain, chosen Port of Trade,
> May Luxury ne'er thy Sons invade;
> Whenever neighboring States contend,
> Tis thine to be the general Friend.
>
> What is't who rules in other Lands?
> On Trade alone thy Glory stands.
> That Benefit is unconfin'd,
> Diffusing Good among Mankind;
>
> That first gave Lustre to thy Reigns,
> And scatter's Plenty o'er thy Plains:
> 'Tis that alone thy Wealth supplies,
> And draws all Europe's envious Eyes.
> Be commerce then thy sole Design:
> Keep that, and all the World is thine.[34]

As a rhetorical key to the *Universal Dictionary,* Gay's poem points to the many
aspects of commerce: economic, cultural, national, and transnational. The
poetic tension between Britain's "Glory" and the benefits it commercially
diffuses throughout the world almost occludes the more fundamental one
over the nature of trade itself. As in *Cato's Letters,* commerce produces forms
of cultural refinement that potentially become enervating "Luxury."

For Postlethwayt, the African slave trade helps to resolve this tension by serving as the negative model of commerce, one which, by implication, legitimates other, more enlightened forms of trade. The *Universal Dictionary*'s entry for "Africa" does acknowledge the "great advantage" of slave-trade profits for the British Empire, but it also goes on to call it an "inhuman commerce" endangering Britain's self-image as a civilized nation. The slave trade inspires the "wars and hostilities among the negro princes and chiefs" who compete to gain captives for sale. This "spirit of butchery" contrasts with the program Postlethwayt proposes of "a fair, friendly, humane, and civilized commerce with the Africans." Framed as a series of rhetorical questions, however, the *Universal Dictionary*'s plan to civilize Africa ("by extending traffic into their country in the largest degree it will be admitted of") reveals in this format more uncertainty than it openly admits. Since these queries reappeared, sometimes verbatim, in the antislavery writings of Anthony Benezet, James Swan, and many others, it in worth citing the text in its entirety:

1. Whether so extensive and populous a country as Africa is, will not admit of a far more extensive and profitable trade to Great-Britain than it yet ever has done?
2. Whether the people of this country, notwithstanding their colour, are not capable of being civilized, as well as those of many other have been; and whether the primitive inhabitants of all countries, so far as we have been able to trace them, were not once as savage and inhumanized as the negroes of Africa; and whether the ancient Britons themselves of our country were not once upon a level with the Africans?
3. Whether, therefore, there is not a probability that those people might, in time, by proper management exercised by the Europeans, become as wise, as industrious, as ingenious and as humane as the people of any other country?
4. Whether their rational faculties are not, in the general, equal to those of any other of the human species; and whether they are not, from experience, as capable of mechanical and manufactural arts and trades, as even the bulk of the Europeans?
5. Whether it would not be more to the interest of all the European nations concerned in the trade to Africa, rather to endeavor to cultivate a friendly, humane and civilized commerce with those people, into the very center of their extended country, than to content themselves

only with skimming a trifling portion of trade upon the sea-coast of Africa?

6. Whether the greatest hindrance and obstruction to the Europeans cultivating a humane and Christian-like commerce with those populous countries, has not wholly proceeded from the unjust, inhumane, and unchristian-like traffic called the SLAVE TRADE, which is carried on by the Europeans?

7. Whether this trade, and this only, was not the primary cause, and still continues to be the chief cause, of those eternal and incessant broils, quarrels and animosities, which subsist between the negro princes and chiefs; and consequently, of those eternal wars which subsist among them, and which they are induced to carry on, in order to make prisoners of one another for the sake of the slave trade?

8. Whether, if trade was carried on with them for a series of years, as it has been with other countries that have not been less barbarous, and the Europeans gave no encouragement whatever to the slave trade, those cruel wars among the Blacks would not cease, and a fair and honourable commerce in time take place throughout the whole country?

9. Whether the example of the Dutch in the East-Indies, who have civilized innumerable of the natives, and brought them to the European way of cloathing, etc. does not give reasonable hopes that these suggestions are not visionary, but founded on experience, as well as on humane and Christian-like principles?

10. Whether commerce in general has not proved the great means of gradually civilizing all nations, even the most savage and brutal; and why not the Africans?

11. Whether the territories of those European nations that are interested in the colonies and plantations in America, are not populous enough, or may not be rendered so, by proper encouragement given to inter-marriages amongst them, and to the breed of foundling infants, to supply their respective colonies with labourers, in place of negro slaves?

12. Whether the British dominions in general have not at present an extent of territory sufficient to increase and multiply their inhabitants; and whether it is not their own fault that they do not increase them sufficiently to supply their colonies and plantations, with whites instead of blacks?[35]

Postlethwayt obviously writes about the conversion of "Africa" within the ideological categories of "Christian" and "heathen" nations. But these categories are not only religious terms but commercial ones as well. The context for our common humanity is commercial exchange. Even more important, the "Christian-like and humane Commerce" he would bring to this presumably uncivilized world implicates as well those Britons and other Europeans who have debased themselves by participating in barbaric trade. To "free" the African trade is to regulate it—and to thereby liberate *everyone* involved.

The Seduction of Africa

The cultural value antislavery activists placed on trade is evident as well in their opponents' response. Because West Indian planters were most often the target of antislavery outrage, they often defended themselves by trying to shift the terms of debate and emphasize the profitability of the sugar, coffee, and indigo trades. During the 1770s, as British and American antislavery politics became more visible, the debate in Philadelphia between the Philadelphia physician Benjamin Rush and the newly emigrated West Indian planter Richard Nisbet demonstrated this clash over commerce itself. In responding to Rush's *An Address to the Inhabitants of the British Settlements in America upon Slave-Keeping* (1773), Nisbet warned his fellow Philadelphians of the danger of "losing her commerce": "The inhabitants of this city will please to recollect, that the West-Indies form a considerable branch of their commerce, and that they ought therefore to listen to every thing that can be said in favour of its inhabitants."[36] Yet antislavery shadows the proslavery apologia. Naturally aware of the antislavery stand, Nisbet at first feigns ignorance by claiming, "I am little acquainted with the method of carrying on the slave trade and, therefore, shall say little on the subject," but then goes on to say that all African slaves "are bought in the fair course of trade, and that the Europeans have seldom, or never, an opportunity of carrying them off by stealth, though they were inclinable. It is, likewise, certain, that these creatures, by being sold to the Europeans, are often saved from the most cruel deaths, or wretched slavery to their fellow barbarians."[37] The appeal to moral value tries to parry Rush's critique on his own terms.

Such a move only testifies to the cultural potency of antislavery. For the condemnation of slave trading emphasized the equivalent danger to *both* Europeans and Africans. If the basic premise of this argument came principally from Montesquieu,[38] it was now cast through the common rhetoric of cultural crisis. An early antislavery tract by the pseudonymous "J. Phil-more," for example, entitled *Two Dialogues on the Man Trade* (1760), argued that West Indian slavery accounted for "that general Depravation of Man-ners, which so much prevails in the Colonies, in Proportion as they have more or less enriched themselves, at the Expense of the Blood and Bones of the Negroes."[39] One of the seminal texts of this era, the English clergyman James Ramsay's *Essay on the Treatment and Conversion of the African Slaves* (1784), also complained of slavery's "ill effect on the manners of the peo-ple."[40] Later, in the early 1800s, as Parliament was poised to abolish the trade, the famous English abolitionist William Wilberforce concluded that slavery "never did nor ever will prevail long in any country, without pro-ducing a most pernicious effect, both on its morals, habits, and manners."[41]

This argument rhetorically depends upon the sentimentalization of com-mercial exchange. Many scholars have viewed sentimentalism in antislav-ery writing with suspicion, as though it either hid economic self-interests or drew attention to British and American capacities for enlightened feeling in and of itself.[42] But sentiment played a crucial rhetorical role in configur-ing the enlightened commercial capitalism that the African slave trade en-dangered. Antislavery depended upon the syncretic language of the moral market.

Take the New Jersey Quaker David Cooper's antislavery sermon, *A Mite Cast into the Treasury* (1772). Two of the key biblical passages it considers come from Proverbs 22.22–23 ("Rob not the poor because he *is* poor: nei-ther oppress the afflicted in the gate") and Micah 6.11 ("Shall I count *them* pure with the wicked balances, and with the bag of deceitful weights?"). The texts are well chosen in that they facilitate the precise meditation on the re-lation between the economies of exchange and feeling. The one from Micah is particularly useful because it recounts how the ancient Israelites were de-luded by their own greed into thinking that divine offerings (the "treasures of wickedness") would stay God's wrath. The sermon certainly makes the common antislavery argument that abolishing the slave trade will be, like the weights of a clock, "the moving cause" behind the end of chattel slavery. Yet the sudden turn from one enlightened trope of balance to another—"the wicked balance, and bag of deceitful weights" used to rationalize slavery—recasts morality in economic terms: "My friend, thy reasoning proceeds from the bag of deceitful weights; the true balance discovers justice to be quite another thing than thou seems to think it, here is no respecter of persons. Justice to thy negroe weighs as heavy as justice to thyself, a small loss in thy interest out in the scale against the freedom of an innocent fellow-creature, weighs but as a feather against mount Atlas."[43]

The typological reduction of slavery to avarice was a staple of antislavery literature. Rather than simply rehearsing the biblical injunction to keep trade out of sacred areas, however, Cooper recasts avarice as a means to distinguish between acceptable and illicit forms of commercial exchange. The trope of weights and measures figures commerce ethically and ethics commercially—that is, moralizing and money changing are equivalent activities.

The trope of balance suggests the importance of preventing what one sermon in the 1790s called "the slavery of vicious passions."[44] As the historian John Brewer has argued, "the formation of a public cultural sphere" in eighteenth-century England theoretically was endangered by "two forces that undercut its impartiality, namely pecuniary gain—acquisitiveness—and sexual passion." Cultural critics feared "the seductiveness and energy of a commercially vibrant, protean and fertile culture suffused with lust and greed."[45] In this context, antislavery writers unsurprisingly placed great importance upon the regulation of both international trade and individual faculties. Both unregulated trade and passions led to what one English emigrant to Massachusetts, James Swan, called the "inhuman Commerce" conducted by "Men-wolves" prowling the West African coast.[46] Such bestial imagery was common and figuratively conveyed the problem of cultural debasement. "Engrossed by one fatal passion," the Philadelphian William Belsham asked in 1790, while Congress was rejecting a Quaker antislavery petition, "the rage of accumulating wealth, how canst thou sympathize with the emotions excited by the various relations of social and domestick life?"[47]

The argument for the "enslavement" of both Anglo-Americans and Africans produced rhetorical strategies wedding irony to the gothic. This was especially true of writers who offered eyewitness accounts of the slave trade such as Alexander Falconbridge, who had served as ship's surgeon aboard an English slave trader. His account of the "scramble" for African slaves depicts the depravity encompassing both subject and object of commercial exchange:

> As soon as the hour agreed on arrived, the doors of the yard were suddenly thrown open, and in rushed a considerable number of purchasers, with all the ferocity of brutes. Some instantly seized such of the negroes as they could conveniently lay hold of with their hands. Others, being prepared with several hankerchiefs tied together, encircled with these as many as

they were able. . . . It is scarcely possible to describe the confusion of which this mode of selling is productive. . . . The poor astonished negroes were so much terrified by the proceedings, that several of them, through fear, climbed over the court yard, and ran wild about the town; but were soon hunted down and retaken.[48]

Not unlike Swan's imagery, Falconbridge's depiction makes much of the fact that supposedly civilized Europeans now demonstrate the "ferocity of brutes." The slave market would appear to problematize the fundamental opposition between "civilization" and "savagery" upon which proslavery writers like Nisbet or Richard Long, for example, defended the removal of Africans themselves.

This antislavery narrative focused particularly upon the trading areas along the West African coast. As David S. Shields has noted, "Great Britain assured itself of the righteousness of its imperial mission by the myth of the *translatio imperii* and the humanist belief that trade engendered the 'arts of peace.'"[49] But accounts of the destructiveness Europeans wrought on these areas went right to the heart of the problem of barbaric traffic. The British antislavery politician William Wilberforce claimed, for example, that "it has been the sad fate of Africa that when she did enter into an intercourse with polished nations, it was an intercourse of such a nature, as, instead of polishing and improving, has tended not merely to retard her natural progress, but to deprave and darken, and, if such a new term might be used where unhappily the novelty of the occurrence compels us to resort to one, to barbarize her wretched inhabitants."[50] This "extraordinary phenomenon" was especially troubling because it violated the principle that trade propelled human "progress from ignorance and barbarism, to the knowledge and comforts of a state of social refinement."[51] The African slave trade undermined the geographical categories of progressive history.

The motif of the violation of Africa has important literary ramifications. It suggests the resemblance between antislavery literature and the seduction novel, or that between the discourses of trade and sexuality. During the late eighteenth century the cultural discourses of seduction, which emphasized the dangers of false appearances, unregulated desire, and uncultivated innocence, circulated throughout political and belletristic literatures. This is critically significant because studies of the early novel recently have recognized the public and political importance of its private and domestic space.[52] Similarly, the novelistic representation of the African slave trade turns on the narrative of seduction wherein the European slave trader assumes the character of the rake whose "arts" equally dissemble African consumers and European competitors.[53] The slave trader symbolizes the disruption of civilized sociability. Consider, for example, the portrait John Atkins provided in the 1730s of the dissembling slave trader: "The Lye did me most Service, and for which I had the Merchant's Dispensation, was informing my good Friend that at *Cobelahon* they had taken a great number of Captives. . . . [T]his I did with an air of diffidence, to make the greater Impression, and at the same time *dashee'd* his Negro Friends to go on board and back it." If the story fails, as Atkins shrewdly notes, "your Reputation is secured by the diffidence of your Report, and you must resolve with him now upon a Price in your Slaves, not to outbid one another; but at the same time make as strong a Resolution not to observe it."[54]

The object of commercial libertinism was the seduced African. Thomas Clarkson described the dynamics of commercial seduction as a process where Europeans "endeavoured, by a peaceable deportment, by presents, and by every appearance of munificence, to seduce the attachment and confidence of the Africans. These schemes had the desired effect. The gaudy trappings of European art not only caught their attention but excited their curiosity: they dazzled their eyes and bewitched their senses."[55] Today we view the image of violated innocence suspiciously, for it depends, after all, on an earlier form of what the historian George Fredrickson has called the nineteenth century's "romantic racialism."[56] Yet the cultural potency of Edenic Africa was powerful enough to elicit African Americans' strategic uses of it. Celebrating the abolition of the slave trade, for example, the New York minister Peter Williams emphasized "the innocent and amiable manners" of West Africans seduced by European invaders: "Ardent in their affections, their minds were susceptible of the warmest emotions of love, friendship, and gratitude."[57] European "pirates" dissemble "the most amicable pretensions . . . and all the bewitching and alluring wiles of the seducer were practiced." Such "wiles" depended upon the luxury goods that Europeans offered for slaves. Hence the "abominable commerce" doubly corrupts the "heroine" by "flattering" her vanity, then creating in her "the same avaricious disposition which they themselves possessed."[58] The West African's seduction, like that of Richardson's Clarissa or Rowson's Charlotte Temple, exposes the danger of latent forms of desire.[59]

Eighteenth-century antislavery writers thus imagine Africans as seduced consumers. Their narratives of seduction did not only recount the licentious desires of miscreant sea captains but metaphorized Africa as a "ravished" woman. Even this highly sentimental trope, however, reflected back upon the virtuous sexuality of Anglo-American women. Commercial seduction in some instances became a way of talking about female virtue. Thus Charles Crawford, who was the son of a wealthy Antiguan planter and went to Philadelphia after an unsuccessful education in England, wrote against slavery, specifically addressing his female readership:

> I would appeal particularly to the sensibility and the virtue of my female readers, many of whom know the beauty, the cleanliness, the healthiness, the peace, the liberty, the dignity, the sanctity of charity, and how preferable it is to the misery, the filth, the unwholesomeness, the servitude, the debasement, the brutality of incontinence. It is impossible but they must feel exquisitely for the condition of any of their sex where their persons can be violated with impunity.[60]

If this appeal suggests the access women readers and writers had to antislavery culture, it also further demonstrates the rhetorical and cultural power of the trope of seduction, which often worked according to the logic of analogy and translation. In this case, the prose translates the dangers of seduction from African to Anglo-American women, thereby both monitoring and reaffirming the state of female manners. In this economy of virtue, however, there is a kind of mercantilist trade-off: the African women's loss, or "debasement," is another's gain.

African Goods

Eighteenth-century antislavery literature registers the dialogue between the languages of cultural manners and biblical authority. If this narrative represents Africans as seduced consumers, it also makes them out to be "stolen goods"—the kind of commodity that poisons civilized society. This conclusion is part of the "consumer revolution" of the eighteenth century, which transformed cultural standards of taste and produced new habits of consumption. The commercialization of British-American societies placed new pressure on the semantic distinction between "luxuries" and "necessities" and eventually redrew the boundaries between illicit and civilizing kinds of commodities.[61] During the Revolutionary era, as T. H. Breen has argued, colonial Americans created a new "semiotic order" of consumer goods as the symbolic medium to resist British authority.[62] While Revolutionary politics certainly shaped the subjects of consumption and enslavement, transatlantic ideologies about the relations among commerce, consumption, and cultural health lent discursive power to these subjects.[63]

Both British and American antislavery writers branded the slave trade as a form of cultural degeneration derived from the consumption of illicit goods. The West Indian export economy—the sugar, rum, tobacco, and indigo that flooded into colonial and metropolitan ports—became their main target. "And why is this cruelty practiced?" asked an antislavery writer in Mathew Carey's *American Museum*. The answer: "That we may have sugar in sweetened tea, that debilitates us—Rum to make punch, to intoxicate us—And indigo to dye our cloths."[64] The corruption of habits of consumption extended as well to West African societies. The antislavery tracts noted that the increase in European demand for slaves further stimulated the sales of luxuries and weapons to African leaders who, seduced by their power, engaged in wars for captives in order to meet this demand.[65] "That soul and body destroying liquor, rum" (in the words of minister Levi Hart) functions as both the corrupt medium of exchange as well as the trope for a form of trade based on the intoxication of one's senses.[66] The New Divinity minister Samuel Hopkins argued that "the inhabitants of the towns near the sea, are taught to exert all the art and power they have to entrap and decoy one another, that they may make slaves of them, and sell them to us for rum, by which they intoxicate themselves, and become more brutish and savage than otherwise they could be, so that there are but few instances of sobriety, honesty, or even humanity, and they who live the furthest from these places, are the least vicious, and much more civil and humane."[67]

This argument focused explicitly on the problem of cultural over-refinement that created new forms of enslavement. The French Catholic antislavery writer, the Abbé Gregoire, who corresponded from France with Jefferson over the problem of slavery, declared: "For three centuries Europe, which calls itself Christian and civilized, has tortured without pity and without remorse, the peoples of Africa whom Europe calls savages and barbarians. In order to obtain indigo, sugar, and coffee, Europe has brought them debauchery, desolation, and disregard of all natural sentiments."[68] This kind of hyperbolic language sometimes swelled to the point of cultural melodrama that staked the fate of "civilized" society on both its commercial relations and habits of consumption. The leading British antislavery politician William Fox, for example, called for English consumption of imports "unpolluted with blood." As members of Parliament dragged their heels in the

1790s on legislation abolishing the slave trade, Fox stated that proslavery interests could force slave sugar "to our lips, steeped in the blood of our fellow creatures; but they cannot compel us to accept the loathsome portion."[69]

The cultural context of consumption is important because it shifts the critical terms for understanding the representation of African humanity. The antislavery argument about consumption effectively recast the African slave as an imported—and dangerous—commodity. This rhetorical process occurred in context of the eighteenth-century Atlantic world's "triangular trade" which included the exchange of African slaves, New England rum, and West Indian sugar. Antislavery writing focused on the pathological nature of this commercial economy and yet became entangled in its representations of Africans as commodities for exchange.

West Indian planters, for example, were accused of buying "stolen goods." Certainly, this effect arose from the antislavery project of defining virtuous commerce and consumption—defining, in other words, what it meant to be a "civilized" consumer. This crucial issue turned on the question of who was responsible for buying stolen goods. One American strategy, apparent in Jefferson's *Declaration of Independence* or Benjamin Franklin's "A Conversation on Slavery" (1770), was to foist responsibility upon the British. More often, Anglo-American writing addresses the morality of consumption in terms of the categories of civilization and barbarity that transcended national terms. This lent new meaning to *caveat emptor.* The Scottish philosopher James Beattie, for example, argued emphatically that "though ignorant and barbarous nations, like those of Guinea, should sell their prisoners, it will not follow, that we have a right to buy them."[70] In "Notes on the Slave Trade," Benezet similarly mocked West Indian planters' pretended innocence when they claimed that their slaves were war captives and destined for bondage anyway: "Indeed, you say, 'I pay honestly for my goods; and I am not concerned to know where they are come by.' Nay but you are: You are deeply concerned, to know that they are not stolen: Otherwise you are partaker with the thief. . . . You know that they are procured by a deliberate series of more complicated villainy . . . than was ever practiced either by Mahometans or Pagans."[71]

Hence the antislavery figure of Africans as dangerous goods.[72] Even though these writers wanted to avoid formulating the antislavery debate on the ideological premises of their opponents, the primacy of the slave trade and the commercial logic underpinning it led almost inevitably into the consideration of Africans as a certain kind of transported commodities. This is apparent, for example, in Thomas Paine's antislavery essay for the *Pennsylvania Journal and the Weekly Advertiser.* Declaring the "wickedness" of a trade in *"an unnatural commodity,"* Paine's persona of the Lockean logician actually put him in the position of arguing about people as goods: "as the true owner has a right to reclaim his goods that were stolen, and sold; so the slave, who is proper owner of his freedom, has a right to reclaim it, however often sold."[73] Notwithstanding his plea for human rights, Paine's reduction of humanity to property, captured in the ethos of owning and buying one another, ends up fighting proslavery on its own terms. The argument unravels along the seams of the uncertain relation between property and humanity, where the African has a natural right to "his freedom"—something that paradoxically can be purchased and yet is an "unnatural commodity."

Antislavery claims for African humanity thus were undermined by its crucial arguments about commerce and civilization. In Volume 5 of *The Philosophical and Political History of the Settlements and Trade of the Europeans in the East and West Indies*, the Abbé Raynal denounces European corruption of African societies:

> Slaves are to the commerce of the Europeans in Africa, what gold is in the commerce we carry on in the New World. The heads of Negroes represent the specie of the state of Guinea. Every day this specie is carried off, and nothing is left them but articles of consumption. . . . Thus the trade for blacks would long since have been entirely lost, if the inhabitants of the coasts had not imparted their luxury to the people of the inland countries, from whence they now draw the greatest part of the slaves that are put into our hands. Thus the trade of the Europeans, by gradual advances, hath almost exhausted the only vendible commodities of this nation.[74]

The passage is representative of the antislavery rhetoric lamenting "vendible commodities" and "articles of consumption" while failing ultimately to recuperate African humanity. Africans are part of a luxury economy that finally depletes local populations and corrupts both the interior and coastal areas. The ironic edge that Raynal provides tends to become so coldly analytical that it all but loses the moral and sentimental appeal to the gross reduction of humans to commodities. This kind of analysis actually goes on at length as Raynal scrupulously surveys increases in slave prices, the costs subsequently passed on to West Indian consumers, and the inevitability of the trade's future decline.

The representational duality of Africans as consumers and commodities appears across a wide array of genres and forms during this era. Antislavery became a prominent theme in the periodicals that appealed to middlebrow readers of the late eighteenth century. In popular periodicals, antislavery expressed many of the same themes—and same problems—as it did in more learned orations and essays, although the former often employed the entertaining medium of satire or even burlesque. Consider a satirical anecdote that appeared in Mathew Carey's *American Museum*—one that was apparently so useful that Lydia Maria Child later recycled it in her *Anti-Slavery Catechism* (1839).

> A Negro fellow being strongly suspected to have stolen goods in his possession, was taken before a certain justice of peace in Philadelphia, and charged with the offense. The fellow was so hardened as to acknowledge the fact, and, to add to his crime, had the audacity to make the following speech: "massa justice, me know me got dem tings from Tom dere—and me tinke Tom teal dem too—but what den, massa? Dey be only a picaninny cork-screw and a picaninny knife—one cost sixpence and tudda a shilling— and me pay Tom for dem honestly, massa."
>
> "A very pretty story truly—you knew they were stolen, and yet allege in excuse, you paid honestly for them—I'll teach you better law than that, sirrah! Don't you know, Cesar, the receiver is as bad as the thief? You must be severely whipt, you black rascal you!"
>
> "Very well, massa—If de black rascal be wipt for buying tolen goods, me hope de white rascal be wipt too for same ting, when me catch him, as well as Cesar." "To be sure," rejoined his worship. "Well den," says Cesar, "here be Tom's massa—hold him fast, constable, he buy Tom as I buy de picaninny knife and de picaninny cork-screw. He know very well poor Tom be tolen from his old fadder and mudder; de knife and the cork-screw have neder."
>
> Whether it was that his worship, as well as Tom's master, were smote in the same instant with the justice or the severity of Cesar's application, we know not: but after a few minutes pause, Cesar was dismissed, and the action discharged.[75]

From the beginning, the comical sketch raises serious syntactic difficulties with the phrase "to have stolen goods." This forecasts the anecdote's thematic turn in reassigning guilt from Cesar to Tom's master. As a comic meditation on the ethics of consumption, its political message is structured upon the typical antislavery opposition between positive law and natural "justice"—at once a satiric personification in the constable and a more serious abstraction underlying the whole piece. Cesar's voice itself only heightens the satiric irony of the debunking proslavery claims to property rights. The sketch argues for racial equivalence: both Cesar and Tom's master are guilty of the same thing; both are human. Yet Cesar's voice just as readily undermines that equivalence. The dialogue in Cesar's voice between "picaninny" black dialect ("massa" and "dem tings") and conventional English ("as well as Cesar" and "Hold him fast, constable") expresses the uneasiness with which the sketch allows African Americans moral authority.

"Not Quite One to a Ton"

In the liberal interpretation, early antislavery writing and ideology oppose slavery on the grounds that it hampers free trade. Yet by "freeing" trade, antislavery did not argue for the unfettered market of laissez-faire capitalism but rather was calling for its regulation in order to make it more enlightened. "Liberty of commerce," Montesquieu argued, "is not a faculty granted to traders to do what they want; this would instead be the servitude of commerce."[76] The complexity of relations between antislavery culture and the emergence of liberalism in this era are apparent as well in the formulations of individual identity and of individual rights that came out of this writing. One of the major features of early antislavery discourse is the regulation of the rights to privacy. Early on, antislavery writers recognized the politics of privacy, and deliberately exposed private scenes of cruelty and abuse on slave ships and West Indian plantations as a way of penetrating these zones of horror. In *The Treatment and Conversion of the African Slaves*, for example, James Ramsay argued,

> And our constitution has such an excessive bias to personal liberty, that in contradiction to the maxims of every well ordered state, it cannot, or will not, meddle with private behaviour. . . . Hence the true secret of police, after having secured the lives, liberties, and properties of the citizens, is to turn the conduct and industry of individuals to public profit, considering the state as one whole, and leaving private persons, each to his own particular happiness in public prosperity, checking every appearance of a wayward disposition, that may make the man injurious to his neighbour, or unprofitable to his country[77]

The antislavery ethos of individual conscience places the very idea of autonomy in highly communal contexts. This is true for William Bell Crafton's summary of the report on the African slave trade that went to Parliament in the early 1790s. "Let no one say, 'my situation of privacy and obscurity precludes all possibility of serving the cause'—for the greatest numbers consist of units, and the most mighty exertions of states and empires are but aggregates of individual ability." Jettisoning the distinction between voting and nonvoting citizens, Crafton skirted the problem of political disfranchisement altogether. The appeal was to private individuals and the "public mind" simultaneously. That is, "individual" identity was regulated by its aggregate context.[78]

The antislavery discourse of regulation entailed the denunciation of "avarice" as the logic of maximizing profit. Perhaps the most vivid expression of the rejection of liberal rationality and utility was the print of the Liverpool slave vessel *Brookes,* which Thomas Clarkson had published in 1789.[79] Soon afterwards, the Philadelphia publisher Mathew Carey reproduced it in his magazine, the *American Museum,* along with an extract commenting on the picture written by the Plymouth chapter of the English antislavery society (see Figure 2). The reprinted image of the overcrowded slave ship testifies not only to the transatlantic traffic of antislavery discourses, but also to their specific repugnance for the logic of rational acquisitiveness. Its depiction of roughly 300 African bodies crammed into the lower deck of the *Brookes*—each figure generic, faceless, depersonalized, and metonymically significant within the context of rational utility—indicts the brutal logic of the capitalist market that is devoid of sentiment. As the British antislavery minister John Newton lamented, "With our ships the great object is, to be full."[80]

The *American Museum*'s preface to the British print appeals to a particular kind of feeling that arises from this economic logic of self-interest. Written presumably by Carey himself, it denounces "the barbarity of the slave trade":

> Here is presented to our view, one of the most horrid spectacles—a number of human creatures, packed, side by side, almost like herrings in a barrel, and reduced nearly to the state of being buried alive. . . . Where is the human being, that can picture to himself this scene of woe, without at the same time execrating a trade, which presents misery and desolation wherever it appears? Where is the man of real benevolence, who will not join heart and hand, in opposing this barbarous, this iniquitous traffic?[81]

Antislavery sentiment in this case arises from the tense identification between "the man of real benevolence" and the generic African slave, the

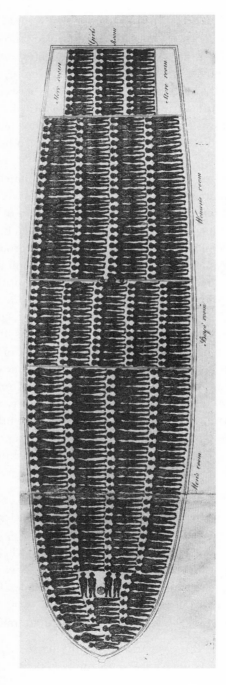

Figure 2. "Plan of an African Ship's Lower Deck, with Negroes, in the Proportion of not Quite One to a Ton." From *The American Museum* (Philadelphia, 1789).

complex process of intimacy and distance that was crucial to contemporary understandings of sympathy. The print's mathematical reduction of people to repeated configurations of space (the "sardine" effect) preserves this tension while highlighting the "horrid spectacle" of rational acquisitiveness. That is, the antislavery appeal depends on a reduction of people to space similar to that of the slave-trading plan for transport. The print's heading reads: "Plan of an African Ship's lower Deck, with Negroes, in the proportion of not quite one to a ton." The British context for this was Dolben's Act (1788),[82] which regulated slave-trading cargo, as the extract from the Plymouth antislavery society states, by the proportion of "five slaves for three tons." So this context raises the question of whether the *Brookes* was representative of the typical slave ship. The Plymouth chapter's commentary responds by claiming that "no ship, if her intended cargo can be procured, ever carries a less number than one to a ton, and the usual practice has been, to carry nearly double that number." (On one particular voyage the *Brookes* actually transported 609 slaves.) Antislavery sentimentalism, then, both denounces and requires the rational calculations of market capitalism.[83]

Antislavery also targeted the slave trade's speculative nature, likening it to gambling. Eighteenth-century cultural critics often stigmatized the practices of "gaming" and "speculation" as illicit activities (see Figure 3).[84] Indeed, gaming served as a trope for all of the precarious, speculative, and passionate qualities of illicit—as opposed to virtuous—forms of commercial capitalism. For example, in eighteenth-century Britain both lotteries and insurance companies were at the very least considered suspect forms of capitalism that were tainted with the vice of speculation. This, in turn, posed the dilemma of how to regulate such capitalist ventures. As one historian of eighteenth-century British society has put it, "How was it possible to draw a line which would outlaw morally dubious forms of insurance without penalizing respectable companies and threatening the legitimate interests of trade and property?"[85]

Antislavery tracts made the most of the negative cultural meanings of "gaming" in order to condemn the slave trade as wild and uncontrollable speculation in the capitalist market. By employing this trope it drew the line between speculative and legitimate—or irrational and prudent—forms of trade. (One British politician during Parliamentary debates claimed that "The African is, or at least was, a speculative trade,"[86] and the Abbé Raynal warned French merchants to "prefer an honest to a more lucrative speculation."[87]) Clarkson pursued the rhetorical potential of the commercial trope

GAMING.

The Diversion of Cards and Dice, however Engaging, are oftner Provocatives to Avarice and Loss of Temper, than mere Recreations and innocent Amusements.

Here Scaramouch and Harlequin, at Gaming can't agree;
They Quarrel, and poor Scaramouch is tumbl'd down you see.

All Cheats at Cards, still gaping for their prey,
Quarrels create; and Mischiefs follow Play:
It loses Time, disturbs y̆ Mind and Sense,
Whilst Oaths and Lies are oft the consequence;
And Murders, sometimes, follow loss of Pence.

John Bickham Scrip:

Figure 3. "Gaming." From *The Universal Penman* (London, 1741).

by puncturing the economic logic of slave trading: "It is evident first, that if a person were to become the proprietor of all the tickets in the wheel, the balance would be greatly against him. So also, were he to be proprietor of all the ships in the slave trade, he would experience a considerable loss, as his disbursements would be then greater than his returns. . . . Why do people engage in *the games of chance?*"[88]

In American writings, the correlation of slave trading with gambling recalled the legislation passed by the Continental Congress during the 1770s.[89] In the early 1790s, for example, the Delaware Quaker Warner Mifflin wrote an address to the U.S. House of Representatives in which he denounced the Constitution's support of an "inhuman traffic" that would surely bring down divine vengeance upon republican hypocrites. Contrasting the nation's present cowardice with its Revolutionary courage, Mifflin noted that the Continental Congress had banned the slave trade. In making his case he shrewdly juxtaposed two parts of the legislative record in the 1770s:

> 2nd Article. "We will neither import nor purchase any slaves imported after the first day of December next, after which time we will wholly discontinue the Slave Trade, and will neither be concerned in it ourselves, nor will we hire our vessels, nor sell our commodities or manufactures to those who are concerned in it."
>
> 8th Article. "And will discountenance and discourage every species of extravagance and dissipation, especially all horse racing, and all kinds of gaming, cock-fighting, exhibitions of shews, plays, and other expensive diversions and entertainments."[90]

The strategic alignment of these two articles defines enlightened commerce by contrasting it with its toxic foil. In this sequence, the two prohibitions assail essentially the same thing. Both the African slave trade and vices such as gaming are equivalent forms of "dissipation." Reading the present moment of Constitutional foundations through the history of the 1770s casts doubt upon the national future. The only way to preserve it is to regulate the passions stimulating barbaric behavior.

The "Hidden Treasures" of Africa

The antislavery project of establishing "free" trade with Africa proposed new forms of imperial control. By "civilizing" Africans, antislavery advocates reimagined Africans as consumers of European goods other than the rum and firearms that presumably had corrupted these societies for centuries. Mary Louise Pratt has noted that the formation of the English Abolition Society occurred at virtually the same time as that of the English Association for Promoting the Discovery of the Interior Parts of Africa. The latter meant to replace the slave trade with supposedly new and enlightened economic relations. Such a program, as she argues, would transform Africa from a source of commodities to a fully developed commercial market. Capitalist ideology's "mystique of reciprocity"—its ideal of "equilibrium through exchange"—legitimated a more profound control over African societies than the slave trade had ever effected.[91] More than the rationale for commercial exploitation, the mystique of reciprocity provided the terms of *cultural* exchange through which eighteenth-century antislavery writing recuperated the "civilized" quality of British and American societies. The antislavery supporters dreamed of new kinds of raw materials within Africa. While Africans would receive the presumably civilizing effects of enlightened trade, so too would Britons and Americans who had divorced themselves from barbaric traffic.

Much of this argument derived from the influential writings by Malachy Postlethwayt and Anthony Benezet. One theme common to both was the financial and cultural profit of establishing "free" trade with Africa. The New Haven minister James Dana, for example, cited Postlethwayt at great length in his "The African Slave Trade" (1791), arguing that "No country is richer in gold and silver. . . . The fruitful rich lands, every where to be found upon the coasts and within the country . . . would produce all the richest articles of the East and West-India commerce."[92] When celebrating the abolition of the slave trade, the orthodox minister Jedidiah Morse's oration concluded by asking an African American audience, "Pardon our accumulated and dreadful guilt, and enable us to repay to Africa that heavy debt which we have incurred by the wrongs we have done to her. May our vessels now sail under thy protection, to bear thither, with a guiltless commerce, the blessings of peace and civilization, and the glad tidings of the Gospel of the Son."[93] The fantasy of "guiltless commerce" imagined a profound involvement in African societies. James Swan invoked Postlethwayt's ideas when he called for "a friendly and humane Commerce with these people" that extended "into the very center of their extended country" rather "than . . . skimming a trifling portion of Trade upon the Coast of *Africa*." Swan envisions the potential for "a great and profitable Commerce" that entailed the "need to travel into the Heart of Africa."[94] For Swan and many like him, the conversion from barbaric to civilized trade re-maps Africa both economically and epistemologically—that is, trade now penetrates the coastal areas inward, enacting another, more subtle, form of seduction.[95]

This vision looked to the improvement of African manners. By the time antislavery movements gained momentum in the 1770s, the very notion of African civilization was highly ambiguous and politically volatile. Both proslavery and antislavery writers were able to draw on a fairly substantial archive of European accounts of West Africa, since many narratives appeared in such multivolume anthologies as *Churchill's Collections* (1704, 1744–46) and *Astley's Collections* (1745–47). These accounts by slave traders, sea captains, factors, physicians, naturalists, and other eyewitnesses to the West African societies provided abundant details about trade, manners, agriculture, family life, social organization, and tribal politics.[96] Antislavery writing selectively culled from these sources evidence of African social and family life. No better example of this exists than the beginning of Equiano's *Interesting Narrative* (1789), much of which was taken the from Anthony Benezet's *Some Historical Account of Guinea* (1771). Roxann Wheeler is right to point out that the ambivalence of antislavery's defenders of African "civilization" helps to complicate the supposed opposition between proslavery and antislavery ideologies.[97] Notwithstanding its refutation of African savagery, antislavery writing allowed for European improvements in African culture through free and enlightened trade. As Postlethwayt rhetorically asked, "Whether Commerce in general has not proved the great means of civilizing all nations, even the most savage and brutal; and why not the *Africans?*" In this newly imagined free exchange of raw materials for commercial goods, Africa would receive the most precious commodity of all—the ability of trade to improve manners.

The self-interest this argument served reveals a particularly antislavery form of commercial speculation. Consider, for example, Joseph Priestley's expectation regarding British exports to West Africa: "In a country of that vast extent, if we favoured the civilization of it, as by our intercourse we might do, instead of contributing to keep it in that state of savage barbarity in which it is at present, the inhabitants, having already a fondness for many of our commodities, would soon arrive at a state in which they would want more of them."[98] Similarly, Thomas Clarkson argued that "free" trade "would soften and polish their manners, and would bring them to a state of refinement. . . . This civilization would be productive of the most beneficial effects to ourselves, for in proportion as we civilize a people, we *increase their wants;* and we should create therefore, from this circumstance alone, another source *of additional consumption of our manufactures.*"[99] Comments of this sort were numerous, and if their appeal to financial profits is transparent to us today, the language of trade and manners ("savage barbarity," "polish," "civilization," and so forth) went a long way in justifying such obvious exploitation of raw materials and potential markets. Antislavery naturalized the arbitrary distinction between "healthy" and "diseased" consumer goods, replacing the African slave with presumably legitimate kinds of raw materials in Africa. It thereby converted former African commodities into new African consumers who, now, were supposedly free from the wiles of commercial seduction.

Eighteenth-century antislavery writing refers to two kinds of enslavement: the persecution of Africans and the cultural depravity of Anglo-Americans. Both peoples are enslaved to the same kind of commercial relations; each finds itself in a kind of "bondage." Antislavery writing made such an evaluation in an era when liberal capitalism was just emerging. It sentimentalized commerce for its own political purposes by dichotomizing civilized and barbaric kinds of trade. It thereby legitimated the larger field of commercial capitalism, especially the imperial activity of "free" trade with sub-Saharan Africa. This narrative of commerce thus regulated commerce culturally and, in a literary context, engendered notable rhetorical conventions and tensions that affected a wide variety of antislavery genres. Thematically, the cultural issues embedded in antislavery writing include the nature of cultural authority (founded upon biblical precept yet giving way to enlightened Christianity); the nature of Africans (as seduced consumer, poisonous consumer goods, and then, again, as civilized consumers); and the nature of commercial language (when "trade" becomes "gaming").

While various literary figures took up the subject of the African slave trade for purposes of addressing the moral state of the nation, they did so through the discourses of commerce, manners, and enlightenment, which circulated widely and vigorously throughout the Atlantic world. The commercial jeremiad is an important part of Anglo-American literary history. Its major thematic and rhetorical features—the sentimental persona, prophetic and apocalyptic overtones, the ideal connection between trade and enlightened manners, its fear of luxury and decadent consumption, and the simultaneous commodification and feminization of African society—significantly shaped literary representations of the African slave trade.

CHAPTER 2

The Poetics of Antislavery

Oh AFRICA, thou loud proclaimer of the rapacity, the treachery, the cruelty of civilized man!

> —Samuel Miller, *A Discourse Delivered April 12, 1797, at the Request of and Before the New-York Society for Promoting the Manumission of Slaves*

Inhuman ye! who ply the human trade,
And to the West a captive people lead;
Who brother, sister, father, mother, friend,
In one unnat'ral hapless ruin blend.
Barbarians! steel'd to ev'ry sense of woe,
Shame of the happy source from whence ye flow:
The time may come, when, scorning savage sway,
Afric may triumph, and ev'n you obey!

> —*Jamaica, a Poem* (1777)

Contemplating the future of America while he was serving as foreign minister to Portugal in the 1790s, the Connecticut Wit David Humphreys wrote *A Poem on Industry*. It generally called for the expansion of both domestic manufactures and the navy, which were resonant subjects as the United States became embroiled in political conflicts with Great Britain. One of the real crises that Humphreys faced, however, was American participation in the African slave trade. The moment the poem turns to this subject, it begins to display some of the major features of antislavery poetics that I take up in this chapter:

AH! ye who love the human race divine,
And fondly wish to cherish all who pine;
In milk of human kindness bless the free,
Which soon shall help to set the bondman free;

> For soon shall int'rest man's fierce wrath assuage,
> And heav'n restrain the remnant of his rage.
>   NOT long shall human flesh be bought and sold,
> The Charities of life exchang'd for gold!
> For soon shall Commerce, better understood,
> Teach happier barter for the mutual good.[1]

In a rather high-handed manner, the passage mobilizes the language of commercial exchange. Such language is premised on the moral and sentimental understanding of commerce as a cultural as well as economic transaction, and it rejects the idea of trafficking in "human flesh." The cultural problem is connected to a metaphysical one. When Americans, Humphreys suggests, decide to engage exclusively in enlightened forms of "barter"—the kind of trade that reconciles "int'rest" with "mutual good"—they will avoid the "rage" of divine vengeance. By renouncing the slave trade, the United States enters the "golden chain" of commercial nations, a cultural ideal upon which both American and British antislavery poetry was founded.[2]

Humphreys' image of commercial civilization, however, relies upon the contrasting one of African savagery. While other Anglo-American antislavery poets such as William Roscoe idealized the affective simplicity of African manners, Humphreys contrasts American culture with what he elsewhere calls the "savage indolence" of "Afric's Sable Sons." The poem might affirm African humanity by condemning the slave trade, but it also partly withdraws that affirmation by re-establishing the hierarchy that slave trading itself unsettles. Hence its ambiguity: "WHAT tho' eternal darkness shades the race, / Tho' grosser features vilify the face / . . . . Are they not made to ruminate the sky? / Or must they perish like the beasts that die?"[3] To our ears, this language sounds patronizingly racist. But rather than simply condemn the poem in those terms, let us pause over its understanding of race. For one thing, the poem spends a lot more time contemplating the cultural enslavement of Americans than it does the physical enslavement of Africans. For another, the "eternal darkness" shading the African race might just as readily reflect the cultural terms of Christianity and Enlightenment as the physical conditions of skin color and appearance.

These mitigating factors are important because much recent work on antislavery literature emphasizes the genre's "racial" bias. Such an argument usually turns on the critique of antislavery sentimentalism as either an aesthetic deformity or the rhetorical means by which Anglo-Americans talk about themselves rather than about suffering African slaves.[4] More recent accounts certainly are more attuned to the complexities of eighteenth-century sentimental culture, but they still emphasize the presumably racial and political limitations of this discourse. Markman Ellis has argued that in early British novels about slavery, "Sentimentalist writers found it difficult to cross certain limits in their portrayal of the victims of social and economic change without endangering the entire system of values by which their world was ordered, and this they were disinclined to do."[5] Sentimental antislavery poetry, Julie Ellison maintains, generally did its best to maintain racial hierarchies: "The literary history of eighteenth-century masculine pathos was demonstrably inseparable from the racial imagination of a colonial and imperial culture. . . . Racial, ethnic and national differences became efficient vehicles for translating sensibility into narratives of inequality. The ideological malleability of sentiment as a relationship available to conservatives, liberals, and radicals of the right and the left, relies on the ubiquity of race."[6]

Here I want to recast the argument emphasizing the problem of racial equality in antislavery writing. Rather than focus upon the African's failure sufficiently to "rise," I turn to the Anglo-American's ability to "fall." Antislavery poetry consistently thematized this problem of cultural declension caused by the African slave trade. Consequently, it considered the rather troubling equivalence between "civilized" and "savage" societies. This motif has important ramifications for how we think about race in this genre. One recent critic has argued that "the debate about the slave-trade was conducted within the parameters of a larger discourse about race."[7] But just the opposite was true. The subject of racial difference was framed by the more flexible categories of savagery, civilization, commerce, and manners. Specifically, in antislavery poetry, the figure of the savage European slave trader confounded racial distinctions between Europeans and Africans. As one English minister declared in 1792, the slave trader "may call himself a *Christian;* or a disciple of Him that *went about doing good;* but the amiable character is profaned by his traffic in man: for it becomes none but a savage, or a votary of Moloch."[8] In other words, the slave trader is the third term of antislavery poetry. He both supplements and undermines the opposition between Europeans and Africans. The story that eighteenth-century antislavery poetry tells is of the collapse and reconstitution of the cultural distance between Christians and Africans. The genre's major literary conventions—the savage slave trader, the pastoral representation of Edenic Africa, the "dying" African speaker, the pathos of the slave's suicide—are the poetic means of accomplishing these dual imperatives.

Noah's Color

During the period in which English and American antislavery movements were gaining momentum, "race" traditionally signified the concept of a group, nation or people, and it suggested, rather loosely, the overlapping relations among family, lineage, and locale in determining identity.[9] Consider, for example, the early antislavery piece, "The Speech of Moses Bon Saam" (1735), which recounts the sentiments of an escaped slave during a rebellion in Jamaica in the 1730s. Lamenting the practice of perpetual bondage, he asks, "But did they also *buy* his *Race?* Must the *Children's Children* of this *Wretch's Children* be *begotten,* and *transmitted* to *Slavery,* because that single Wretch himself was unsuccessful in a Battle, and had been put to *Sale* instead of *Slaughter?*"[10] The possibility that race designates either one's family or one's African heritage—or perhaps the uncertain combination of the two—suggests the kind of semantic instability characterizing the term.[11]

During the latter part of the eighteenth century, the concept of race gradually came to signify differences in physical appearance.[12] In this transitional period, writers were still able to challenge proslavery assertions about African inferiority, though, as Roxann Wheeler has argued, these debates often produced ambiguous, overlapping arguments.[13] Challenges to racial ideology abound in antislavery writing. In *Letters on Slavery* (1789), William Dickson, the former secretary to the governor of Barbados, proclaimed: "I call colour (the principal difference in the varieties of men) a very equivocal mark of superiority. . . . The white man reasons thus, The negro's *colour* is different than mine, *ergo* I am naturally superior to the Negro. Might not the copper-coloured man, or an olive-coloured man, or a tawney man, or a *black* man thus demonstrate the natural superiority of men of *his own colour,* to all others?"[14] In post-Revolutionary Connecticut, the minister Jonathan Edwards, Jr., similarly argued that "Their colour is indeed different than ours. But does this give us the right to enslave them? The nations from Germany to Guinea have complexions of every shade from the fairest white, to a jetty black: and if a black complexion subject a nation or an individual to slavery; where shall slavery begin? Or where shall it end?"[15]

Thomas Clarkson's *Essay on the Slavery and Commerce of the Human Species* (1786) attacked the biblical justification for racial inferiority. Clarkson went right to the heart of the proslavery argument by attacking the racial exegesis of Genesis 9, which recounted Noah's curse upon the Hammites, the presumed ancestors of all Africans. Mocking the smug assurance with which his adversaries maintained the "whiteness" of Old Testament patriarchs, Clarkson theorized "that the complexion of Noah and his sons, from whom the rest of the world were descended, was the same as that, which is peculiar to the country, which was the seat of their habitation. This, by such a mode of decision, will be found a dark olive; a beautiful colour, and a just medium between white and black." Europeans should "be cautious how they deride those of the opposite complexion, as there is great reason to presume, that *the purest white is as far removed from the primitive colour as the deepest black.*"[16] This argument, taken to its extreme, questioned the semiotics of race in general. Clarkson's contemporary James Ramsay, for example, did just this, claiming "that these signs [of skin color] are mere arbitrary impressions, that neither give nor take away animal or rational powers."[17]

During the period between the 1760s and 1790s, the categories of culture and Christianity still carried enough ideological weight for antislavery writing to contest effectively the emergent modern understandings of racial difference. As Paul Gilroy put it, "Notions of the primitive and the civilized which had been integral to pre-modern understanding of 'ethnic' differences became fundamental cognitive and aesthetic markers in the processes which generated a constellation of subject positions in which Englishness, Christianity, and other ethnic and racialised attributes would finally give way to the dislocating dazzle of 'whiteness.'"[18] Gilroy's commentary is particularly compelling in light of the contested nature of such terms as "Englishness," "Christianity," and "manners" during this era. English culture in this period tried to dichotomize the cultural meanings of "politeness" and "barbarity" in order to distinguish "between modernity and the past, between England and the Continent, and between the 'western' and the 'non-western.'"[19] But, as a barbaric activity, the slave trade undermined this project, while destabilizing the semantics of cultural key words directly associated with racial identity.

The contingency of race upon the category of culture facilitated complex identifications—or misidentifications—of Anglo-Americans and African slaves.[20] As Karen Halttunen has argued, the dynamics of most forms of sentimental identification in the wake of Adam Smith's *Theory of Moral Sentiments* (1759) simultaneously required intimacy and distance from sympathetic observers. "Although spectatorial sympathy claimed to demolish social distance, it actually rested on social distance—a distance reinforced, in sentimental art, by the interposition of written text, stage, or canvas between the virtuous spectator and the (imaginary) suffering victim."[21] The antislavery strategy of role reversal heightened the emotional effects of political writing while ultimately preserving that cultural distance. But in order to pursue the logic of the humanitarian argument, it called upon readers to "see" themselves as African slaves. The Dissenting minister Joseph Priestley, for example, urged readers to imagine Africans "who have the same feelings with ourselves" and to consider their suffering "as we should do, if any [of us] were violently seized, conveyed away from all our friends, and confined to hard labour all our lives in Africa."[22] Similarly, the Connecticut minister Levi Hart projected his audience onto the shores of West Africa, where, "from you a race of abject slaves will, probably, be propagated down for hundreds of years!"[23]

This rhetorical strategy took on another form as well. Acting on the general assumption (theorized so influentially by Montesquieu) that slavery corrupted everyone involved, antislavery writers often collapsed the distinction between "civilized" and "savage" cultures. This argument significantly jeopardized the belief in historical progress. Noah Webster, for one, associated the despotism of slavery with a process "that in its operation . . . not only checks the progress of civilization, but actually converts the civilized man into a savage; at least so far as respects the humane affections of the heart."[24] Similarly, the English minister John Newton argued that those repeatedly exposed to the slave trade "are liable to imbibe a spirit of ferociousness, and savage insensibility, of which human nature, depraved as it is, is not, ordinarily, capable."[25] In this spirit, the Pennsylvanian William Belsham mocked the United States Congress for its refusal to hear petitions against the slave trade, "which is itself the most flagrant of all abuses which the annals of the world exhibit, would disgrace the understandings, and detract from the dignity even of a Convention of Hottentots."[26] Yet such irony actually cuts both ways. Satire depends upon the "savage" presence of the African, creating tonal ambiguities; while the slave trade makes us savage, we are more civilized than heathens. Antislavery writing inscribes these dual identities, enforcing the identification with poor Africans and with barbaric, heartless traders. Asking readers to imagine themselves as Africans, it reproaches them for having become "savage" themselves. The poetics of antislavery is about exploiting and containing these enforced identifications across cultural borders.

Savage Trade

Early antislavery poetry represents the slave trade as a cultural crisis in enlightened civilization. Like narrative forms of antislavery, the poetry denouncing the African slave trade was premised on a modern understanding of Christian behavior. As a poem written for Harvard's commencement in 1792, "The Nature and Progress of Liberty," lamented, "Blush, Despots, blush! Who fir'd by sordid ore, / Like pirates, plunder AFRIC's swarming shore, / To western worlds the shackled slave trepan, / And basely traffic in 'the souls of man!'"[27] In the attempt to resuscitate Christian civilization, antislavery poetry consistently sets the slave trade outside the parameters of civilized trade and the slave trader himself outside civilized society. In Thomas Morris's *Quashy, or the Coal-Black Maid* (1797), for example, the speaker exhorts:

> Say what the gains thro' all these dangers sought:
> Why, from black princes men are cheaply bought;
> And those for cruelty and av'rice known,
> Joy to find hearts as savage as their own?
> O Liverpool, O Bristol, brave not fame;
> Bid your youth feel, and hide their fathers' shame;
> Extend their commerce; trade where'er they can;
> But never more presume to deal in man.[28]

These lines make use of the thematic conventions of what I have called the commercial jeremiad, particularly the intentional confusion of the categories of civilization and savagery. In this case, Morris does just that. Obviously, he indicts the major commercial of centers of British slave trading, but he also more subtly suggests the cultural equivalence between African princes and English merchants who "deal in man."

The poetic expression of this unfortunate misalliance often takes the form of bestial tropes conveying the theme of dehumanization. This poetry confounds the Christian/savage dichotomies. This certainly is the case for British West Indian Bryan Edwards, whose antislavery sentiments were at best ambiguous.[29] In "Ode on Seeing a Negro Funeral," for example, Edwards prophesies to his fellow Jamaicans that their inhumanity will lead inevitably to slave rebellions. Only planter compassion can avert the "avenging rod" of "Africk's god":

> Soon, Christian, thou, in wild dismay,
> Of Africk's ruthless rage the prey,
>   Shalt roam th'affrighted wood:
> Transform'd to tygers, fierce and fell,
> Thy race shall prowl with savage yell,
>   And glut their rage for blood![30]

This image suggests not only providential violence but (as in Alexander Falconbridge's depiction of the West Indian slave market) a *particular* kind of cultural crisis. Notably, the poem imagines the transformation from men into beasts, but its awkward syntax confuses the subject of this transformation. The lines would seem to depict the slave rebellion as newly transformed African "tygers" hunting English "prey." Yet, following the colon, the singular "Thy race" could refer to the "thou"—the Christian addressee—preceding it. Is there any difference, in other words, between those who "roam" and the ones who "prowl"—between English and African beasts?

Such equivalence is a major argument in British women poets writing against slavery in this era. Either ignored or undervalued by traditional accounts of British literary history, poets like Ann Yearsley, Anna Letitia Barbauld, and Hannah More were politically quite influential at this time.[31] The recent critical recovery of their importance, however, generally has focused on the sexual politics of equating the position of British women with that of African slaves.[32] But the cultural significance of women's antislavery writing extends beyond sexual politics per se.

Known as "Lactilla," the famous milk-woman of Bristol, Ann Yearsley and her family were on the brink of starvation (as contemporary lore had it) when sympathetic patrons rescued them.[33] Bristol was one of the leading slave-trading centers in the world, and Yearsley would have witnessed the same abundance of material signs—ships, advertisements for runaways, and captains' slaves—that inspired, for example, Samuel Taylor Coleridge's antislavery writings.[34] Deeply invested in both Christian piety and cultural reform, Yearsley put them both to use to manipulate the many meanings of "enslavement" at the beginning of her well-known *A Poem on the Inhumanity of the Slave Trade* (1788):

> Bristol, thine heart hath throbb'd to glory.—Slaves
> E'en Christian slaves, have shook their chains, and gaz'd
> With wonder and amazement on thee. Hence
> Ye grov'ling souls, who think the term I give,
> Of Christian slave, a paradox! to *you*
> I do not turn, but leave you to conception
> Narrow; with that be blest, nor dare to stretch
> Your shackled souls along the course of *Freedom*.[35]

Yearsley plays off spiritual and physical forms of slavery in order to tweak her local audience's epistemological limitations, which in effect constitute another important form of cultural enslavement to debased custom. In this way, she turns her back on "thou slave of avarice" (p. 4) and focuses instead on "more enlightened beings." Yet such a distribution of readers has left a troubling third term in its wake: the "Christian slave," who is figured ambiguously in two guises: as the spiritually innocent slave, and the spiritually depraved (or "shackled") Christian of the antislavery imagination.

The poem then goes on to connect the potentially unregenerate reader with the corrupted slave trader in order to explode all of the false pretenses of Christian civilization. Structurally, the poem combines the antislavery convention of the broken African (or, in this case Indian) family with abstract philosophical meditations on the nature of commerce, culture, and civilization. The story of the captive Luco, who is separated from his family and his amour Incilanda, services these meditations. Yearsley's main target is the Bristol slave trader, the "crafty merchant" whose face lights up in "horrid joy" as "he grasps / The wish'd-for gold, purchase of human blood!" (p. 6). She exposes the hypocrisy of the slave merchant who hides behind the rationale of making a living for his own children by pointing to the scene of "human woe, / Tho' drest in savage guise!" (p. 3). Asking the slave trader to imagine his own children stolen by foreigners, Yearsley advances the poem's chief indictment: "Curse on the toils spread by a Christian hand / To rob the Indian of his freedom! Curse / On him who from a bending parent steals / His dear support of age, his darling child" (p. 5). Enforced identification thus ultimately facilitates the poem's grander theme of "social love" that ideally liberates Bristol society from the "fetters" of "avarice" (pp. 28–9).

Yet this imaginative reconstruction of trade founders on the representation of Lady Commerce:

> Advance, ye Christians, and oppose my strain:
> Who dares condemn it? Prove from laws divine,
> From deep philosophy, or social love,
> That ye derive your privilege. I scorn
> The cry of Av'rice, or the trade that drains
> A Fellow-creature's blood: bid Commerce plead
> Her publick good, her nation's many wants,
> Her sons thrown idly on the beach, forbade
> To seize the image of their God and sell it:—
> I'll hear her voice, and Virtue's hundred tongues

Shall sound against her. Hath our public good
Fell rapine for its basis? Must our wants
Find their supply in murder? Shall the sons
Of Commerce shiv'ring stand, if not employ'd,
Worse than the midnight robber? (pp. 25–6)

Structured as a rhetorical question, the passage addresses the very nature of commerce with some uncertainty. This is stylistically expressed in the poetic enjambment disrupting the rhythm of the speaker's voice. The task for the speaker is to distinguish between commerce and "Av'rice." Yet what of Lady Commerce's sons, thrown idly upon the west coast of Africa and forbidden to barter for human souls? She would seem to be culpable. So to address her possible duplicity, the speaker invokes the "hundred tongues" of virtue. If this collective voice overwhelms the slave-trade apologists, the passage nevertheless raises questions that resist easy solutions. What, for example, is economic "necessity" as opposed to "luxury"? How does one define the "publick good"?

One way of addressing these dilemmas was to recast them in an imperial context of cultural relations between metropole and colonies. As the historian Seymour Drescher has argued, British society traditionally deflected the problem of slavery as a flawed institution that lay safely "beyond the line" of metropolitan society.[36] Antislavery poetics shorten this distance. A notable example of this is Anna Letitia Barbauld's "Epistle to William Wilberforce, Esq. On the Rejection of the Bill for abolishing the Slave Trade" (1791).[37] Written in the wake of a major political defeat for the abolitionists in the early 1790s, the poem directly connects metropolitan and colonial manners rather than contrast them, recasting the West Indies from Britain's foil into its cultural metonym. The poem is structured as a comparative analysis of dual societies connected by egregious forms of commerce, and it argues that the corruption of Parliamentary politics—particularly the proslavery and sugar interests—finds both its parallel and cause in the corruption of the West Indies.

The poem initially considers Wilberforce's failed effort to end the slave trade. Skeptical as it is about the prospects for English abolitionism, it still emphasizes Wilberforce's moral stature, which highlights the proslavery lobby's "flimsy sophistry" and "artful gloss."[38] Especially infuriated about the "jests unseemly" and "horrid mirth" that occurred during Parliamentary debates over the slave trade bill, Barbauld begins to make the connection between metropolitan and colonial corruption by suggesting that the crisis in national politics is a crisis in national culture. With Yearsley, Barbauld laments Britain's "shrinking soul" (l.10). Hence the bill's defeat means much more than political failure, for Barbauld warns: "Forbear!—thy virtues but provoke our doom, / And swell th'account of vengeance yet to come" (ll.41–2). After condemning Parliament, the poem shifts scenes and transatlantically extends the contexts for cultural declension.

Such a connection is forged primarily through the discourses of disease. (Thus writers about Philadelphia's yellow fever epidemics during the 1790s represented the slave trade as a physical and cultural pathology.) In the "Epistle to Wilberforce" Barbauld engages in a similar strategy. In crucial passages the poem simultaneously critiques both West Indian culture and the "nabobs of the East India Company."[39] Both are plagued by "voluptuous ease" that endangers the health of metropolitan culture.[40] This in itself, as many recently have noted, associates disease with effeminacy:[41]

> Nor less from the gay East, on essenc'd wings,
> Breathing unnam'd perfumes, Contagion springs;
> The soft luxurious plague alike pervades
> The marble palaces, and rural shades. . .
> The manners melt—One undistinguished blaze
> O'erwhelms the sober pomp of elder days;
> Corruption follows with gigantic stride,
> And scarce vouchsafes his shameless front to hide:
> The spreading leprosy taints ev'ry part,
> Infects each limb, and sickens at the heart.
> Simplicity! most dear of rural maids,
> Weeping resigns her violated shades:
> Stern Independence from his glebe retires,
> And anxious Freedom eyes her drooping fires;
> By foreign wealth are British morals chang'd,
> And Afric's sons, and India's, smile aveng'd. (ll.86–9, 94–105)

This kind of characterization of West Indian corruption of planters was typical of the antislavery perspective from London. In *The West Indies* (1809), for example, James Montgomery similarly debunked the "dull Creole" as the embodiment of aristocratic effeminacy: "Voluptuous minions fan him to repose / Prone on the noonday couch he lolls in vain."[42] Barbauld recasts the critique as a disease that, by implication, infects Britain through the medium of commerce: the "foreign wealth" that "melts" manners and morals alike. The feminization of such a pathology, however, is further complicated by the equally potent image of feminized "Simplicity," the return to pastoral origins about which the poem fantasizes. Moreover, these gendered images actually describe the difference between the benevolent affections and the unregulated passions—the boundary that, after all, the commercial jeremiad meant to police.

The "Epistle to Wilberforce" generally neglects the plight of African slaves. It is addressed to a famous British political activist, scorns its complacent British audience, and extends its purview into the West Indies chiefly as a way of considering what is wrong with British culture in the 1790s. I have argued that the problem of commodification—the association of Africans with transported goods—is endemic to antislavery literature. But did colonial poets, who lived more intimately with the realities of slavery, share Barbauld's metropolitan vision—did they similarly displace chattel with cultural forms of enslavement?

Philip Freneau's status as the first American poet to write extensively about the West Indies makes him a viable candidate for exploring this question. Since much of Freneau's antislavery work postdates American independence, the context shifts from a colonial to a national category. But I want to consider Freneau in the larger context of the cultural discourses about the slave trade circulating throughout the late eighteenth-century Atlantic world. His numerous poems on the West Indies derived from his personal experiences there, beginning in the 1770s, when (much to the damage of his reputation later on) he escaped the American Revolutionary war to the island of Santa Cruz (now St. Croix). There he lived for two years and learned to be a mariner, a vocation he later took up seriously during several periods of his life in the 1780s and early 1800s. This body of poetry covers standard Freneauvian themes: the mutability of existence in "Lines Written at Port Royal"; the sublime forces of nature in "The Hurrricane"; the tension between his appreciation for West Indian beauty and his repugnance for despotic power, which shapes, for example, "The Beauties of Santa Cruz."

First published in 1791 as "The Island Field Negro," Freneau's most famous antislavery poem was later retitled "To Sir Toby, a Sugar Planter in the Interior Parts of Jamaica, Near the City of San Jago de le Vega, 1784."[43] Like Barbauld's "Epistle to Wilberforce," it focuses upon the West Indies as the site of bodily violence and cultural corruption. The initial image of the slave's branding, for example, not only suggests his new identity, or name, but connects such brutality to the debased habits of consumption engendered by the West Indian export economy: "But kindled RUM too often burns as blue; / In which some fiend, whom nature must detest, / Steeps Toby's brand, and marks poor Cudjoe's breast" (p. 192). Freneau does not include a scene from the United States (as did Barbauld for England, in depicting Parliament) with which to measure and compare West Indian corruption. In fact, Freneau's poem goes out of its way to localize African slavery in the West Indies. Its subtitle takes the reader into the "interior of Jamaica," and its footnotes clarifying Jamaican customs, manners, and places —slave staples, maroons, Jamaican legal codes—strengthen the point. One should note that Freneau was not the only American antislavery writer to foist the problem onto the West Indies as a way of deflecting American guilt. The Connecticut Federalist Timothy Dwight, for example, in Part II of *Greenfield Hill* (1794), emphasized the relative mildness and humanity of Connecticut slavery. Ignoring the situation at home, Freneau voices republican hostility against the aristocratic trappings of the British empire, focusing his scorn exclusively on West Indian "despots" associated with "nature's plagues."[44]

Yet the poet's consideration of the plantation's larger commercial connections makes this localizing strategy untenable. Trade expands the scope and meaning of slavery. Whereas most antislavery writing during this era was structured upon the logical sequence of placing the slave trade before slavery—the idea being that abolishing the one would end the other—Freneau reverses this structure. The poem's dissection of the brutality of the representative plantation segues into its consideration of the commercial Atlantic. As the speaker indicts the planter's illicit wealth ("Angola's natives scourged by ruffian hands, / And toil's hard product shipp'd to foreign lands"), the poem significantly turns from slavery to the slave trade:

> Here Stygian paintings light and shade renew,
> Pictures of hell, that Virgil's pencil drew:
> Here, surly Charons make their annual trip,
> And ghosts arrive in every Guinea ship,
> To find what BEASTS these western isles afford,
> Plutonian scourges, and despotic lords:— (p. 193)

As Freneau's footnote makes clear, these lines are his version of the Virgilian underworld found in Book 6 of *The Aeneid*. Yet his use of the classical gothic, the myth of the underworld, actually deflects the kind of direct responsibility for Americans in the slave trade which Barbauld, by comparison, readily admits. The U.S. Constitution extended the life of the slave trade for at least another twenty years. In light of this blemish on American character *vis-à-vis* Britain, the poem abstracts the Middle Passage, romanticizing it as an archetypal journey into hell, as opposed to the actual journey across very real trade routes on ships chartered in real cities like Bristol, Liverpool, and Newport, Rhode Island.

African Manners

The land of "BEASTS" in which Freneau's Africans find themselves suggests the cultural debasement produced by slave trading. In order to highlight and manage this problem, antislavery often resorted to the contrast between such debasement and the relative simplicity of African social and domestic manners. The affect of poetic scenes of African home life served primarily to condemn cultural over-refinement—the kind of refinement which marked the continuum between commercial sophistication and savage avarice. This became something of a rhetorical formula. It invoked a particular version of the "noble savage" that had extensive antecedents in eighteenth-century sentimental writing, including the work of such figures as Chateaubriand and Rousseau. Like the noble (American) Indian that these writers romanticized, the image of the noble African often blended child-like innocence and aristocratic bearing, and the poets focused on domestic and romantic plots to highlight those affections through which "native" peoples staked the claim to full humanity. The literary genealogy for such eighteenth-century figures as *The Royal African* or Sarah Wentworth Morton's "The African Chief," of course includes Shakespeare's *Othello* and Aphra Behn's *Oroonoko*, both of which make pathos and tragedy contingent upon the hero's royal status.[45]

Notwithstanding the continued presence of the royal African in antislavery imaginative writing, during the 1770s and 1780s the desire to condemn the cultural decadence associated with slave trading generally democratized scenes of African social and domestic life. If poems like Thomas Branagan's *Avenia* (1805), for example, continued to romanticize royal and aristocratic Africans, a good deal of antislavery poetry emphasized the affective simplicity of African social and domestic relations as a foil for the decadence traditionally associated with aristocratic society. The cultural poetics of antislavery idealized everyday life in West African societies disrupted by barbaric trade—even the royal or aristocratic family is made to be affectively "representative" of the kind of African manners that highlight the destructive capacities of barbaric traffic. Prominent examples of this kind of poetic ethnography are found in William Roscoe's *The Wrongs of Africa* (1787), John Singleton's *A General Description of the West Indian Islands* (1767), and Hannah More's poem "Slavery" (1788), which was alternatively entitled "The Slave Trade."

One of the central figures in Liverpool's artistic circles, Roscoe not only founded the city's Athenaeum but also was involved in banking and politics, and later, as a Member of Parliament, opposed the slave trade.[46] Contrasted with his rather tempered *A General View of the African Slave Trade* (1788), which promotes abolition "under proper cautions" that protect West Indian planters,[47] *The Wrongs of Africa* takes a more confrontational approach to the slave trade. Its preface begins by reconsidering the very meaning of "free" trade and its relation to British manners. "The spirit of trade," it states, "may degrade the national character, and endanger our sacrificing the principles of justice and the feelings of humanity to the acquirement of wealth. It becomes us therefore to guard against the introduction of those base and sordid maxims which represent everything as fair that is lucrative."[48] This rejection of market-driven ethics is consistent with the poem's argument that the "traffic in the human species" arises "from the noisy haunts/Of Mercantile confusion, where thy voice [of "Humanity"] / Is heard not; from the meretricious glare / Of crowded theatres. . . ." (p. 9). Later on, this critique becomes a full-blown commercial allegory about "the dread spirit of commercial gain" (p. 23) where Roscoe, like Yearsley and Barbauld, tries to unmask "unrelenting avarice" that would pawn itself off as "soft compassion" (p. 23). As in Barbauld's poem, the slave trade is figured pathologically:

> And like the fever's rage,
> Sought but precarious victims for their prey:
> But soon the epidemic madness swell'd
> To pestilential fury, and involv'd
> Surrounding nations in one general doom. (p. 18)

The trope of disease poetically culminates in the "wild contagion" with which the slave master infects the "fainting wretch" (p. 24). But it is an expansive figure that includes all "nations" "involv'd" in the trade, either as agents or victims, which are implicated in the "one general doom."

The reverse of doom is an idealized African social life uniting civilized manners to sentimental affections.[49] In Roscoe, African manners possess the depth of sentimental feeling that emphasizes the artifice of cultural refinement. The poem tactfully deploys the image of Edenic innocence in Africa—an image available through many European travel narratives written early in the eighteenth century—that composes a prelapsarian place corrupted by "European avarice" (p. 13). Forestalling the slave owners' views of African indolence, Roscoe's Africans are "Strangers alike to luxury and toil, / They with assiduous labour never woo'd / A coy and stubborn soil" (p. 13). By situating African manners in the cultural position somewhere between aristocratic and bourgeois norms, the poem offers negative praise— Africans "are" in terms of what they "are not." In this way, the poem can both idealize and subordinate their "unperverted taste."[50]

Perhaps Roscoe was familiar with John Singleton's *A General Description of the West Indian Islands* (1767), a work that puts Africans in a similarly indeterminate cultural position. This reveals the problem for Anglo-American writers of equating Africans with "civilization." A member of Lewis Hallam's theatrical group, which toured the West Indies in the 1760s, Singleton composed a blank-verse poem which, if not an antislavery work per se, still contains extended passages on the severity of West Indian planters and the barbarity of the slave trade.[51] At one important moment in Book II, the speaker fantasizes about the history of a particular slave he sees abused by the plantation overseer:

> By treach'rous scheme of some sea brute entrap'd,
> When the steel-hearted sordid mariner
> Shap'd out his wat'ry course for traffic vile,
> Commuting wares for baneful dust of gold;
> Or, what is worse, made spoil of human flesh.
> Accursed method of procuring wealth!
> By loading free-born limbs with servile chains,
> And bart'ring for the image of his God.
> Deal Christians thus, yet keep that sacred name?
> Or does the diff'rence of complexion give
> To man a property in man?—O! no:
> Soft Nature shrinks at the detested thought,
> A thought which savages alone can form.[52]

In this context, the simplicity of African manners would appear to contrast with the slave-trading society of "Christians" who have become "savages." Condemnation of the excesses of commercial society is implicit, for example, in the poet's detailed and sentimental descriptions of the funeral rites of West Indian slave societies. Alternatively, however, the poem satirizes the "crafty slave," whose peddling of false nostrums "Draws the credulous, un-thinking crowd, / To venerate his art, and fill his purse" (II, 337–8).

The poem's many oscillations are never quite resolved. If it finds any normative position for Africans at all, this occurs in Book II where the Ebon king—the father of the imagined slave mentioned above—becomes religiously consoled to his misfortune. He had entrusted his child to his European guests, who sold him into slavery "for a little trash" (l.57). Their purpose of "vile commercial gain" comes with the pretense of enlightened civilization—of European "culture" itself—that is the seductive allure for the "untutor'd slave": "Hoping 'ere yet he reached th'approaching grave, / To see the youth return, with science stor'd, / And such accomplishments as Britain's sons / Had oft display'd before the Ebon king" (II ll. 67–70). If the poem exposes the frailty of affective innocence, it ultimately accepts that as the normative quality of African life. That is, the royal African must come to understand the trappings of European commercial society, and fall back upon his own moral and religious virtue. Hence his "calm deportment puts to shame / The boasted reason of the polish'd world" (III ll.499–500). This ensures his place in "bliss eternal."

Because of its more rigorous antislavery position, Roscoe's poem more emphatically proclaims civilized African manners. But this only raises questions about the very nature of manners themselves. Unlike, say, James Thomson's portrayal of Africans in *The Seasons*, Roscoe's poem actually accounts for African politeness:

> Nor yet unknown to more refin'd delights,
> Nor to the soft and social feelings lost,
> Was the swart African: whenever man
> Erects his dwelling, whether on the bleak
> And frozen cliffs of Zembla's northern coasts,
> Or in meridian regions—Love attends
> And shares his habitation; in his train
> Come fond affections, come endearing joys,
> And confidence, and tenderness, and truth,
> For not to polish'd life alone confin'd
> Are these primaeval blessings: rather there
> Destroyed, or injured. . . . (p. 14)

By following the conventional strategy of sentimentalizing the African fam-ily, the poem seems to erase difference in the name of universal humanity. If this strategy winds up dramatizing yet another version of patriarchal feeling, it also raises the question of what "refin'd delights" really are, for Africa would appear to reduce civilized manners themselves to "fond affections." What, then, is the right cultural relation between "primaeval blessings" and "polish'd life"?"

Much the same formula arises in Hannah More's "Slavery, a Poem," which she wrote under the auspices of the English Abolition Committee to influence Parliamentary opinion. Literary bluestocking, evangelical moralist, and conservative social critic, More inhabited social and literary circles that included such figures as Samuel Johnson and Lady Montagu, corresponded eagerly with other antislavery poets such as William Cowper, wrote poems (like this one) specifically to help the newly formed English Abolition Society, and even campaigned with eminent abolitionists like Wilberforce. Commentators on More's poem typically focus on her attitudes toward race and class, and find her falling short on both counts.[53] I want to emphasize instead that More's poem represents the "savage" slave trader in ways that press at the borders of racial and cultural categories. As the embodiment of unregulated passions, the slave trader disrupts traditional cultural assumptions about the superiority of Euro-Americans. The slave trader is the third term—the undesired supplement—that the poem employs yet must contain.

"Slavery" (alternatively titled "The Slave Trade") dismantles and then reconstructs the cultural distance between Britons and Africans. It thus unsurprisingly makes the immediate case for African humanity: "Revere affections mingled with our frame, /In every nature, every clime the same."[54] Yet the language with which More humanizes Africans simultaneously makes her poem's cultural commentary problematic.[55] Her representative Africans are true to "keen affections," "active patriot fires," and "rude energy" (ll. 69, 71). Such language is not simply racialized, for it appears as well in her characterization of the European slave trader. Even more forcefully than Roscoe, she assails the slave trade by dismantling the distinction between civilized Europeans and savage Africans:

> Barbarians, hold! th'opprobrious commerce spare
> Respect *his* sacred image which they bear.
> Tho' dark and savage, ignorant and blind,
> They claim the common privilege of kind;
> Let Malice strip them of each other plea,
> They still are men, and men shou'd still be free. (ll. 135–140)

These lines begin to suggest the unsettling possibility for cultural equivalence, a theme that later reaches an indignant crescendo: "And thou, WHITE SAVAGE! Whether lust of gold, / Or lust of conquest rule thee uncontrol'd!" (ll. 211–121) More thus pushes to its logical end the grudging acknowledgment by earlier poets like Singleton, who were forced to admit the depravity of slave-trading "white savages" in the West Indies. More here strategically juxtaposes English "Barbarians" with the "dark and savage" African whose humanity is nevertheless affirmed. This implicitly raises the question that looms over and against much of this early antislavery poetry: What is (or is there?) the essential difference between these two cultures?[56]

This question is left unresolved for much of the poem. Yet More appears anxious about the equivalence her poem's assault on the slave trade suggests. Like Roscoe, she resurrects the distinction between "civilized" and "savage"—or British and African—cultures and exploits the ambiguous potential of the very meaning of "culture" and "refinement." Her poem at once abandons and recovers these concepts by imbuing them with Christian and sentimental meaning. Like Roscoe, More distinguishes Christian virtue from cultural refinement, a thematic move which, even as it condemns all those involved in the slave trade, implies the superiority of British manners:

> Tho' wit may boast a livelier dread of shame,
> A loftier sense of wrong refinement claim;
> Tho' polish'd manners may fresh wants invent,
> And nice distinctions nicer souls torment;
> Though these on finer spirits heavier fall,
> Yet natural evils are the same to all. (ll. 151–156)

The passage crucially debunks "wrong refinement" and "polish'd manners" only to suggest their enduring relevance to the meaning of civilized culture. By divesting African humanity of these qualities and reducing it to forms of suffering from "natural evils," More seems to place it within the context of Christian feeling: "The nerve, howe'er untutor'd, can sustain / A sharp unutterable sense of pain" (ll. 159–160). Yet neither the passage nor the poem can abandon completely the categories of wit and refinement that are associated with "fresh wants," or new forms of consumption. Put another way, only the more refined sensibilities of British readers bring suffering Africans into visibility. The poem thematizes slavery by placing the category of race in the context of the larger and more fluid category of culture, and by mobilizing culture to reframe the relations among trade, refinement, and sympathy.

Cowper, Wheatley, and White Slavery

Antislavery poetry engages in the project of cultural and commercial reform. It turns on a number of resonant questions about the exact relation between trade and civilization.[57] Who are more "savage," these poems ask, both righteously and anxiously, heathen savages or savage Christians? What is the relation between cultural refinement, consumption, and the benevolent affections? The poetic emphasis upon the brutality of the European slave trader generated these questions, thereby precluding the opposition between "self" and "other" in colonialist criticism.[58] The questions themselves also extend the issue of slave trading beyond that of national identity, since the poetic and cultural figure of commercial savagery circulates throughout British-American antislavery writing.[59] Put another way, eighteenth-century Britons and Americans contemplated the perils of slave trading for national virtue within transnational ideologies deliberating the proper relations among commerce, wealth, and civilization.

The subject of barbaric traffic produces the poetic dynamic of the speaker's identification with—and withdrawal from—uncivilized yet suffering Africans. One good example of the poetic tensions and shifting cultural subject positions this creates may be found in William Cowper's poem "Charity." As the author of *The Task* and "The Negro's Complaint," Cowper would seem to hold secure antislavery credentials, though his private writings belie an underlying indifference to antislavery politics.[60] Regardless of his devotion to antislavery politics, however, "Charity" does express the difficulty of maintaining the sanctity of a British identity easily distinguishable from the "savagery" of Africans. Cowper referred to the poem as a critique of "the diabolical traffic" of "Man-merchandize."[61] This is why early passages emphasize the ideal of enlightened commercial exchange:

> God, working ever on a social plan,
> By various ties attaches man to man:
> He made at first, though free and unconfin'd,
> One man the common father of the kind,
> That ev'ry tribe, though plac'd as he sees best,
> Where seas or desarts part them from the rest,
> Diff'ring in language, manners, or in face,
> Might feel themselves allied to all the race.

Later, Cowper amplifies the themes of progressive history and international coherence that fall within the domain of civilized trade:

> Again—the band of commerce was design'd
> T'associate all the branches of mankind,
> And if a boundless plenty be the robe,
> Trade is the golden girdle of the globe:
> Wise to promote whatever end he means,
> God opens fruitful nature's various scenes,
> Each climate needs what other climes produce,
> And offers something to the gen'ral use.[62]

By universalizing the "race" of mankind—the staple of antislavery arguments—through the "social plan" that itself is predicated upon the "genial intercourse" of enlightened trade, the poem first offers the ideal of commercial sociability corrupted by the slave trade. As though the implications of such an argument about the loss of civilization were too radical, Cowper returns to the importance of cultural difference. There are distinctive "tribes" and "branches of mankind" in a world where enlightened trade ideally serves as the "golden girdle of the globe." The imperial subtext that other readers have recognized becomes all but transparent when the poem argues for the civilizing capacity of trade to refine Africa's "unsocial climates" and "wasted regions." It is "an herald of God's love, to pagan lands."

The speaker's tenuous cultural authority contributes significantly to the poem's unsteady articulations of the meanings of racial and cultural "difference." His ability, moreover, to maintain a smug cultural tone depends upon the representation of African manners. Like Roscoe and More, Cowper humanizes the African slave by domesticating African manners: "The tender ties of father, husband, friend, / All bonds of nature in that moment end" (p. 284). Yet the object of the antislavery sentimental economy just as readily exhibits (as in More) the unregulated passions—those passions that typically describe the slave trader as well. One wronged African is "The sable warrior, frantic with regret / Of her he loves, and never can forget" (p. 284). Removed from domestic affections during the Middle Passage, the African slave "Puts off his gen'rous nature, and to suit / His manners with his fate, puts on the brute" (p. 285). There is a suggestion of a rough equivalence between the brutality of the slave trader and the African slave, the debasement of British manners in those who "gage and span" or speculate in slaves and then imprison them. The equivalence between subject and object of the slave economy is again apparent in the bestial imagery characterizing them both. Cowper likens, for example, the African's natural love of freedom to a horse's; the slave trader is called a wolf. Both are debased, dehumanized.

The poem invokes the evangelical need for conversion as a way of managing this troubling equivalence. Such a move rhetorically shifts the context for the very meanings of "liberty" and "slavery." British identity is recovered through Cowper's version of the voice of the converted African:

> Oh 'tis a godlike privilege to save,
> And he that scorns it is himself a slave.—
> Inform his mind, one flash of heav'nly day
> Would heal his heart and melt his chains away;
> "Beauty for ashes" is a gift indeed,
> And slaves, by truth enlarg'd, are doubly freed:
> Then would he say, submissive at thy feet,
> While gratitude and love made service sweet,
> My dear deliv'rer out of hopeless night,
> Whose bounty bought me but to give me light,
> I was a bondman on my native plain,
> Sin forg'd, and ignorance made fast, the chain;
> Thy lips have shed instruction as the dew,
> Taught me what path to shun, and what pursue;
> Farewell my former joys! I sigh no more
> For Africa's once lov'd, benighted shore;
> Serving a benefactor I am free,
> At my best home if not exil'd from thee. (p. 287)

By moving mellifluously from cultural to bodily to spiritual slavery, the poem recovers the hierarchy between true Christians and "submissive" Africans for whom "service" is now "sweet."[63] Yet readers focusing on this hegemonic move tend to miss the importance of both the African's *and* the British reader's conversion to *true* Christianity. The spiritual freedom of one implies the cultural freedom of the other. If the passage's opening lines suggest the complexity of "slavery" through the ambiguous referents "he" and "his," it ultimately works out the poem's imaginative emancipation of both Africans and Britons by staging the concurrent passage from darkness to light.

Cowper's persona of the pious African cannot help but recall Phillis

Wheatley's well-known poetic account of slavery and freedom in "On Being Brought from Africa to America." Published in *Poems on Various Subjects Religious and Moral* (1773), the poem actually predates "Charity," but it also exemplifies the alternative ideological direction that such a persona could take. Recognizing the subversive potential of her work, critics now read Wheatley in the context of what Henry Louis Gates, Jr. has called Enlightenment debates about "the nature of the Negro."[64] They emphasize, for example, "the complex process of black Americanization" that her poetry publicly performs.[65] Yet Wheatley's most famous poem unfolds in unexpected ways when read together with the transatlantic antislavery discourses of trade and consumption. Like Wheatley herself, these discourses criss-crossed the Atlantic world.[66]

"On Being Brought from Africa to America" subtly interrupts the hierarchical project in antislavery writing that one finds in the work of Cowper and More. It does so by exposing the fragility of Anglo-American "civilization." The poet begins as follows:

> 'Twas mercy brought me from my *Pagan* land,
> Taught my benighted soul to understand
> That there's a God, that there's a *Saviour* too:
> Once I redemption neither sought nor knew.

Like Cowper's converted African, Wheatley would at first appear to offer the conventional argument that spiritual emancipation more than compensates for physical enslavement. (This is certainly the argument of the African-American Jupiter Hammon's poetic address to Wheatley, which reads "Thou has left the heathen shore, / Thro' mercy of the Lord, / Among the heathen live no more, / Come magnify thy God.")[67] Certainly, the poem's opening is in keeping with the staple antislavery theme, extending from early critics of colonial American slave owners who failed to Christianize their slaves (Morgan Godwyn), to eighteenth-century New Divinity ministers who attacked the hypocrisy of West Indian planters in much the same terms (Samuel Hopkins). In these opening lines Wheatley's voice mimics the kind of African piety that, for example, in "Charity" makes "service sweet." It also uncannily prefigures the very language Cowper's African persona uses to describe his own journey: "I sigh no more / For Africa's once lov'd, benighted shore."

Mimicry becomes all the more important in light of the second quatrain's reconfiguration of the Christian geography of civilization. These next four lines press upon the meanings of and contexts for Anglo-American commerce and consumption, thereby revising the entire diasporic situation of the poem.

> Some view our sable race with scornful eye,
> "Their colour is a diabolic die."
> Remember, *Christians*, *Negros* black as *Cain*,
> May be refin'd, and join th'angelic train.

James Levernier points out that Wheatley's poem rhetorically manipulates key words to expose the economics of the proslavery argument. With an eye towards West Indians, Wheatley effectively puns on "Cain" / sugar cane and "diabolic die" / indigo dye.[68] Such wordplay recalls the widespread proslavery biblical citations: Genesis 4, which sanctions the curse of Cain's "blackness," and God's curse of perpetual bondage upon the Hammites in Genesis 9.

But such wordplay becomes even more startling in light of the antislavery critique of the depravity of West Indian (and, according to Barbauld, British) habits of exchange and consumption. The play upon "Cain," then, suggests the cultural enslavement to consuming West Indian "blood sugar." Wheatley's strategic use of "refinement" addresses the relation between the corrupt commodity and its manufactured derivative: the poem bitterly, albeit subtly, contrasts the claims of Christian "refinement" with the slave economy's distillation of rum. Such a contrast further suggests that cultural refinement ideologically connects commerce and Christianity. As in "To Sir Toby," the product of refinement or distillation—the "demon rum"—emphasizes the passions endemic to slavery. By association, then, Wheatley's poem debunks the very notion of western cultural refinement through the transatlantic economic context the poem unfolds. This, moreover, undermines the spiritual geography juxtaposing the realms of savagery and civilization upon which the speaker's diasporic journey is premised. By simultaneously punning on biblical texts and creating the *double entendre* between distillation and cultural refinement, Wheatley finally debunks the cultural myth of blackness. She exposes the limitations of the trope of "civilization" by highlighting the point where commercial refinement actually degenerates into barbarity. "On Being Brought from Africa to America" is thus the first instance in Black Atlantic literature of the self-conscious meditation on the relations between African and Anglo-American enslavement. It is finally a poem about Anglo-American enslavement.

"Negroish Accents"

The comparison of Cowper and Wheatley begins to suggest the varying uses of the African persona in antislavery poetry. I want to explore further the poetic convention of the African speaker in the context of established rhetorical patterns of identification in antislavery writing. This writing enacts dual kinds of identification simultaneously. For purposes of eliciting sympathy, it asks readers to see themselves as African slaves "stolen" from home;[69] for purposes of cultural chastisement, it forces the identification between readers and European slave traders. The complexity of such identifications and misidentifications, however, derives from the crisis in cultural—that is, civilized and Christian—rather than in racial identity. The African speaker here speaks in multiple voices that alternatively fix and transgress the cultural boundary between "savage" and "civilized" peoples. The dialogue among these voices reveals some uncertainty over this boundary.

What did it mean for British and American antislavery poets to imaginatively assume the voice of the African slave? The "whiteness" studies proliferating in the field of American studies address this question by focusing upon transgression—what Eric Lott, for example, has called the "symbolic crossings of racial boundaries."[70] This argument, however, is more suitable for historical periods in which race was a pseudo-scientific category.[71] In early antislavery poetry the figure of the African is drawn from within the fluid historical context where race and culture coexisted, however uncomfortably. The genre sentimentalizes Africans and redeems them for Christian civilization. After accomplishing this goal, antislavery poems often erase the African presence by employing the pathos of the slave speaker's suicide.

A good deal of antislavery writing disrupted the silence of slavery by lending the persecuted African a public voice. To do this meant to imaginatively "become" the African, to assume his, or her, identity. This poetic act foundered upon prevailing fears of linguistic and cultural contamination. The orthodox New England minister Jedidiah Morse, for example, complained that "The children, by being brought up, and constantly associating with the negroes, too often imbibe their low ideas, and vitiated manners and morals; and contract a *negroish* kind of accent and dialect, which they often carry with them through life."[72] Across the Atlantic, the Scottish philosopher James Beattie similarly claimed "that the children of our slaves could not learn to speak well, because they associated from infancy with people . . . among whom a barbarous dialect had long prevailed."[73]

To resolve this problem antislavery writing often anglicized the African voice. The English antislavery cleric James Ramsay's retelling of the famous legend of Quashi, the noble African slave who refuses to be whipped by the master with whom he has been a life-long companion, performs this sort of rhetorical ventriloquy. Like Roscoe and More, Ramsay emphasizes Quashi's "elevation of sentiment" to denounce the brutality of the West Indian slave system. But he does so by removing language two or three steps away from the vernacular directness of slave dialect. Ramsay frames the tale by announcing, "As I had my information from a friend of the master's, in the master's presence, who acknowledges it to be genuine, the truth of it is indisputable. The only liberty I have taken with it, has been to give words to the sentiment that inspired it."[74] Such a maneuver implies the dissonance between the refinement of African feeling and the capacity of African-American language to convey it. Hence at the tale's sentimental climax Quashi paradoxically gains and loses his voice: "Master, I was bred up with you from a child; I was your play-mate when a boy; I have loved you as myself; your interest has been my study; I am innocent of the cause of your suspicion; had I been guilty, my attachment to you might have pleaded for me. Yet you have condemned me to punishment, of which I must ever have borne the disgraceful marks; thus only can I avoid them."[75]

And then he dies. Yet even in death—and perhaps because of it—the sentimental tale raises important questions about the relations among sympathy, language, and cultural refinement. One wonders immediately, for example, why the slave's "grandeur of mind," which, after all, surpasses the arts of "polished society," would need Ramsay's polished voice in the first place. Such "authentic" language would seem to be inadequate to the task of capturing slave feeling.

Ramsay's awkward position begins to describe the problem of the African speaker in antislavery poetry. Looking to the African slave for true and unmediated feelings, these poets nevertheless refine them through the anglicized voice. This is not so much a racist withdrawal as it is part of the process of defining cultural refinement itself. Indeed, the initial separation of sentiment from refinement, and their recoupling in newly creative ways, goes far in describing the poetics of antislavery. The aversion to slave dialect, moreover, is not simply a matter of poetic decorum. Though not known as an antislavery poet per se, William Shenstone shows the kind of poetic maneuvers that the assumption of the African voice necessitated. As the headnote to his "Elegy XX" states, the speaker "compares his humble fortune with the distress of others; and his subjection to DELIA, with the miserable servitude of an *African* slave."[76] The distraught speaker at once utilizes and satirizes the poem's premise about the nature of enslavement. On the one hand, it authenticates the identity of sincerity he wishes to cultivate. His feeling for Delia is part of a larger sentimental scheme eschewing luxurious "pomp" and "costly art" for the virtue of "simple friendship." On the other, the speaker, claiming that enslavement to Delia's beauty is "even bliss to bear," suddenly wakes up to the hyperbole of his own metaphor. The poet's interrogation of his own premise leads to its consideration of the African slave voice:

> See the poor native quit the Lybian shores,
>   Ah! not in love's delightful fetters bound!
> No radiant smile his dying peace restores,
>   Nor love, nor fame, nor friendship heals his wound.
>
> Let vacant bards display their boasted woes,
>   Shall I the mockery of grief display?
> No, let the muse his piercing pangs disclose,
>   Who bleeds and weeps his sum of life away!
>
> On the wild beach in mournful guise he stood,
>   Ere the shrill boatswain gave his hated sign;
> He dropt a tear unseen into the flood;
>   He stole one secret moment, to repine.
>
> Yet the muse listen'd to the plaints he made;
>   Such moving plaints as nature could inspire;
> To me the muse his tender plea convey'd,
>   But smooth'd, and suited to the founding lyre.
>
> "Why am I ravish'd from my native strand?
>   What savage race protects this impious gain?
> Shall foreign plagues infest this teeming land,
>   And more than sea-born monsters plough the main?[77]

The poem's short discourse on chattel slavery depends upon its assumption of the African's point of view. While realizing the gulf that exists between the imagined slave and himself, the speaker nevertheless is unable, or unwilling, to cross it. By smoothing over the slave's language, the speaker appropriates him sympathetically, thereby resolving the contradictions underlying the poet's negative view about the decadence of commercial civilization. In this way, the poem both claims and abandons identification with the African slave. Smoothing over that voice inoculates writer and reader alike from *both* the "savage race" of slave traders and the savage wilds of Africa (which, we later learn, are filled with such dangers as "dire locusts" and "prowling wolves"). Indeed, the refined African voice recognizes the barbarity of over-refinement: "What fate reserv'd me for this christian race? / O race more polish'd, more sever than they?"

This poetry manipulates the African persona in order to navigate thematically between alternative forms of savagery. Such a tenuous relation with the African voice often expresses itself dialogically. In this way, the African voice becomes the site of cultural debate about the nature of Anglo-American commercial society. Hannah More's "The Sorrows of Yamba" demonstrates the power and limitations of this dialogic voice. The poem was probably intended for a young audience, and it employs the convention of the slave's lament, which verges on suicide. It employs African dialect to produce "authentic" emotion; the rhetorical refinement of that voice temporarily erases primitive differences marked by dialect in order to highlight the theme of barbarity in the Anglo-American slave trade. Stolen from "Afric's golden coast," the speaker finds herself a slave in St. Lucia, pining away for the family she left behind.[78] In light of the didactic spirit of virtually all of More's writing, the poem emphasizes the barbarity of slavery only to subordinate liberty and slavery, as in Cowper's "Charity," to Christian metaphysics. In despair, the speaker encounters the "English missionary good," and eventually comes to learn that "t'was the Christian's lot, / Much to suffer here below."[79]

Yet this thematic transformation is notably incomplete. In working through the sentimental story of the slave's separation, sale, transport, and bondage, the speaker's voice oscillates between dialect and refinement, registering her fluid cultural positions that sometimes change line-by-line:

> Whity man he came from far,
>   Sailing o'er the briny flood;
> Who, with help of British Tar,
>   Buys up human flesh and blood. (p. 2)

As the poem progresses, however, it tends to anglicize the African voice as a way of specifically highlighting the slave trade based on a "love of filthy gold":

Naked on the platform lying,
   Now we cross the tumbling wave;
Shrieking, sickening, fainting, dying!
   Deed of shame for Britons brave!

At the savage Captain's beck,
   Now, like brutes, they make use prance;
Smack the cat about the deck
   And in scorn they bid us dance. (p. 3)

Having shifted cultural authority to the suffering African, More returns to the normative relation between British and African cultures by again pronouncing slave dialect ("Massa hard," "Which poor me no understood"). This voice again changes during the speaker's climactic realization about the ever present "slavery" of sin. Disavowing thoughts of vengeance, her conversion to Christianity enfolds her voice back into the evangelical one assuming the moral and cultural high ground: "Cease, ye British sons of murder! / Cease from forging Afric's chain; / Mock your Saviour's name no further, / Cease your savage lust of gain."[80]

The refined slave voice marks the limitations of antislavery dialogics. Whatever understanding More shows of African cultures—indeed it is precious little—the African speaker's conversion forecloses it altogether.[81] The general obtuseness, moreover, that antislavery poetry demonstrates to cultural differences makes the genre's most meaningful dialogue not between African dialect and English language, but between competing definitions of the meaning of "slavery" itself. One finds this in William Cowper's "The Negro's Complaint" (1788), a poem that was commissioned by the English Abolition Society, and sung as a popular ballad in the streets of London. It had an American audience as well, for it was reprinted widely in early national magazines during the 1780s and 1790s.[82]

"The Negro's Complaint" makes an important shift in the poetic situation: instead of a British or American speaker lamenting African enslavement, it offers an African speaker denouncing British enslavement. The poem is premised on the slave trade's violation of universal humanity: "Skins may differ, but affection / Dwells in white and black the same."[83] The opening metaphors ("stranger's treasures," "paltry gold"), along with the speaker's complaint, "Minds are never to be sold" (l. 8), offer conventional protests against the slave trade. Yet the poem gradually shifts the very meaning of slavery from chattel to cultural and spiritual bondage. To accomplish this translation, it sentimentalizes not just familial but commercial and labor relations. Like Farmer James's image of slave labor in Crevecoeur's *Letters from an American Farmer* (1782), where slaves water southern crops with their own tears, it sentimentalizes the sugar cane's cultivation: "Sighs must fan it, tears must water, / Sweat of ours must dress the soil" (ll. 19–20). The poem then connects this image to depraved forms of consumption that, as in Barbauld, collapse the difference between metropolitan and West Indian manners: "Think how many backs have smarted / For the sweets your cane affords" (ll. 23–24).

By using the African speaker to translate chattel slavery into cultural and spiritual forms of enslavement, the poem concludes with the apocalyptic imagery that characterizes the commercial jeremiad. Imagining the "wild tornadoes" and "whirlwinds" that might beset the British commercial empire, the speaker associates divine wrath with the failure of British civilization:

> Slaves of gold, whose sordid dealings
> >   Tarnish all your boasted pow'rs,
> Prove that *you* have human feelings,
> >   Ere you proudly question ours. (ll. 53–56)

This completes the redefinition of slavery. The idea of "sordid" trade arises from the dissonance between commerce and sentiment ("dealings" and "feelings"), one that both empowers and distorts the African's voice.

The thematic confusion in these poems over the nature of Anglo-American civilization goes a long way in explaining the striking motif of the African speaker's suicide. This motif extends at least as far back as the English dramatist Thomas Southerne's dramatic version of Aphra Behn's *Oroonoko*, whose tragic hero dies by his own hand. This poetic convention fulfilled the evangelical project of much antislavery writing by juxtaposing secular and spiritual modes of "freedom." As the slave speaker in Samuel Jackson Pratt's *Humanity; or the Rights of Nature* puts it, "'Ah! give me death, / Give the last blow and stop the hated breath, / To arm this hand were holy innocence, / I call on suicide as self-defence."[84] Even more significant was the poetic use of the slave suicide to resolve troubling questions that the genre raised about the quality of civilization. Such issues—the suggestion that slave traders were more savage than the Africans they enslaved; the designation of Anglo-Americans for both the slave traders and Africans themselves; the position of "Africa" within the spectrum of "civilized" and "savage" manners—all serve as contexts for the ultimate erasure of the African voice engaging in cultural critique. The convention of African suicide helps to manage cultural fears of degeneration, removing the African who unsteadily has assumed the moral high ground.[85]

The slave dies, in other words, because he has to. Theodore Dwight's poem below, for example, which appeared in 1789 in the *American Museum*,[86] exemplifies the poetic pattern of sorrow, moral outrage, and suicidal despair. The poem's headnote called it "an attempt to represent the anguish of a mother, whose son and daughter were taken from her by a ship's crew belonging to a country where the God of justice and mercy is owned and worshipped."

> "Help! Oh, help! thou God of Christians!
>   Save a mother from despair!
> Cruel white-men steal my children!
>   God of Christians hear my prayer!
> From my arms by force they're rended
>   Sailors drag them to the sea;
> Yonder ship at anchor riding,
>   Swift will carry them away.
> There my son lies, stripp'd and bleeding;
>   Fast, with thongs, his hands are bound.
> See, the tyrants, how they scourge him;
>   See his sides a reeking wound!
> See his little sister by him;
>   Quaking, trembling, how she lies!
> Drops of blood her face besprinkle;
>   Tears of anguish fill her eyes. . . ."
> "Christians, who's the God you worship?
>   Is he cruel, fierce, or good?
> Does he take delight in mercy?
>   Or in spilling human blood?
> Ah, my poor distracted Mother!
>   Hear her scream upon the shore."—
> Down the savage Captain struck her,
>   Lifeless on the vessel's floor.
> Up his sails he quickly hoisted,
>   To the ocean bent his way;
> Headlong plung'd the raving mother,
>   From a high rock, in the sea.[87]

The pathos of the African family's destruction thematically exceeds the argument that the slave trade is simply brutal. Rather, it poetically disrupts the readers' common distinction between civilized "Christians" and savage Africans. In a series of eyewitness accounts, first the mother's, and then her daughter's, the scene defines the savagery of slave trading and also suggest an alternative—and "African"—norm for humanity. The poem, and many others like it during this era, then erases that voice of African authority, either through sale or suicide, once it has served its purpose.[88]

The prototype for the genre is of course Thomas Day's *The Dying Negro* (1773). Co-authored by Day and his roommate at Middle Temple, John Bicknell,[89] the poem was very popular in its day. Equiano cites it from memory in his *Interesting Narrative*, and it was reprinted widely in American magazines. As its Advertisement states, the poem was founded on a real incident about an African slave: "preferring death to another voyage to America [where he would not only return to plantation slavery but be separated from his beloved in England], he took an opportunity of shooting himself."[90] The preface also makes clear the poem's thematic concerns about the inhumanity of the slave trade and the corruption of modern British manners. This context helps to explain the poetic trope of the dying Negro.

The poem is dedicated to Jean-Jacques Rousseau, and the preface rounds up the usual suspects of the antislavery imagination. "How should I rejoice to see a cause like this rescued from my weak pen . . . to see that insolence, that successful avarice confounded, which, under the mark of commerce, has already ravaged the two extremities of the globe!" (p. v). The authors ponder the problem "of the refinement of modern manners" (p. iii): "But if our boasted improvements, and frivolous politeness, be well acquired by the loss of manly firmness and independence, if in order to feel as men it be necessary to adopt the manners of women, let us at least be consistent, nor mingle the exercise of barbarism with the weakness of civilization" (p. vii). Throughout, the preface unsuccessfully negotiates the opposition between republican austerity and modern over-refinement. Rousseau thus strategically serves Day as a model for the former virtue, which further enables him to deplore modern British corruption. Yet even this central complaint reveals some indecision about the very term "cultural" with which the poem is dealing. Day finds himself only able to define culture negatively. While the preface resists with equal vehemence extreme forms of courtly refinement and primitive barbarity (recognizing, for example, that the ancient Greeks were guilty of slavery), it fails to offer a precise norm for modern Britain that

lies somewhere between them. Instead, the language tends to oscillate between denunciation of the primitive past ("savage and gloomy liberty") and
the decadent present (the "swift infection" of "commerce and prosperity").
What's an enlightened reader to do?

That norm the poem finds only in the African speaker—and that is why
he must die. Published the same year as Wheatley's *Poems on Various Subjects,
Religious and Moral*, *The Dying Negro* impersonates the Black Atlantic spiritual
autobiographer who simultaneously laments physical bondage and cele-
brates Christian emancipation. In Day's poem, the slave speaker recounts
both of these journeys, which articulate (as in the work of More and Roscoe) the theme of African civilization. Borrowing from source materials
that were reprinted in eighteenth-century England—travel narratives like
Michel Adanson's *Voyage to Senegal, the Isle of Goree and River Gambia* (1759),
and John Barbot's *Description of the Coasts of North and South Guinea* (1732)—
Day represents a similar duality of innocence and barbarity in Africa.[91]

By mediating between these extremes, *The Dying Negro* thematizes the
proper balance of cultural refinement for its *British* readers. The speaker's lament, for example, about the irony of himself, a Gambian hunter who now
has become the hunted—"To human brutes more fell, more cruel far than
they" (p. 8)—highlights the common trope of British savagery. Yet the "liberty" he once enjoyed in Africa was extremely primitive. Given these
equally untenable alternatives, the poem turns to the African's conversion
to Christianity to find the norm for civilized manners. In his opening speech
the speaker marks the cultural distance between the poetic present and his
African past:

> Arm'd with thy sad last gift—the pow'r to die,
> Thy shafts, stern fortune, now I can defy;
> Thy dreadful mercy points at length the shore,
> Where all is peace, and men are slaves no more;
> This weapon, ev'n in chains, the brave can wield,
> And vanquish'd quit triumphantly the field.
> Beneath such wrongs let pallid Christians live,
> Such they perpetrate, and may forgive. (p. 1)

The process of grafting Christian refinement onto African simplicity occurs
through the poem's deft handling of the romance plot. Rhetorically, it makes
the speaker's beloved the poem's immediate audience. Her tears provide the
proper model for the extensive audience in Britain (or America, for that

matter).[92] But the sentimental power of British womanhood is little more than a vehicle for the cultural equilibrium the poem urgently wants to dramatize.

In the spirit of Rousseau, the poem's image of Africa represents the superiority of primitive virtue. "Descended from yon radiant orb, they claim / Sublimer courage, and fiercer flame. / Nature has there, unchill'd by art, imprest / Her awful majesty on ev'ry breast" (p. 16). Yet the poet, through the African speaker, ultimately appears to seek a harmony of primitive passions and refined affections. As the speaker admits,

> Then my lov'd country, parents, friends forgot;
> Heav'n I absolved, nor murmur'd at my lot
> Thy sacred smiles could ev'ry pang remove,
> And liberty became less dear than love. . . .
> Not such the mortals burning Africa breeds,
> Mother of virtues and heroic deeds! (pp. 15–16)

After the African speaker assumes such moral and cultural superiority, the poem realizes the antislavery logic of environmentalism, and the slave speaker dies because of that realization.

The Dying Negro was written in the immediate aftermath of the landmark Somerset case in England in 1772, in which Lord Mansfield ruled, albeit reluctantly, that slavery was incompatible with the principles of British liberty. The Mansfield decision did not end British slavery overnight, but it did establish judicial precedent against the transport of slaves out of Britain, and it significantly raised the prospect of the expansion of Britain's free black population. *The Dying Negro* symbolically responds to that political context by embodying the voice of principle *in* the African slave (who, like Somerset, resists returning to abject slavery in the West Indies), and then erasing him from the British social landscape. Hence the poem does not so much embrace African manners as re-contextualize them into an uncertain norm for contemporary British readers to contemplate.[93] Embodying the "sublimer courage" that is leavened by love's "soft emotions," the slave metaphorizes the form of enlightened masculinity calibrated carefully to find the right measure of both "liberty" and "love." Once that norm is established in the African, the poem removes him safely to the confines of heaven. He is converted from passive slave to active Christian warrior bent on his own emancipating self-destruction. As in Cowper (and as opposed to Wheatley), heaven becomes the final destination of the African diaspora.

Persons and Property

The alternative, poetic means for managing the cultural hierarchies disrupted by the savage slave trader was to turn Africans back into property. This poetic trope in antislavery writing reveals unexpected similarities between antislavery and proslavery sensibilities. This was nearly a literary convention of early antislavery prose, and antislavery poetry likewise oscillates between the representations of Africans as seduced consumers and poisonous goods. The English poet Frances Seymour's "The Story of Inkle and Yarico" (1726), based on the tale of a ship-wrecked Englishman who betrays his Indian savior (see Richard Ligon's *A True and Exact History of the Island of Barbados* of 1657 and Addison and Steele's *Spectator* #11), emphasizes this theme of commercial seduction. "*Negro* Virgin" is susceptible to Inkle's "alluring grace" as he promises her "softest silks" back in Europe, "While she on his enticing accents hung, / That smoothly fell from his persuasive tongue."[94]

In other poems, however, the African consumer just as easily becomes the unnatural commodity itself, as in "Charity"'s depiction of the Middle Passage: "For merchants rich in cargoes of despair, / Who drive a loathsome traffic, gage and span, / And buy the muscles and the bones of man?"[95] Another of Cowper's antislavery poems, "Pity for the Poor Africans," similarly imagines slaves as stolen goods. Written from the perspective of the false Christian who feigns pity for the poor Africans, the poem satirizes the consuming addiction to West Indian luxuries ("For how should we do without Sugar and Rum?"[96]). It then recounts the tale of a schoolboy named Tom—the allegorical figure for England—who is tempted to rob the apple orchard of a "good Neighbor." By reducing slavery to the slave trade and deploying the trope of theft to condemn that trade, the poem finds the right kind of conceit with which to assail the particular arguments offered by Britain's proslavery advocates. It exposes, for example, the hollowness of the mercantilist rationale for the African slave trade, to the effect that if Tom abstains from theft, others will profit at his (or rather Britain's) loss. The apple's symbolic power, moreover, invests "bad" commerce with biblical significance, equating the trade with the sinful Fall. But the argument works poetically only by equating, in turn, slaves themselves with stolen goods. They are "plunder"—forbidden fruit—a metaphor suggesting the very loss of its status *as* metaphor.

These discourses of seduction, consumption, and human commodities coalesce in Roscoe's *The Wrongs of Africa* at the very moment of the Africans' "fall" from innocence:

> Thou to their dazzled sight disclosest wide
> Thy magazine of wonders, cull'd with care,
> From all the splendid trifles that adorn
> Thine own luxurious region; mimic gems
> That emulate the true; fictitious gold
> To various uses fashion'd, pointing out
> Wants which before they knew not; mirrors bright,
> Reflecting to their quick and curious eye
> Their sable features: Shells, and beads and rings,
> And all fantastic folly's gingling bells,
> That catch'd the unpractis'd ear and thence convey
> Their unsuspected poison to the mind. (p. 13)

Roscoe's image of commercial exchange brilliantly captures the complexity of reflections connecting consumers and goods. In his imagination, the "poison" of luxuries seduces innocent Africans and, in a post-Lockean context, corrupts their senses. Emphasizing the artificiality of the appeal of goods ("fictitious gold," goods that "emulate the true"), Roscoe links sensual consumption to the diseased imagination. The passage proceeds inward, starting from the consumer's "dazzled sight" and moving into his poisoned "mind." The mirror, moreover, symbolizes the capacity for discovering self-identity in the goods one consumes. Hence it symbolically transforms Africans from deluded consumers into goods themselves—or the "magazine of wonders." This process involves the poem's historical readers as well. (Think, for example, how easily the passage in isolation might offer a commercial critique of 1780s London or Philadelphia, instead of the Gold Coast.) In an extension of this scene, the "mirror" of antislavery reflects upon Anglo-American manners, unsettling its readers' distance from the scene, forcing them to see themselves in context of the slipperiness of civilized identity.

Barlow and the Limits of Sympathy

I have argued that the poetics of antislavery—the thematic emphasis upon Anglo-American barbarity, the disruption of the African family, the use of the African speaker, and the poetic "resolution" of cultural problems through the sentimental trope of African suicide—arose chiefly from the cultural dislocations produced by the slave trade. Early antislavery poetry represents one artistic and generic response to the cultural crisis in eighteenth-century enlightened identity based on the complex relations between commerce and manners. Such a crisis often was expressed as the failure of Christian civilization. (This, after all, is the main thrust of the African speaker's suicidal lament).

The language of antislavery contains cultural tensions worth exploring. Rather than see the cultural project of antislavery as a kind of consensual program meant to fulfill the codes of Enlightenment, we might see it as a site in which contested claims to cultural authority took place. In an illustrative example, in Revolutionary America the ministry contributed to the political cause, and yet the political sermons that justified the Revolution ironically promoted the secularization of cultural authority. As Robert Ferguson has argued, these political sermons, which tethered "Enlightenment conceptions of law to a religious frame of reference," contributed as well to the process whereby the ministry lost "the proprietary hold over a national covenant."[97]

Evangelical versions of antislavery writing certainly resisted such a trend. Antislavery ministers like Samuel Hopkins and James Dana selectively culled from scriptural texts to argue, especially in light of evidence for Hebrew slavery in Exodus and Leviticus, that the covenant of grace precluded the Old Testament practice of chattel slavery. Claiming that slavery violated the precepts of Christian charity found, for example, in Acts 17.26, Matthew 7.12, and other key passages, antislavery ministers applied biblical hermeneutics to the contemporary problem of slavery. Just as readily, however, the antislavery pulpit could drop its appeal to enlightened sensibilities and employ the apocalyptic potential of the jeremiad. The Baptist minister Elhanan Winchester, for example, shamed his audience by declaring, "Blush, O ye christians, to think that ye are the supporters of a [savage] commerce." "Alas," he concluded, "I would choose to be in the situation of the slaves, rather than in that of their masters; for if there is a just God, he will punish those who sin against his authority; and who is able to endure his displeasure?"[98]

The evangelical project of shoring up religious authority helps to explain the secular version of antislavery polemic that Joel Barlow offers in his well-known epic poem about the progress of both America and mankind, *The Columbiad* (1807). Published at the time where England and the United States each were abolishing the slave trade, Barlow's poem not only castigates Americans for continuing to enslave Africans but also significantly intervenes in the subject of antislavery *writing* itself. *The Columbiad* debunks the religious tenor of antislavery such that epic/antislavery poetry becomes the site of a particular contest over the terms of cultural authority. The poem accomplishes this by interrogating the sentimental languages that evangelical antislavery used to wed social reform and religious piety and indeed the very nature of Enlightenment—it points out the potentially "enslaving" capacities of antislavery discourse.

Barlow's poem derives from an earlier version of his epic of American progress, *The Vision of Columbus* (1787). That poem's dedication to the King of France and its generally uncritical belief in divine providence reveal the more conservative sensibility Barlow displayed early in his career. His exposure to the radical ideas of the French Revolution changed his political beliefs, however, and eventually alienated him from the Yale-bred Federalists with whom he had collaborated earlier. Both *The Vision of Columbus* and *The Columbiad* are poems that celebrate the moral and material progress of America, though the latter significantly takes a broader perspective and situates such progress within the larger context of the entire western hemisphere. It thus dramatizes the encounter between Hesper—the Angel of the West—and the historical Columbus, who despairs his life's failure while in prison. Even though the poem went through numerous American editions, as well as French and British ones, it was critically panned in both the United States and Britain.

Rather than try to recover the aesthetic merits that critics might have missed, I focus on Barlow's critical revision of the rhetoric and ideology of antislavery culture. The increasingly secular worldview that Barlow embraced serves to empower *The Columbiad*'s full-scale assault upon the regressive forces of superstition, aristocratic privilege, monarchical traditions, and the corruption of the Catholic Church.[99] Indeed, this is main object of the poet's understanding of enslavement. In Book 4, for example, he unsurprisingly situates the Protestant Reformation in light of the Enlightenment history that devolves upon the leadership of republican America: "From slavery's chains to free the captive mind, / Brave adverse crowns, control the pontiff's sway / And bring benighted nations into day."[100] The poem's thematic emphasis upon political and cultural enslavement actually subsumes its critique of the chattel enslavement of Africans because, as Barlow would have it, the latter merely derives from the former; it is the functionary.[101]

The Argument prefacing Book 8 of *The Columbiad* suggests as much. Indeed, this book takes up the problem of slavery in the United States and is perhaps the most significant addition to the earlier *Vision of Columbus*. The Argument summarizes the process whereby Americans themselves have become enslaved: "Freedom succeeding to Despotism in the moral world, like Order succeeding to Chaos in the physical world." Slavery thus imaginatively impedes the precarious trajectory of progressive history, the enlightened path of which America is both measure and propulsion. "Hesper, recurring to his object of showing Columbus the importance of his discoveries, reverses the order of time, and exhibits the continent again in its savage state" (p. 680). Book 8 thus begins by charting the extent of such regression and celebrating the end of the Revolutionary war: "Hail holy Peace, from thy sublime abode / Mid circling saints that grace the throne of God" (ll. 1–2). The fallen Titan Atlas, however, the "Great brother guardian of old Afric's clime," intrudes upon the self-righteousness of early republican America by directly pleading the case of the enslaved: "But thy proud sons, a strange ungenerous race, / Enslave my tribes, and each fair world disgrace" (ll. 211–212). Atlas only echoes the dire warning that Barlow himself, now speaking in his own voice, offers about the precarious nature of republican liberty: "Think not, my friends, the patriot's task is done, / Or Freedom's safe because the battle's won" (ll. 79–80).

The poem's suggestion that chattel slavery is a symptom of "the fell Demon of despotic power" (l. 158) thus places the burden on the American reader for a particular kind of "conversion." Barlow writes in Book 8 with complete familiarity with the conventions of the commercial jeremiad. Atlas ventriloquizes the apocalyptic cant of antislavery:

> Nor shall these pangs atone the nation's crime;
> Far heavier vengeance, in the march of time,
> Attends them still; if they dare debase
> And hold inthrall'd the millions of my race;
> A vengeance that shall shake the world's deep frame,
> That heaven abhors and hell might shrink to name. (ll. 261–66)

In this case Atlas is certainly not a satirical figure, but his exhortation begins to emerge as the metacritical subject of the poem. For the ensuing description of the eruption of the earth's bowels in a "wallowing womb of subterranean war" (l. 276) is an exercise in evangelical excess. "Two oceans dasht in one! That climbs and roars, / And seeks in vain the exterminated shores" (ll.

287–88). By depicting "a ruin'd world" Barlow mimics the literary conventions of evangelical antislavery, implicitly offering the alternative between
prophetic dread and rational analysis.

The parody becomes more forceful as Barlow addresses the nature and future of liberty in America (as opposed to merely American liberty). In the
following passage from Book 8—which I quote at such length because of its
importance—Barlow defamiliarizes the literary and ideological conventions
of antislavery:

>   Fathers and friends, I know the boding fears
> Of angry genii and of rending spheres
> Assail not souls like yours; whom science bright
> Thro shadowy nature leads with surer light;
> For whom she strips the heavens of love and hate,
> Strikes from Jove's hand the brandisht bolt of fate,
> Gives each effect its own indubious cause,
> Divides her moral from her physic laws,
> Shows where the virtues find their nurturing food,
> And men their motives to be just and good.
> You scorn the Titan's threat; nor shall I strain
> The powers of pathos in a task so vain
> As Afric's wrongs to sing; for what avails
> To harp for you these known familiar tales;
> To tongue mute misery, and re-rack the soul
> With crimes oft copied from the bloody scroll
> Where slavery pens her woes? Tho tis but there
> We learn the weight that mortal life can bear.
> The tale might startle still the accustom'd ear
> Still shake the nerve that pumps the pearly tear,
> Melt every heart and thro the nation gain
> Full many a voice to break the barbarous chain.
> But why to sympathy for guidance fly,
> (Her aids uncertain and of scant supply)
> When your own self-excited sense affords
> A guide more sure, and every sense accords?
> Where strong self-interest join'd with duty lies,
> Where doing right demands no sacrifice,
> Where profit, pleasure, life-expanding fame
> League their allurements to support the claim,

Tis safest there the impleaded cause to trust;
Men well instructed will always be just. (309–40)

Book 8 brilliantly establishes the cultural politics of sentimental antislavery. The above passage rather presumptuously simply assumes the enlightened reader's innate capacity of human rationality, which is expressed structurally in its overall movement from "boding fears" to "just" "self-interest." Just as evangelicals appropriated the language of political liberty to promote the cause of pious reformation, Barlow reassigns the religious language of "souls" to signify the "light" of reason. Dispelling the irrationality of anxieties about the impending doom of divine displeasure, Barlow goes on to link evangelical religion to the "powers of pathos." He is equally aware of slave "misery" and the sentimental conventions, or "known familiar tales," which shake the nerves, pump one's tears, and melt every heart, thereby enslaving the sensibilities of readers. Writing at the conclusion of a thirty-year period that witnessed the political and literary assault upon the slave trade, Barlow rejects both slavery and the sentimental rhetorical conventions of antislavery—"that bloody scroll/Where Slavery pens her woes."

Barlow's warning about antislavery's potential for excessive sentimentalism is somewhat ironic in light of his own poem's use of feeling to argue against slavery. More importantly, it suggests the issues that literary antislavery raised about the relations among sympathy, imaginative writing, and the aesthetic imagination. The era, after all, was characterized by intensive political agitation in both Britain and America against the slave trade, as well as by the historical development of what we now identify as romantic aesthetic and cultural ideologies that were themselves the partial outgrowth of sentimental culture. The major epistemological questions facing antislavery imaginative writers and political activists at the time involved the ability of antislavery representations to reconcile "truth" and "imagination." The literary politics of antislavery writers necessitated the claim to truth, because so much proslavery writing criticized their imaginative excesses. So activists like Thomas Clarkson countered, "Some people may suppose, from the melancholy account that has been given in the preceding chapter, that we have been absolutely dealing in romance: that the scene is rather a dreary picture of the imagination than a representation of fact."[102]

The aversion to "romance" raised particular questions about the epistemological reliability of poetry. In his summary of the London Abolition Committee's evidence offered to Parliament against the slave trade, William

Bell Crafton concluded that some readers simply relished "the perusal of pathetic poetry" for all "its tales of human woe."[103] Citing the fame of poets like Cowper and Day, Crafton lamented that prosaic, factual accounts like his did not wield the same rhetorical power as antislavery verse: "Yet the evidence delivered before the House of Commons, containing a true and faithful account of the miseries and wickedness attendant upon the traffic of their fellow creatures, unembellished by the flourishes of rhetoric, undecorated with the splendid habiliments of poetry, is almost in vain recommended to their notice." This kind of complaint—and it certainly was not exceptional—aimed to distinguish between "true" and "false" sympathy, or the appeal to the "mind" as opposed to the "nerves." The result, in Crafton's case, is a version of the aesthetic imagination in which sympathy is masculine: true sympathy resists the "effeminacy of manners" or "extreme DELICACY."[104] His objection might appear at first to be curiously self-defeating. Why, after all, lament the sentimental means by which antislavery was gaining popularity? Yet the complaint is consistent with the antislavery motif of regulation, which controls both the aesthetic imagination and commerce.

The antislavery position on the imagination was in fact highly ambiguous. Lurking within Crafton's argument is the irrepressible sense of the importance of the imaginative faculties and discourses to spread the antislavery Word. Antislavery poets themselves recognized how, especially by the time the slave trade was abolished, sentimental conventions had themselves become so formulaic as to rob them of affective power for readers. In 1810 the British poet James Montgomery, for example, noted that there was no "subject so various and excursive, yet so familiar and exhausted, as the African slave trade,—a subject which had become antiquated, by frequent, minute, and disgusting exposure; . . . which public feeling has been wearied into insensibility, by the agony of interest which the question excited, during twenty-three years of almost incessant discussion."[105] Such a realization is premised upon the epistemological ambiguity of "truth" and "imagination," the mutually animating relation of these abstract terms that Crafton, for example, is unable to recognize fully. If not the historical, then the political truth—or reality—of antislavery depends upon the power of sentimental discourse to mobilize the passions of readers.

Moreover, the prose literature of antislavery politics was itself highly sensationalist. It made use of what Crafton (or Clarkson) identify as poetic and imaginative discourses that might obscure the factual realities of the African slave trade. Antislavery politicians, ministers, and humanitarian reformers from Anthony Benezet onward apparently recognized the rhetorical necessity of imaginative writing to further political needs. As one minister put it in 1774, "Now transport yourselves in imagination to Africa, and see two armies assembled to battle. . . . Oh, the dying groans! The cries of the wounded! The shrieks of the women and children who have lost their friends in battle, and are now being seized and sold!—But the scene is too shocking to describe to this assembly—let imagination conceive of the rest if possible!"[106] This observation blurs even the generic distinction between antislavery prose and poetry. Well-known antislavery pamphlets, such as Benjamin Rush's *An Address to the Inhabitants of the British Settlements in America, upon Slave-Keeping* (1773), made use of statistical data, eyewitness accounts, biblical citation and exegesis, moral abstraction, testimony from abolitionist authorities, the philosophy of Montesquieu and others, and economic theory. But at crucial moments they also embraced the rhetoric of sensational melodrama:

> Think of the bloody wars which are fomented by it, among the African nations. . . . Think of the many thousands who perish by sickness, melancholy and suicide, in their voyages to America. Pursue the poor devoted victims to one of the West India islands, and see them exposed there to public sale. Hear their cries, and see their looks of tenderness at each other upon being separated.—Mothers torn from their daughters, and brothers from brothers, without the liberty of a parting embrace. . . . But let us pursue them into a sugar field and behold a scene still more affecting than this—See! The poor wretches with what reluctance they take their instruments into their hands. . . . But, let us return from this scene, and see the various modes of arbitrary punishments inflicted upon them by their masters. Behold one covered with stripes, into which melted wax is poured—another tied down to a block or a stake—a third suspended in the air by the thumbs—a fourth obliged to set or stand upon red hot iron—a fifth,—I cannot relate it.[107]

Asking readers to identify with the plight of Africans, Rush and many like him resorted to titillating scenes of violence and violation that appealed directly to heightened imaginations. In Rush (and the passage cited above it) the representation of African suffering ends ("I cannot relate it," "if possible") where the imagination exclusively begins. Left to their own sympathies, readers complete the gothic horror that imaginative identification creates. The next chapter turns to a different kind of enslavement where Americans were subjected to North Africans. The dynamics of both imaginative identification and cultural representation would change altogether.

CHAPTER 3

American Slaves in North Africa

E notes are enemies—Savage, Briton, and Algier
Who plunder our shipping, or scalp on the frontier.

—"Political Alphabet; or Touch of the Times," *Boston Gazette and Weekly Republican Magazine* (1794)

The literature of Barbary captivity expanded significantly between the 1780s and 1810s, when hundreds of American mariners were imprisoned during the naval wars the United States fought with Algiers and Tripoli.[1] As Americans complained about the "enslavement" of its citizens, they simultaneously called attention to the moral inconsistency between republican principles and the participation of their country in slavery and the slave trade.[2] "Barbary captivity," as Paul Baepler recently has put it, "served as a mirror with which to critique the integrity of democracy in the new republic, just as it was used to question the practice of slave holding in a newly freed nation."[3] Needless to say, antislavery writing exploited the irony of Americans enslaved to Africans to the point where it virtually became a rhetorical convention. During the Constitutional debates of 1787–88, for example, one anonymous writer for a New England newspaper complained, "We reprobate the conduct of the Algerines; their conduct truly is highly reprehensible—they enslave the Americans—the Americans enslave the Africans; which is worst [sic]? Six of one and half a dozen of the other."[4]

This kind of equivalence thickens the complexity of cross-cultural identifications in antislavery works. During this era, these writers urged American audiences to "see" themselves as North African slave-holders or as African slaves. While ministers like Samuel Hopkins drew upon typological language to condemn slave-holders as "Egyptian taskmasters,"[5] satirists like Benjamin Franklin, writing in one of his final pieces under the persona of "Sidi Mehemet Ibrahim," humorously identified American proslavery supporters with Islamic despotism. Antislavery writing enforced as well the sympathetic identification between enslaved Africans in America and enslaved Americans in Africa. In the early 1790s, for example, one petitioner to the U.S. Congress lamented that far too many Americans "should be so enslaved by illiberal prejudice, as to treat with contempt a like solicitude for another class of men [Africans] still more grievously oppressed. . . . I feel the calls of humanity as strong towards an African in America, as to an American in Algiers, both being my brethren; especially as I am informed the Algerine treats his slave with more humanity."[6]

The complexity of identification and misidentification is significant, especially in light of the recent critical tendency to emphasize Barbary captivity genre's racial and cultural oppositions.[7] The historian Joanne Melish summarizes the relation between American and African slavery: "This potential mutability of whites into slaves/people of color in Africa offered as great a symbolic challenge to the American social order as the actual mutability of blacks into freemen/whites at home; both could be read symptomatically to evaluate the potential political, social, and perhaps biological consequences of democracy and emancipation." The Barbary captivity genre tested "the durability of republican whiteness" and ultimately naturalized "the stability of whiteness and blackness in the face of [U.S.] enslavement."[8] This is consistent with the argument that these works of captivity and enslavement "were polemically structured around raced and gendered distinctions between liberty and slavery, morality and licentiousness—the dualistic rhetoric feeding omnivorously on the discourse as it had been sketched in the cultural imaginary."[9] Hence canonical literary works such as Royall Tyler's *The Algerine Captive* (1797) fantasize about "a race uniquely American": "The metaphor of Algerian captivity provided a chance at resolving the conflicts of American society through the invention of a composite threat [of "Indian, African American, savage slave master, British, and French"] that would both chastise and unify the nation through the dichotomous metaphors of race: dark and pure, corrupt and chosen."[10]

What *is* an "American" race? In these accounts, it becomes a form of whiteness that ultimately racializes the new American nation. I would argue, however, that the literature of American enslavement produces more pointed meditations on the nature of American culture than on race per se. My argument rests on the third term of the equation, so to speak, which seems to have got lost in discussions of the politics of American antislavery literature during the 1790s: Great Britain. During this era, after all, the

United States was embroiled in political and maritime conflict with both Britain and Algiers—indeed, many Americans blamed their Mediterranean woes on British diplomatic intrigue. The popular resistance to British barbarity against Americans further suggests the cultural focus of American antislavery literature. Notwithstanding the rhetoric of political propaganda, this popular trope during the 1790s problematizes the correlation of civilization with whiteness or even with Christianity. It raises crucial questions about the nature of cultural refinement in civilized societies, questions that underlie American literature about enslavement in North Africa.

As Raymond Williams has argued, for much of the eighteenth century the categories of "civilization" and "culture" were interchangeable, but their meanings eventually diverged. Part of the reason for this, Williams claims, "was the attack on 'civilization' as superficial; an 'artificial' as distinct from a 'natural' state; a cultivation of external properties—politeness and luxury— as against more human needs and impulses."[11] This certainly was not an exclusively American historical development. The historian John Brewer has argued that the commercialization of British culture in this period produced ongoing debates over the nature of aesthetics, refinement, and gendered identity. In an early number of the *Spectator,* for example, Richard Steele proclaimed that "the most polite Age is in danger of being the most vicious."[12] Much later in the eighteenth century, Americans faced the dual adversaries of Britain and Algiers, which forced their confrontation with the ambiguities of civilization.

In this chapter I intend to unsettle the critical paradigm for Barbary captivity literature that racially juxtaposes Americans and North Africans, by placing this literature in the generally overlooked historical context of Britain's role in these maritime and naval conflicts. Between the 1780s and 1810s American writings about North African captivity consistently blamed Britain not only for preying on American commerce but urging Muslim nations in the Mediterranean to do so as well. Contemporary commentators generally vilify these political enemies, and further make the argument that each represents the cultural extremes of barbarity and over-refinement— extremes which actually resided along an ideological continuum. Like the African slave trade, the American one led to condemnation of barbaric practices in civilized states. Hence I will examine the Barbary political crisis in the context of debates about the generally unpopular Jay's Treaty between the United States and Britain, and through the important literary works about Barbary captivity by Susanna Rowson, Royall Tyler, and Washington

Irving. Each in unique ways dramatizes the problem of American enslavement in context of America's transatlantic relations; each meditates on the
nature of Anglo-American cultural ties; each articulates the problem of slavery with an eye towards the equivalent savagery of Muslims and Britons.

Intimate Relations

During the post-Revolutionary era the United States became involved in political conflicts with Great Britain and the North African states of Algiers and
Tripoli, which stood at the frontier of the Ottoman Empire. After the Revolution the American carrying trade no longer enjoyed the protection of the
British navy in the Mediterranean. The states of Algiers, Morocco, Tripoli,
and Tunis had been seizing European vessels and ransoming hostages for
hundreds of years; the first crisis for the United States occurred in 1785,
when an Algerian xebec captured the Boston schooner, *Maria*. Over the next
decade Algiers seized more than a dozen American vessels and captured
about 150 American mariners, who languished in prison for over a decade
largely because of diplomatic confusion and lack of national funds to pay
their ransom. Eventually, in 1795, the United States signed a treaty with Algiers, and the following year American captives were released. Several years
later, after the Jeffersonian administration refused to pay tribute to the
Tripolitan pasha, the Americans got embroiled in another maritime conflict
with Tripoli, which declared war on the United States in 1801. With the capture of the American frigate *Philadelphia* in 1804, over three hundred American mariners were held captive until the war ended in an American victory
the following year.[13]

During the early 1790s, American foreign relations with Algiers were directly related to those with Great Britain. Both were strained to the point of
war. The Jay Treaty of 1794–95 avoided war with Britain, but it by no means
addressed all of the major issues angering the United States at that time.
These included Britain's unwillingness to evacuate the northwest posts and
thereby open up the Native American trade; its seizure of "contraband" on
American ships headed for France; its impressment of American mariners
into the British navy during its wars with France; and its commercial restrictions on American trade to British ports, especially in the West Indies. The
power of the British navy tilted the terms of the treaty. It delayed evacuation
of the posts, put severe limits on the American West Indian trade, and contained no guarantees whatsoever of American neutral rights.[14] When the

treaty was finally made public in the summer of 1795, it met with widespread, even violent, opposition, and the Federalists were accused of sacrificing the nation's interests and its reputation. But Washington's support lent the treaty credibility; it passed in Congress because it simply was the best the United States could do.

The treaty exacerbated anti-British popular opinion and highlighted important cultural issues about the relations between the two nations. In an era in which domestic and foreign relations were inextricably bound, both Federalists and Republicans fought vehemently over both the terms and future implications of the treaty. According to two of the most influential historians of the late eighteenth century, the conflict with Britain posed "a deep crisis of spirit" for Americans. Those who opposed the treaty believed "the manners and morals of the Republic needed protection—protection against British money, British consumer goods, and British ideas: that was what [James] Madison really meant by 'commerce.'"[15] As one critic asked at this time, "To stand in this intimate political relation with the old, corrupt, and almost expiring government of Great Britain—that government which stands foremost in the wars of Europe . . . accords not with the spirit and principles of the free constitution and government of the United States, or with the genius, temper, and feelings of the republican citizens of America."[16]

The debate over the nature of Anglo-American cultural relations often expressed itself through the figure of the national—or transnational—body. This trope went right to the issue of national health. Federalists imagined the national body as still figuratively connected to Britain. Assessing the terms of the treaty, for example, one South Carolinian supporter wrote: "But it was observed, on the other side, that these restrictions [i.e., import duties on British goods] would probably widen the breach between us and Britain instead of closing it; would irritate rather than heal the wound."[17] Republican opponents objected not only to the regulations imposed on American trade in the British West Indies but also to the free circulation of British goods and citizens *within* the body of the United States itself.[18] Anti-treaty rhetoric alienated Britain by figuring it as a foreign—and toxic—substance to the national body. As one letter to the *Boston Gazette and Weekly Republican Journal* put it, "We ought with the lancet to have extracted all the British from our COUNTRY, to appease the manes of the patriotic who have died for this Country's liberties."[19]

Thus the treaty's explicit call for a "true and sincere friendship" between the two nations elicited rather polarized responses from Americans. In his famous speech before Congress, the New England Federalist Fisher Ames sardonically contemplated the Republican fantasy of England "sinking into the sea": "[W]here there are now men and wealth and laws and liberty, there was no more than a sand bank for sea monsters to fatten on; [there would be instead] a space for the storms of the ocean to mingle in conflict."[20] Republicans countered the argument emphasizing British stability by recasting it as a nation whose very commercial prosperity had made it corrupt. "Had *we* robbed Great Britain?," Atticus asked. "Had we kept possession of a part of her territory, that was to have been surrendered by positive stipulation. . . . Had *we* impressed her seamen, contrary to every rule of justice, and obligation of humanity?"[21] As another opponent argued in the *Newport Mercury,* the treaty tried "with unwearied pains to bind with adamantine chains the Commerce of this Country to the arbitrary power and control of GREAT-BRITAIN." The writer urged readers to remember the "atrocities" committed against the United States, and to "behold every brutish action, that disgrace the dignity and humanity of man—exercised by a merciless crew upon the defenseless Inhabitants, and enormities and barbarities too shocking to be mentioned . . . Can you wish yourself connected with such a power?"[22]

The treaty's antagonists naturally invoked Revolutionary memories to inflame Anglophobic feelings. Political propaganda aside, the strategy raised important cultural issues about Anglo-American relations. Even the most pedestrian literary productions reveal these. For example, the anonymously published "A Poem on Jay's Treaty" (1795) lampooned the treaty and vilified Jay by contriving a political typology connecting the 1770s and 1790s:

> Ye Patriots true, that's brave and bold,
> That stood the "times that try'd the soul";
> That guarded well the public weal,
> Once more to you we now appeal—
> Is't Britain's pow'r—or is it gold?
> Are we conquer'd? or are we sold?
> Must we submit, or war, the fate?
> Or caught like fish, with gold for bait?[23]

The allusion to the opening of Thomas Paine's *The Crisis* (1776) contextualizes the present moment. As the passage goes on, however, the fantasy of a second Revolutionary *rage militaire* rhetorically collapses into a series of nervous questions. The juxtaposition of "pow'r" with "gold" leaves open the question of whether America is "conquer'd" (from without) or "sold" (from within). Who is the real enemy, the speaker wonders, Britain or American society itself?[24]

All the more galling was the popular belief that Britain had worked behind the scenes to encourage Algiers to sabotage American trade. One writer claimed, for example, that "the intrigues of the British cabinet" conspired to establish a truce between Portugal and Algiers, which subsequently exposed American ships to the latter's "piratical rapacity."[25] As the Virginia jurist St. George Tucker argued, the agreement "does not stipulate that Great Britain (instead of exciting the Algerines to annoy our commerce, and enslave our citizens, as we have too much reason to believe she has done) should use her good offices with them in favor of the United States."[26] In his *Short Account of Algiers* (1794), the Philadelphia printer Mathew Carey, an Irish immigrant known for his anti-British feeling, similarly argued that Britain "adopted the miserable expedient of turning loose the Algerines, [so] that these execrable ruffians *might plunder our property, and plunge our fellow-citizens into slavery.*"[27]

This accusation did not merely catalogue British politics but lampooned British culture. Specifically, it likened Britain to Algiers, since both were guilty of waging "piratical warfare" against innocent Americans. The preface to the novel *Humanity in Algiers: or, the Story of Azem* (1801) declared that "A vile, piratical set of unprincipled robbers is the softest name we can give them."[28] Carey claimed that both the British and Algerians "plundered" shipwrecked crews on their respective coasts and "treated [them] with the utmost savageness."[29] The war with Tripoli produced much the same rhetoric. William Ray's patriotic poem, "To the Memory of Commodore Preble," began by scourging Britain and Tripoli as equivalent menaces to American liberty:

> While war, fierce monster, stained with guiltless blood,
> Roars, threats, and rages round the infuriate flood,
> While hostile Britons murdering fleets employ
> To infest our harbors and our ships destroy,
> Impress our tars in their inglorious cause,
> In base defiance of all nation's laws;
> When each bold veteran, in his country's name,
> Is called to save her freedom and her fame;

When few whose bravery and whose nautic skill
Can duly execute her sovereign will;
What sighs of sorrow waft from shore to shore,
With these sad tidings—"*Preble is no more!*"
    Erst when mad Tripoli, in prowess vain,
With her rapacious corsairs blocked the main;
Poured round our ships in predatory swarms,
With purple banners and audacious arms—
Our neutral cargoes plundered on the waves,
And made our free-born citizens her slaves.[30]

The parallel crimes of impressment and enslavement produce the argument equating "hostile Britons" with "mad Tripoli." Neither nation respects enlightened trade. Such equivalence, moreover, rhetorically *conflates* Christian and Muslim nations. For the poem's accusation that Britain's "murdering fleets" destroy American ships more fittingly describes the Tripolitans during its war with the United States, while its claim that Tripoli violates "neutral cargoes" better describes British naval policy.[31]

The poet's language certainly resembles what Kenneth Silverman has called "Whig sentimentalism," which during the Revolutionary era sensationalized the British ravishing of American innocence.[32] By the 1790s, however, the literary conventions of antislavery reshaped the particular language and imagery of this political propaganda. One kind of antislavery discourse, in other words, significantly affected another. Likening the British to North African infidels—and both to "savage" slave traders preying upon West Africa—the literature of Barbary captivity unsettled the cultural borders between Europeans and North Africans and between Christians and Muslims. Consider, for example, St. George Tucker's denunciation of the Jay Treaty:

Of all the injuries to which mankind are exposed, those committed on the *high seas* are most easily perpetrated, and most difficult to be prevented or punished. The conduct of *privateersmen* differs in nothing from that of *pirates*, except in circumstances of obtaining a previous license to exercise their *nefarious practices*. That of the commanders of ships of war but too often partakes [more] of the insolence of the bashaw than that courtesy of a soldier of honor.[33]

The main rhetorical components of antislavery literature about the African slave trade are all here: the universal context for morality, the epithet of "nefarious" commerce, the correlation of such commerce with piracy, the bogus kind of refinement that language falsely draws between such piracy and privateering. Tucker's language recalls Thomas Clarkson's argument in *An Essay on the Slavery and Commerce of the Human Species* (1786), that the piracy of the ancients marks the point from which the progress of "civilization" may be charted.[34] As a commercial trope, piracy enables the cultural critique of both Christian and Muslim slave traders, and helps to produce the damning equation of a British officer and the Algerine bashaw.

The ideological association of barbarity and over-refinement helped to create the rhetorical British Muslim. This is not an instance of cultural hybridity, as cultural theorists today conceive of that category, but rather a figure in the service of the cultural project of writing nationalist satire. The trope, in other words, emphasized not creative syncresis but ironic resemblance—specifically, how and why a presumably civilized nation like Britain had been reduced to Muslim barbarity. If this did not let the United States off the hook for trading in slaves, it still located the greater villain across the Atlantic. As Carey bitingly put it, "For this practice of buying and selling slaves, we are not entitled to charge the Algerines with any exclusive degree of barbarity. The Christians of Europe and America carry on this commerce a hundred times more effectively than the Algerines. It has received a recent sanction from the immaculate *Divan* of Britain."[35]

The satiric potential of such a conflation led to imaginative debunking of Britons. Like this era's antislavery writings about the abuse of Africans, this subgenre too deliberately jeopardized the sanctity of Christian identity. One newspaper in 1795 published a "Letter from an English Slave-driver at Algiers to his Friend in England" that employs the common antislavery strategies of inversion and exaggeration:

By the Blessing of God, I have now got into a very good birth [*sic*]. I have the command of twenty slaves, some Spanish, some English, and some American. I get my victuals, and equal to one shilling a day besides, and all for driving the slaves to the field, and keeping them to work when they are there. To be sure, it went hard with me at first to whip my country folks; but custom, as the saying is, is second nature. . . . People may say this or that about the infidels; but sure am I they do not deserve to be extirpated any more than the English themselves. For one white slave that we have here the English have ten black ones in the West Indies, and they use their slaves much more cruelly than we do ours.[36]

Identifiable literary conventions of antislavery—the association of slave-holding with avarice, the commodification of humanity, the emphasis upon religious hypocrisy—satirize the fictional British narrator. Not only does the passage uncouple race and slavery, since American, African, Spanish, and British slaves are mentioned, but it also detaches "Englishness" from "civilization."

One purpose of this and other narratives of British savagery was to distract attention from the obvious national embarrassment over American involvement in the African slave trade. The strategy included not only political speeches and public documents but belletristic writing as well. Thus the anonymously authored poem, *The American in Algiers; or the Patriot of Seventy-Six in Captivity* (1797), called for relief of American citizens who were enslaved in North Africa. Rather than ignore the issue, the poem directly contrasts American slavery abroad with African slavery in America. Divided into two cantos, it employs two speakers: an American war veteran once enslaved in Algiers, and an African now enslaved in America. If this points to the ethical paradox of a slave-holding republic, its opening canto skirts this issue, emphasizing instead the equivalence between British and Algerines: "vile scourges of the human race," "hoard of pirates," "unfeeling butchers"[37]

In the second canto, however, the African speaker turns around the argument about the barbarity of Christian manners to highlight this same problem in the United States. Reminiscent of the persona of the sympathetic African employed in so much Anglo-American antislavery poetry, this speaker asks the "gentle reader" to compare "that piratic coast" of Algiers with Columbia's "widespread empire throng'd with slaves" (p. 21). Yet the poem then works to manage this ethical inconsistency and recover the ethical high ground. To do so it commercializes the issue of slavery. Not unlike Philip Freneau's "To Sir Toby," this one elides national culpability by invoking Jefferson's argument in the original draft of the *Declaration of Independence* blaming the British empire for foisting vicious commerce upon America:

> To call forth all the vices of the cane,
> Confusion's fire, and friendship's mortal bane;
> To introduce luxurious rules of art,
> To sink the genius and enslave the heart
> To make mankind in vicious habits bold,
> By bart'ring virtue for the love of gold. (pp. 21–22).

Patriotic as it is, *The American in Algiers* ultimately establishes the transatlantic theme of slave trading, a rhetorical and political move that both complements and competes with its national indictment of the slaveholding republic. Moreover, by at once locating, and then displacing, American culpability, the poem implicitly queries the proper relations the United States should maintain with Britain.

The American condemnation of British aristocracy exploited the ideological proximity between refinement and barbarity. No better example of this appears in this literature than William Ray's *Horrors of Slavery* (1808), a captivity narrative in poetry and prose, combining the discourses of sentiment, seduction, and reform, written by an American mariner aboard the *Philadelphia* when it ran aground off the coast of Tripoli in 1803. The narrative directly responded to Dr. Jonathan Cowdery's *American Captives in Tripoli* (1806), an account of the relative ease which Cowdery, a privileged gentleman, enjoyed in Tripoli. Long before he experiences "despicable bondage" of "Turkish servitude," Ray emphasizes the mistreatment he and other common "tars" undergo in the U.S. navy. Indeed, *Horrors of Slavery* unfolds the theme of captivity in ways that make it a proto-Jacksonian polemic against the antidemocratic—and highly British—privilege of class. Whereas autobiographies like *The Journal of the Travels and Sufferings of Daniel Saunders* (1802) or James Cathcart's *The Captives, Eleven Years in Algiers* (1899) likened North African and British forms of enslavement,[38] Ray expands upon this analogy to philosophize more vigilantly about the barbaric nature of all aristocratic traditions. At the outset, he declares

> that petty despotism is not confined alone to Barbary's execrated and piratical shores; but that base and oppressive treatment may be experienced from officers of the American, as well as the British and other navies; that our countrymen, as well as those of other nations, when invested with the robe and cockade of authority, can act the insolent tyrant, inflict tortures for petty offenses . . . and with a contemptible pride and brutal ferocity, that would disgrace the character of a savage despot, stamp an indelible stigma on the nature of an American officer.[39]

Ray's denunciation of social hierarchy draws on the Federalist symbol of the "cockade of authority"—a move that cannot fail to recall the image William Dunlap employed in his highly controversial drama *Andre* (1798), about Washington's decision to execute a British spy. Throughout, Ray savages American social pretensions by associating them specifically with British and Algerian vices. This kind of antidemocratic behavior is both effeminate and brutal. The "cruel, vain, and magisterial coxcomb of an officer," for example, wields "the authority of a West-Indian slave-driver, and inhumanity of a Tripolitan or Algerine."[40] Like the English slave driver satirized above, who loses his civilized "Englishness," Ray's American officers engage in "emulous imitation" that sacrifices their "Americanness."

The larger antislavery themes of seduction inform the presentation in *Horrors of Slavery* of a particularly democratic form of sympathy. Certainly, the denunciations of the Jay Treaty also provide a context for this, for they represented Jay himself as alternatively the victim and agent of British seduction. In order to dramatize the abuse of innocent American workingmen, Ray emphasizes their vulnerability (à la Clara Wieland to Carwin) to double-tongued, haughty officers of the U.S. navy. Likening the process of American recruitment to British impressment, Ray offers a sociological exposé of post-Revolutionary urban America. Just as antislavery writers like William Roscoe were sensitive to the seductive power of new consumer goods upon African sensibilities, Ray sympathizes with newly arrived rubes to the American city who are undoubtedly out of their league. The recruiting officer-as-rake is "armed with a whinyard of enormous length and huge dimensions"; he wears "a large harness buckle, polished and glittering like the shield of Achilles; on his snow powdered-sconce [is] a cap; on the front of which a large brass plate, with the American spread eagle, like the Helmet of Hector, dazzling all the eyes with the effulgence of its beams."[41] Like the Africans of the Anglo-American antislavery imagination, these poor white men are intoxicated by the power of consumer goods.

Criticism of cultural refinement begs the question of whether there was a viable alternative for Americans to follow. The impossibility of adequately theorizing "civilized" commercial society in the face of slavery led some critics of the Algerian crisis to doubt the foundations of progressive history. Thus James Wilson Stevens, in his *Historical and Geographical Account of Algiers*, called both North African and European forms of slavery "incontestable evidence of the remains of barbarism in those nations who sanction so diabolical a principle."[42] Stevens contemplated a future where

the more general diffusion of science will teach them the true principles of justice and humanity. But the grand science of universal benevolence must be reserved for future ages; for though many modern nations imagine themselves to be eminently enlightened, yet they are in fact just beginning

to emerge from the intermediate state between barbarity and true refinement.

> For the practice of slavery we are not to reprobate the Algerines alone; for
> the divan of Great Britain are equally reprehensible, and have more emi-
> nently distinguished themselves in this nefarious commerce. From them we
> have adopted the execrable practice, and the United States, emphatically
> called the land of liberty, swarm with those semi-barbarians who enthrall
> their fellow creatures without the least remorse. With what countenance
> then can we reproach a set of barbarians, who have only retorted our own
> acts upon ourselves in making reprisals upon our citizens?[43]

Britain plays the role of cultural foil—that is, Stevens blames Britain for the
"nefarious practice" of U.S. slave trading. By employing a particular kind of
ironic language ("the divan of Great Britain"), the passage collapses the
boundary between civilized and savage nations, a move that is compounded
by the uncertain distinction between the "barbarians" trading in American
slaves and the "semi-barbarians" trading in African ones. Whereas William
Ray understands aristocracy to be essentially brutal, Stevens views the Euro-
American world as poised precariously between "barbarity and true refinement." However, he is able only to define the problem rather than articulate the solution. For the passage (and the entire work) fails to specify the
nature of "true refinement." What does it mean to be "eminently enlightened"? Can the United States continue to engage in commercial and cultural forms of exchange with Britain and maintain its cultural integrity?
How does one judge the proper balance of Anglo-American "trade"?

Reuniting the British-American Family

Susanna Rowson's play *Slaves in Algiers; or a Struggle for Freedom* engages such
questions through a plot involving a British-American family. First performed on June 30, 1794, at the Chestnut Street Theater in Philadelphia,
Rowson's play appeared during the time when the United States was engaged in diplomatic negotiations with both Britain and Algiers. Indeed, the
play's appearance coincided with the beginning of John Jay's diplomatic
mission to Britain—making it seem that political theater and American diplomatic politics are performing parallel missions. While U.S. envoy John Jay
was negotiating perhaps the best terms that his country could expect from
Britain, the British immigrant playwright Susanna Rowson was imagining

newly restored cultural relations between the two nations. Put another way, Rowson's play spins its own version of Alexander Hamilton's optimistic vision of the "unfolding mutual advantages" between the United States and Great Britain.[44]

Slaves in Algiers rehabilitates Anglo-American relations through the dramatic lens of the transatlantic domain. Traditional readings of the play highlight its nationalist sentiments as well as Rowson's role in the development of early American drama.[45] Revisionist readings emphasize more subversive meanings, which produce a feminist critique of domestic relations in the early American republic. Cathy N. Davidson, for example, calls the play "a historical drama crossed with a not completely satiric feminist tract," while another critic claims it is "an important text of feminist political ideology in American drama."[46] Both critical approaches remain within nationalist parameters.[47] They both lose sight of the transatlantic historical and biographical contexts for the play, ones that suggest a far more complex dramatic meditation on American identity.

Rowson's early life itself resembles that of the uprooted protagonist (such as Moll Flanders, Roderick Random, Charlotte Temple) of the eighteenth-century novel. Born in 1762 in Portsmouth, England, Rowson never knew her mother, who died shortly after the birth. At age five, she went to live in Nantasket, Massachusetts, with her father, William Haswell, a British naval officer who had resettled and remarried there. Life was generally pleasant for the family until the American Revolution disrupted its world. Haswell's neutrality eventually became untenable in patriotic Massachusetts, and in 1775 he and his family were removed from their home and placed under arrest. Three years later, in 1778, they finally were able to leave America for London, where poverty forced the teenage girl into the role of provider, which she fulfilled by teaching, songwriting, and acting. In 1786 she made an unfortunate marriage to the hardware merchant and hack actor (and perpetual drunk) William Rowson. The couple obtained acting jobs in provincial town companies outside London and eventually in Edinburgh, but their financial position was uncertain enough to make them receptive to Thomas Wignell's offer in 1793 to join his New American Company in Philadelphia. They spent two years there before moving to Boston, where Rowson eventually abandoned the theater and returned to writing and the education of girls.

Rowson's biography informs not only the transatlantic plot but also the new cultural identity imagined in *Slaves in Algiers*. Notwithstanding the play's patriotic cant, it ultimately dramatizes an Anglo-American identity made possible by reunification of the Constant family. Some critics tend to read *Slaves in Algiers* for "the overt comparison it makes between marriage and slavery and between patriarchal power and the power of a ruling despot."[48] That is, the political context of Algerian slavery comments on the nature of domestic, or conjugal, relations. I want to consider instead how the domestic context of the Constant family—"constant in every sense"—provides audiences in the 1790s with political and cultural solutions to Anglo-American relations.

The historical scope of *Slaves in Algiers* covers a good part of the Revolutionary period. Between 1780 and 1794—"fourteen years of deep affliction"[49]—the Anglo-American family has fallen apart. The play's most important familial plot, focusing on the Constant family, actually prefigures the literary conventions of historical romances of the American Revolution that appeared in the 1820s. James Fenimore Cooper's *The Spy* (1822) and Catharine Maria Sedgwick's *The Linwoods* (1835), for example, contain romance plots that confound patriotic and loyalist allegiances. In *Slaves in Algiers,* the romance plot between an American woman and a British officer symbolizes not only national divisions produced by the Revolution but international ones as well. Rebecca and her husband Constant represent the cultural bond between British and American citizens.

Act I stages the captivities of three important female characters. Each captivity is related to the divided Constant family. Each, moreover, might be said to reflect the American audience's own captivity to nationalist ideology—until the play's final scene liberates them from it. Who are these female captives? The play's maternal heroine, Rebecca Constant, is held captive by the Jewish moneylender Ben Hassan, who wants to marry her; Fetnah, Hassan's daughter and Rebecca's protégé, is one of the wives of the Dey, Muley Moloc; and Olivia suffers as the favorite of the Dey, who eventually agrees to free her father if she will marry him. Much of the plot revolves around the planned escape of the American captives in Algiers, most notably Henry (who is in love with Olivia) and Frederick (who is in love with virtually everyone else). Eventually, Rebecca is able to secure the release of her son Augustus, and in the final scene learns that Olivia and her imprisoned father, Constant, are Rebecca's own long-lost husband and daughter, from whom she and her son were tragically separated during the Revolutionary war. The slave rebellion is successful, and the Anglo-American family reunites to return to America.

The family trope for Anglo-American relations was not unique to either Rowson or the early American stage. In 1795, for example, the Massachusetts minister Isaac Story published two sermons that aimed to raise money for American captives. Taking his text from Exodus 2.11, Story rehashed the history of Jewish enslavement (the shopworn parallel for that of republican Americans), and focused in particular on the discovery of the infant Moses by Egyptians. The tale of a mother forced to abandon her child in order to save him, and of the surrogate who cares for him, forges the sentimental appeal to Americans for their enslaved brethren abroad.[50] Yet this story of two mothers confuses the terms for the affective nation. While the eventual reunification of the son with his Jewish mother allegorizes (or typologizes) the American Israel, Moses, standing in for George Washington, enjoyed the benevolence of both mothers. The sermon asks implicitly, what is the "American" family?

The complexity of the Anglo-American family is the theme that *Slaves in Algiers* fully pursues. Who is part of the true American family? This is the central context for the play's dramatization of a series of false, or hopelessly corrupt, familial relations. It also shapes the play's representation of captivity: Rebecca's potentially mercenary marriage to Hassan, Olivia's decision to prostitute herself to Muley as his "wife," and the role Zoriana must play as the despot's dutiful daughter. If these captivities highlight patriarchal foibles, they also introduce the important thematic tension between affective and bloodline relations. This tension is at the heart of the issue of the true family, and it dominates the drama from its very beginning. In the opening scene, Fetnah tells Selima how important her surrogate mother, Rebecca Constant, is to her. "It was she who nourished in my mind the love of liberty and taught me woman was never formed to be the abject slave of man" (p. 60). Most readers recognize Fetnah as the most complex, ambiguous character, chiefly because her English, Jewish, and Muslim identities resist racial oversimplification. Her declaration of loyalty to Rebecca introduces the play's gendered concerns, but it also inaugurates the revision of the figure of the British Muslim, which circulated widely during the early 1790s as the United States became embroiled in maritime conflicts with both Britain and Algiers. In this case, the symbolic American mother—Rebecca—morally redeems the British daughter, who is not quite British. As in Story's sermon, the play intermingles the roles of natural and surrogate families, which in both cases converge upon the figure of the feeling mother. In Rowson's play, the "natural" family consists of the American mother who reunites with her

British husband and daughter; the newly constructed family excludes the Jewish father, Ben Hassan, but includes his British-Jewish daughter whom Rebecca embraces.

Leonard Tennenhouse has argued that in post-Revolutionary United States popular British seduction novels—including Rowson's *Charlotte, a Tale of Truth* (1791)—helped to maintain a cultural form of "Englishness" for politically independent Americans. Abridged American reprintings of such novels as *Pamela* (1740) and *Clarissa* (1748) displaced the importance of the heroine's sexual purity with her ability to construct a home based on "the rules of good conduct." This shift proposed the genre's fundamental question of cultural identity: "Are you Anglo-American because you are born of an English family, or are you Anglo-American because you live your life according to an English model?"[51] The issue was particularly volatile during the political crisis with Britain over commercial policy in the middle 1790s. *Slaves in Algiers* turns the cultural metaphor of Englishness into literal fact by maintaining the bloodline of the English father. But the play does not reduce enlightened morality to English genealogy; its familial plot forges a political and cultural solution by claiming "constant" affections for the true family. By reuniting the Constant family, it relocates the future of Anglo-American culture in America, for, as Henry says in Act II, the family will return to its "native land." Proponents of the Jay Treaty could not have hoped for a more appealing resolution.

The ongoing meditation upon the family and American identity in *Slaves in Algiers* leads to numerous pairings and doublings of the main characters. Act I immediately presents the affective contrast between Fetnah and her father Ben Hassan. The stereotype of the Jewish moneylender was actually a common trope in Barbary captivity literature. It appears in fictional works such as Tyler's *The Algerine Captive* and James Ellison's *The American Captive* (1812) and in Jonathan Cowdery's autobiography, *American Captives in Tripoli* (1806). Hassan's status as a comic ethnic stereotype, however, tends to obscure the importance of his British background, especially for audiences in the 1790s. His Jewish/British traits equally explain his "avarice, treachery, and cruelty" (p. 92). Hassan is, after all, the play's chief slave trader, and he embodies the blend of commercial sophistication and barbaric inhumanity for which Americans faulted the British. Able to manipulate documents (Rebecca's bills of exchange), Hassan testifies to the association of artifice and paper credit at this time. (Think of *The Memoirs of Stephen Burroughs* [1798] and Brown's *Arthur Mervyn* [1798–1800].) His avarice, moreover, feminizes him. In Act III he appears on stage in drag, and Sebastian mistakes him for his would-be lover. "Consider the delicacy of my nerves" (p. 86), Hassan complains, trying to maintain his sexual disguise that is really no disguise at all. Whereas William Ray would later cast the coxcomb's brutality as the logical end of effeminacy, Rowson symbolically feminizes brutal avarice.

Yet the play goes on to redeem and reclaim British manhood, recasting it, however, within the thematic context of a new kind of American identity. This makes Hassan Constant's double, for the two men are, in effect, Rebecca's "true" and "false" British husbands. The play initially exploits the comic potential of the British Muslim, and then finds a cultural alternative in the enlightened British American. So, as the plot abandons burlesque comedy (contrived plot devices, sexual impersonations, and the confusion of identities), the former British officer, Constant, becomes the mouthpiece for American republicanism in the final scene. One of the few good lines he gets is the lecture he gives the Dey on the virtues of enlightened authority: "Open your prison doors. Give freedom to your people. Sink the name of the subject in the endearing epithet of fellow citizen. Then you will be loved and reverenced; then will you find, in promoting the happiness of others, you will have secured your own" (p. 93). Rowson—the childhood victim of Revolutionary violence—does not so much democratize as sentimentalize political authority. Indeed, the restoration of Constant's "ruined constitution" (both bodily and political) could be read as the symbolic embodiment of post-Revolutionary cultural norms of authority.[52]

The play's sentimentalization of political authority is commensurate with its reconsideration of the nature of citizenship. The dramatist does not merely show subjects turned into citizens—a thematic move that would be firmly within the fold of Revolutionary patriotism—but explores the wider meanings of citizenship. Act III stages a series of cultural and political conversions in Algiers, which raise the question of the proper field of attention for republican citizens. How far do their moral and political duties extend?

One of the ways that the play suggests the limitations of national identification is by repossessing the very language of Whig patriotism. When Rebecca, for example, calls Olivia "a daughter of Columbia and a Christian" (p. 91), the play implies the collateral necessity of national identity and humanitarian benevolence. Rebecca, the moral center of the play, declares, "I am an American; but while I only claim kinship with the afflicted, it is of little consequence where I first drew my breath" (p. 90). Such hedging lightly unsettles the patriotic cant based on the fundamental distinction between citizens and noncitizens, and it provides an important counterpoint to the mini-American Revolution against tyranny staged in the climactic scenes in Act III. Critics miss the complexity, for example, with which the play interrogates patriotic masculinity and at the end weds patriotism to Christian benevolence. Consider the final sequence: Frederick preaches Christian mercy in place of vengeance; Rebecca declares that "By the Christian law, no man should be a slave" (p. 92); Constant offers his solution for enlightened order; and the "freedom" Olivia proclaims symbolically fuses the American eagle with "the dove and the olive branch" (p. 93).[53]

This humanitarian form of nationalism is contingent in Act III on a flexible model of racial identification. Notwithstanding the caricatures of Muley and Hassan, race is a motile term largely synonymous with culture. The fate of each character depends upon his or her ability to embrace the enlightened form of Christianity that is the thematic focus of the play. This has the effect of confusing racial designations. The *Dramatis Personae*, for example, lists Fetnah as a "Moriscan," but, curiously enough, she later declares to Frederick, "Lord, I'm not a Moriscan. I hate 'em all. There is nothing I wish so much as to get away from them" (p. 73). What, then, *is* a "Moriscan"? A religious follower of the Koran's teachings? Or a regional designation (in an era generally observing the connection between physical and moral environments)? Fetnah's capacity for Christian humanity is unambiguous; she is doubled with Olivia and Zoriana, the Dey's daughter, who also declares, "I am a Christian in my heart" (p. 67). The play suggests that "Moriscan" and "Christian" identities are less a function of genealogy than of sensibility. Put another way, all racial and national identifications become the function of feeling—the only category, it would appear, that the play naturalizes. When the Dey finally asks Fetnah to stay in Algiers to morally uplift him, *Slaves in Algiers* suggests the potential for Muslim despots to undergo this kind of conversion: "I fear from following the steps of my ancestors, I have greatly erred. Teach me, then, you who so well know how to practice what is right, how to amend my faults" (p. 93). The roles of masters and slaves are thus reversed.

The distinction, then, between civilized and barbaric identities is firm but flexible, allowing for both moral and cultural regeneration. As a consequence of this thematic preoccupation, the language of Christian identity saturates the play. Recall that Henry is a "young Christian" who loves "this Christian maid"; to Ben Hassan, Frederick is "that wild young Christian" (p. 64) who has just ransomed himself from slavery; Zoriana wishes "to be a

Christian" and later exemplifies "Christian duty"; Rebecca is "the beautiful Christian" (p. 74); Frederick romantically seeks a "good-hearted Christian" (p. 76) and, in turn, is a "charming young Christian" (p. 77) to Fetnah; the Algerian Dey labels his enemies "Christian dogs" (p. 92); the Dey demands only that Olivia renounce her faith; the play ends with the possibility of re-generation for Hassan and the Muley.[54]

Why, then is Fetnah excluded from the reconstituted Anglo-American family? This question might very well raise the issue of Rowson's view of race,[55] but I contend that Fetnah's *de facto* exclusion is consistent with the play's final rejection of romantic conventions, particularly their direct asso-ciation with the dangerous faculty of the passions.[56] Indeed, Rowson's han-dling in Act III of the numerous romantic subplots thickens the thematic of antislavery—specifically, they dramatize the enslavement to the passions. Muley's uncontrollable desires, for example, epitomize the problem of self-regulation, which, to lesser degrees, plagues Ben Hassan, Frederick, Sebas-tian, and even Fetnah herself. Although many scenes treat the unregulated passions comically, the problem significantly crosses racial, cultural, and gendered borders. The danger of the lack of regulation is, after all, a com-mon theme in this era's antislavery literature. Rowson's unwillingness to find Fetnah a (white) romantic lover stems as much from antislavery politics of the 1790s as it does from either feminist concerns (for female indepen-dence) or racial bias (against intermarriage). Fetnah's fate is commensurate, moreover, with the sketchy and sometimes discarded love plots of *Slaves in Algiers*. The relationship between Henry and Olivia, for example, is notably muted; Zoriana and Sebastian virtually drop out of sight; and Fetnah re-nounces romantic passion in the name of a more altruistic—and balanced—ideal of benevolent love. No one is left on stage who is a slave to the pas-sions.

This ideal of balanced regulation extends as well to commercial relations. The play's many movements—from false to true husband, from captivity to restoration, and from the unregulated passions to regulated affections—is commensurate with its displacement of the slave trade with enlightened commerce. *Slaves in Algiers* regulates many forms of "commercial" exchange, and, like the literature about African slave trading, the play puts commercial capitalism under sentimental revision. Here the author resorts to cultural stereotypes. The Jew Ben Hassan becomes the symbolic locus of the play's commercial commentary, particularly the bills of exchange he secretly holds that keep Rebecca Constant his slave. "She does not know I got her pocket-book, with bills of exchange in it. She thinks I keep her in my house out of charity as if she was in her own country. . . . Yesh, here is the letter: ransom for Rebecca Constant and six other Christian slaves. Vell, I vill make her write for more. She is my slave; I must get all I can by her" (p. 64). Hassan's mastery of Rebecca stems from his manipulation of paper credit (a standard "republican" vice in the Pocockian sense), which amplifies the corruption of slave trading.

The question is whether the play offers an alternative model of virtuous commerce. *Slaves in Algiers* sentimentalizes capitalism, at least on the level of language, by manipulating the language of debts, credits, and exchange. This occurs, first, during the early conversation between Hassan and Rebecca, where all of the verbal irony arises from the rhetorical conflations of humanity and property. Hassan inquires about Rebecca's "ransom"; she guarantees her ability to "repay" him for her value as a slave; "I have kept you in my own house at my own expense," he tells her, noting secretly "for which I have been more than doubly paid" (p. 63). But as she wishes to "return [his] kindness," this language begins to suggest instead sentimental forms of exchange. The contrived plot device of Hassan's lost notes, now in Rebecca's possession, converts slave capitalism into virtuous commerce, since Rebecca plans to redeem the American slaves. "My child will soon be free," she exclaims, declaring her "gratitude for this unexpected blessing" (p. 84). In an ironic inversion of the economic logic of the slave trade, the mother unwittingly aims to buy back her daughter, whom she calls "a Christian maid" (p. 89). Rebecca thus brings together the play's sentimental and capitalist economies.

The tension between the two finally gives way to the value Rowson places on sentimental forms of exchange. In the climactic scene, where Olivia sells herself to Muley, she effectively removes the register for her own value from the context of slave capitalism. She offers herself to the Algerian in order to purchase the freedom of Christian slaves, a decision whose significance Muley altogether misses because, being a "heathen," he responds only to sexual appetite. Ironically, his passion also makes Olivia invaluable to him. "Woman," he tells Rebecca, "the wealth of Golconda could not pay her ransom" (p. 90). The deal Muley and Olivia tentatively strike represents the exchange of sexual passion and selfless benevolence; yet, in light of Olivia's plan to take her own life,[57] this nullifies the force of passion, bringing the play from its initial denunciation of inhumanity to its fantasy of a purely sentimental economy of credit and debt. By offering herself as collateral,

Olivia puts virtually everyone in the debt of gratitude to her—at least until the slave rebellion succeeds and the plot finally is resolved.

Rowson was not alone to deplore American Anglophobia of the early 1790s. One of the key diplomatic players in the release of the American captives, David Humphreys, also wrote poetry that reformulated the transatlantic context for American patriotism. As one of the Connecticut Wits, Humphreys served as minister to Portugal in the mid-1790s, and his efforts in securing the release of the American prisoners earned him such regard that Royall Tyler dedicated *The Algerine Captive* to him. Sent to Europe in the 1780s as secretary to a commission negotiating commercial treaties, Humphreys took an aggressive position on naval and commercial issues. Yet his most accomplished work during this period, *A Poem on the Happiness of America,* refrains from equating Britain with Algiers, and instead urges the United States to emulate British naval strength.[58] William Dowling has argued that Humphreys' vision of America is premised on the *ricorso* of civic humanism—the recovery of the pastoral and communal ideal.[59] This overestimates the republican sensibility of a poet whose enthusism for both commerce and manufacturing belie his fascination with modern registers for national greatness.

Humphreys views the Algerian conflict as a commercial crisis. After recounting the story of the American Revolution, his poem turns to America's potential position in the world of free and enlightened commerce. Like Rowson, Humphreys at once nationalizes and universalizes the Algerian conflict, representing it as part of a larger one between "enlightened" and "barb'rous" forces. Consider the stanzas which Mathew Carey reprinted as one of the appended materials to his *Short Account of Algiers* (1794):

> O ye great pow'rs, who passports basely crave,
> From Afric's lords to sail the midland wave—
> Great fall'n pow'rs, whose gems and golden bribes
> Buy paltry passports from these savage tribes . . .
> Would God, would nature, would their conqu'ring swords,
> Without your meanness, make them ocean's lords?
> What! Do ye fear? nor dare their pow'r provoke,
> Would not that bubble burst beneath your stroke?
> And shall the weak remains of barb'rous rage,
> Insulting, triumph o'er the enlighten'd age?
> Do ye not feel confusion, horror, shame,

> To bear a hateful, tributary name?
> Will ye not aid to wipe the foul disgrace,
> And break the fetters from the human race?[60]

The passage significantly echoes Carey's complaint that the Algerian pirates have jeopardized free trade and enlightened commerce for Americans. Moreover, Carey uses the passage as a marketing device—it appears not only in the *Short Account*'s appendix but also in an advertising section of Carey's recent publications. In other words, Humphreys' poetic summary of free trade itself becomes marketable.

Like *Slaves in Algiers*, Humphreys' poem symbolically reunifies the Anglo-American family. If this is in keeping with the Wits' well-known Federalist sympathies, it also recasts the poem's earlier nationalism as a transatlantic commercial-cultural alliance:

> In freedom's voice pour all thy bolder charms,
> Till reason supercede the force of arms . . .
> Albion! Columbia! soon forget the past!
> In friendly intercourse your int'rests blend!
> From common sires your gallant sons descend;
> From free-born sires in toils of empire brave—
> 'Tis yours to heal the mutual wounds ye gave;
> Let those be friends whom kindred blood allies,
> With language, laws', religion's holiest ties!
> Yes, mighty Albion! Scorning low intrigues,
> With young Columbia form commercial leagues:
> So shall mankind, through endless years, admire
> More potent realms than Carthage leagu'd with Tyre.[61]

The call for economic reconciliation (the purpose, after all, of Humphreys' residence in England) is premised on trade as both economic and cultural exchange. Like the conclusion of Rowson's play, the passage imagines the Anglo-American family in terms of the "holiest ties" of "kindred blood." Historical precedent legitimates historical progress. American "happiness" historically comes full circle to reconnect with its British origins, recalling the imperial alliance between Carthage and Tyre. The poem, in other words, "forgets the past" by remembering it. Whereas Humphreys skirts the associ-ation of Britain with imperial Rome, Rowson brings it up through the figure of Rebecca's son "Augustus" (August Caesar). As the emasculated republican ("Oh, how I wish I was a man!" [p. 84]), Augustus recovers his manhood only upon finding his long-lost British father.

"Lord Deliver Me from Such Politeness"

Slaves in Algiers thus repairs Anglo-American ties by linking commerce with familial feeling. Rowson certainly employs nationalist sentiment, but invests it with transatlantic meanings. The play confronts the argument that U.S. commercial relations with Britain would eventually corrupt the young country—an argument that accompanied the antislavery critique of the commercial barbarity of civilized societies. Indeed, this apparent paradox, whereby cultural refinement eventually produced its own forms of barbarity, lay at the heart of the cultural condemnation of the African slave trade. The paradox provides, moreover, a point of thematic convergence between the literatures of African and American slavery. The literary and cultural ramifications of such an argument appear in such well-known works as Royall Tyler's *The Algerine Captive* and Washington Irving's *Salmagundi* Papers (1807–8). Both Tyler and Irving play upon the multiple levels of enslavement by weighing the relations between bodily and cultural enslavement. Their works thematize the latter by equating the brutality of aristocratic and primitive cultures.

Tyler's critics generally view *The Algerine Captive*'s Anglophobic features as symptomatic of his attempts to stimulate a fledgling national culture and literature.[62] The novel is framed by a prefatory complaint about cultural contamination. Tyler's fictional persona, Updike Underhill, laments New England's taste for British literature, including the exoticism of Mediterranean travel writing as well as the gothic novel, so that "the New England reader is insensibly taught to admire the levity, and often the vices of the parent country. While the fancy is enchanted, the heart is corrupted."[63] Yet such rhetoric not only comes from an often unreliable narrator, but also tends to obscure the larger dimensions of the novel itself. *The Algerine Captive* is, after all, an antislavery novel ranging across the Atlantic: Updike travels the African slave's diaspora just about in reverse. Read in the larger context of late eighteenth-century antislavery writings, *The Algerine Captive* similarly obsesses on the cultural ramifications of commercial exchange. This issue provides some thematic consistency throughout a fast-paced, rather chaotic work blending the forms of comic picaresque, captivity narrative, ethnography, and international travel.

Part One's picaresque movement exposes not only the false pretenses but also the violence of American claims to cultural refinement. Starting by deflating in scene after scene Updike's aristocratic pretensions, it goes on to show the fallacy and even the brutality of Anglophilic gentility. This particular characterization is apparent, for example, in the scene where Updike finds himself challenged to a duel. Having abandoned teaching in rural New England, Updike embarks on a worldly career in medicine, in which he can simultaneously act out the role of gentlemanly man of letters. When he inadvertently insults one of the town's ladies by writing her an overblown ode, filled with "all the high sounding epithets of the immortal Grecian bard" (p. 66), he is forced into the duel. Out of his depth, Updike consults a colleague and finally realizes the severity of the cultural refinement to which he has aspired all along:

> "You have been bred in yankee land," replied my fellow student. "Men of honor are above the common rules of propriety and common sense. This letter, which is a challenge, bating some little inaccuracies of grammar and spelling, in substance, I assure you, would not disgrace a man of the highest honor; and, if Mr. Jasper T— acts as much the man of honor on the wharf as he has on paper, he will preserve the same style of good breeding and politeness there also. While, with one hand, he, with a deadly lunge, passes his sword through your lungs, he will take his hat off, with the other, and bow gracefully to your corpse."
>
> "Lord deliver me from such politeness," exclaimed I. "It seems to me, by your account of things, that the principal difference between a man of honor and a vulgar murderer is that the latter will kill you in a rage, while the former will write you complaisant letters, and smile in your face, and bow gracefully, while he cuts your throat." (p. 69)

Notwithstanding its comic excesses, the exchange rather cynically comments on the necessity for cultural performance in post-Revolutionary America.[64] Updike begins to realize that these new "circles of polished life" (p. 65) are not all that he imagined they would be. Indeed, the very distinction between civilization and barbarity appears to collapse. The superficial cant, gesture, and intonation of polite culture are nothing but style and appearances. At these moments, *The Algerine Captive* does not express so much specific American fears of British culture as longstanding Anglo-American anxieties about forms of politeness devoid of sentimental feeling. These extend at least as far back as the Shaftesburyan project of investing courtly forms of *politesse*, or the art of pleasing, with genuine feeling.[65] The problem of savage refinement, moreover, could take a variety of national and cultural directions. In William Ray, it becomes the means to criticize aristocratic, or "un-American," barbarity; in Rowson, the "vastly pretty" palace imprisoning Fetnah highlights the ironies of patriarchal rule; in Tyler, it deflates American claims to cultural purity.

Yet *The Algerine Captive* does not simply debunk British manners in order to safeguard American culture.[66] Perhaps revealing the same ambivalence that runs through Hugh Henry Brackenridge's *Modern Chivalry* (1792–1815), Tyler unveils the equivalent brutality of democratic and aristocratic cultures. To this end, the novel stylistically oscillates between them. For every jibe at Updike's silly pretensions, the novel debunks the backcountry rubes antagonizing him. Very rarely do figures like Benjamin Franklin (a man "simple in his manners and style" [p. 91]) strike the proper balance between the two extremes. Updike's subsequent flight to the "liberal, enlightened people" (p. 94) of the South reveals yet another society where gentility is marked by violence, most notably during the scenes where the parson beats the slave. Finally, Updike flees to England as the last refuge of cultural refinement, but there he finds London's abject squalor.

The thematic conflation of barbarity and refinement culminates in the African slave trade in Part One. As a ship's surgeon on board the ironically named *Sympathy*, Updike soon witnesses the horrors of slavery, denouncing it in the language of the time: "this infamous, cruel commerce," "this execrable traffic," "this inhuman transaction," a trade based on "wanton barbarity" and "the Christian thirst for gold" (pp. 108–112). Here the novelist begins to trace dual thematic trajectories about the nature of "slavery." If the language metaphorizes chattel slavery by emphasizing its cultural ramifications, it also literalizes Updike's cultural enslavement by foreshadowing his future condition.

The novel, then, is not nearly as disjointed as most readers claim: Part Two's ethnography of savage refinement echoes and amplifies its earlier thematic focus.[67] The cultural categories that Tyler brings to bear do not make Algiers merely a "disturbing reflection" for the United States.[68] Rather, his focus on Islamic despotism raises the problem of how to interpret "culture" itself. British writings about the Islamic world, like William Guthrie's *A New System of Modern Geography* (reprinted by Carey and consulted by Tyler), emphasized the tumultuous nature of despotic forms of government. But *The Algerine Captive* addresses its cultural ramifications. During Updike's enslavement, the novel consistently emphasizes the apparent paradox that cultural refinement breeds its own forms of barbarity and violence. "The higher his rank in society, the further is man removed from nature. Grandeur draws a circle round the great and often excludes them from the finer feelings of the heart" (p. 126). In contrast, the wretched slaves, who come from various nations, nevertheless are knitted together in "fraternal affection" speaking "the universal language of benevolence" (p. 126).

The cultural dimensions of slavery contribute as well to the novel's dissociation of race and slavery—and, indeed, to its interrogation of the reliability of visual, aesthetic signs of race. Updike's own status as the "white slave" of course is part of this movement. But even his earlier observations about the African slave trade unsettle his preconceptions about racial differences. During one scene, when the *Sympathy* stops at a Portuguese factory on the Guinea coast, Updike encounters the fluidity of racial boundaries:

> The day after our arrival at Cacongo, several Portuguese and Negro merchants, hardly distinguishable however by their manners, employments, or complexions, came to confer with the captain about the purchase of our cargo of slaves. . . . To hear these men converse upon the purchase of human beings with the same indifference, and nearly in the same language, as if they were contracting for so many head of cattle or swine shocked me exceedingly. (p. 108)

Notwithstanding his well-known lapses in reliability, Updike is made to confront the ambiguity of racial difference. Indeed, the difference in "manners" and "complexions" is "hardly distinguishable." European and African slave traders look alike because they *are* alike—their mutual participation in the slave trade reduces them all to "this scene of barbarity." Race, culture, and commerce: these categories are woven into one another.

The Algerian captivity further interrogates the racial distinction between Europeans and Algerians. It is worthwhile noting that the problem of the unreliability of appearances was certainly a widespread motif in early Barbary captivity literature. Contemporary narratives like *The Journal and Suffering of Daniel Saunders* (1794) and *A Journal, of the Captivity and Sufferings of John Foss* (1798) contain episodes in which their protagonists struggle unsuccessfully to distinguish between Christians and Muslims. In Peter Markoe's *The Algerine Spy in Pennsylvania* (1787), the protagonist Mehemet exclaims at the end of Letter XI, "When I survey my person in a mirror, I rejoice for two reasons: first that I resemble a Christian, and secondly, that I am not observed by an Algerine. I have so much the air of a Christian slave on his first landing at Algiers, that if Fatima were to see me in this dress, I should risk the loss of her affection."[69] Accounts by William Ray and James Cathcart take this problem one step further by interrogating Christian identity; they tell of Neapolitan slaves, for example, cheating their fellow Christians in blackmarket trading.

Updike similarly tries to interpret the visual signs of racial difference and to maintain the traditional ethical distinctions between Muslims and Christians. Both endeavors periodically fail and leave ambiguous results in their aftermath. Perhaps the most profound probe in this regard is the altercation between Updike and a *renegado,* or Christian apostate to Islam. Updike's initial impression of him suggests the unreliability of visual markers of difference:

> As I was drooping under my daily task, I saw a young man habited in the Turkish dress whose clear skin and florid cheek convinced me he was not a native of the country. Yet his mild air and manners betrayed nothing of the ferocity of the renegado. The style of his turban pronounced him a Mahometan; but the look of pity he casts towards the Christian slaves was entirely inconsistent with the pious hauteur of the Mussulman. (p. 133)

What, then, does it mean to be "native"? Is it a matter of birth or belief? The subsequent scene, where Updike prepares to see the Mollah, manages to further question the reliability of the visual and aesthetic marks of racial difference:

> I was then anointed in all parts, which had been exposed to the sun with a preparation of gum called the balm of Mecca. This application excited a very uneasy sensation. . . . In twenty-four hours, the sun-browned cuticle peeled off and left my face, hands, legs, and neck as fair as a child's of six months old. This balm the Algerine ladies procure at a great expense and use it as a cosmetic to heighten their beauty. (p. 137)

First white, then brown, then white again: Updike's appearance is uncannily and significantly protean. It prepares him to meet the Mollah, who, we learn, originally comes from Antioch and was a member of the Greek Orthodox Church. This European-Muslim priest oversees both native Muslims and European converts like the renegado. The mutations in Updike's skin thus suggest not only the instability of such racial designations, but also the flexibility of cultural identities subject to conversion. One does not have to be born but can become a Muslim.

The instability of cultural boundaries—and hierarchies—becomes even more pronounced during the subsequent debate between Updike and the Mollah. Here the novel expresses contemporary concerns among antislavery writers about the state of "civilized" and "Christian" identity. The ambivalence with which Tyler handles the scene—Updike never really gains the moral high ground—is consistent with the entire novel's thematic treatment of slavery. As a former participant in the slave trade, Updike is never going to win the moral argument with the Mollah, who in effect becomes the voice speaking against Christian hypocrites. He gets most of the good lines: "We leave it to the Christians of the West Indies, and Christians of your southern plantations, to baptize the unfortunate African into your faith, and then use your brother Christians as brutes of the desert" (p. 142). His status, moreover, as a convert to Islam challenges the cultural categories that Updike holds sacred. Embodying both the humanitarian principles of the European Enlightenment and Islamic theology, the Mollah is a hybrid figure, defined not by what he is but what he thinks.

The dismantling of this cultural opposition occurs on the level of language as well. As David Porter has argued, "Commerce emerges as the universal language of the mercantile age, with its promises of reciprocal advantages for trading partners, smoothing over the potential for conflict in much the same way that the schemes for a lingua franca tirelessly promoted by seventeenth-century language projectors were to have defused religious discord in Europe."[70] At first Updike is obtuse to such a concept. Earlier in the novel, while visiting London, he criticized the lack of racial and cultural purity there: "A motley race in whose mongrel veins runs the blood of all nations; speaking with pointed contempt of the fat burgomaster of Amsterdam, the cheerful French peasant, the hardy tiller of the Swiss cantons, and the independent farmer of America" (p. 99). This forecasts his repugnance for the absence of linguistic purity in Algiers, which supposedly confirms their savage state: "I had by this time acquired some knowledge of their language, if language it could be called which bade defiance to modes and tenses, appearing to be the shreds and clippings of all the tongues, dead and living, ever spoken since the creation" (p. 144). Yet he immediately admits the historical and commercial context behind this linguistic hodge-podge, recognizing that the "LINGUA FRANCA" of the Mediterranean arises from "the awkward endeavors of the natives to converse with strangers from all parts of the world" (p. 144). Hence this pastiche language is the sign not of cultural barbarity but of a Mediterranean cosmopolitanism, which itself resists reduction to simplistic racial and cultural categories. When Updike admits, "I the more readily acquired this jargon as it contained Latin derivatives" (p. 144), he begins to recognize how languages, like cultures, engage in complex processes of reciprocal exchange.

Updike's insights, however, are ephemeral at best. Like the works by James Wilson Stevens and Mathew Carey, this "Sketch of the History of the Algerines" asserts American political and cultural superiority in the midst of the political crisis in North Africa. Updike blames the Algerians "for the constant violation of the laws of nations and humanity" (p. 166), and he further upbraids the "avarice and rapacity of a people who live by plunder" (p. 167). Yet Tyler undermines this smugness by suggesting that, as Updike admits, western Europe might have defeated the Muslim world in the Mediterranean, except that "the narrow politics of Europe seek an individual not a common good" (p. 166). The base fact of commercial self-interest crosses national, cultural, and racial borders. By universalizing this theme, the novel reveals its skeptical outlook on *le doux commerce:*

> Whoever turns the pages of history with profit will perceive that sordid passion is the impulse of action to the greatest states. Commercial states are also actuated by avarice, a passion still more baneful in its effects. . . . Hence it is, that while every European power is solicitous to enrich and aggrandize itself, it can never join in any common project. . . . Hence it is that Christian states, instead of uniting to vindicate their insulted faith, join the cross and the crescent in unholy alliance, and form degrading treaties with piratical powers. (p. 189)

The thematic preoccupation with "piratical" commerce supports an ironic reading of its heavily patriotic conclusion. Because of the uneven reliability of its narrator, it is difficult to ascertain his moral progress by the time he returns to "the freest country in the universe" (p. 224). While Rowson recast such patriotic cant in context of the reconstituted Anglo-American family, Tyler shadows nationalist enthusiasm with the specter of the African slave trade. The route by which Updike returns to the United States subtly maps out the history of the slave trade—or at least major points of Euro-American participation in it. During his final captivity on board a Tunisian vessel, Updike wants more than anything to find a "Christian coast" (p. 222). His final journey takes him through Port Logos, Portugal, Bristol, England, and the Chesapeake Bay. Extolling the virtues of America as a newly "free" man, Updike, once enslaved, unknowingly reminds readers of the moral inconsistency of lamenting the Muslim enslavement of American citizens. His story, in Tyler's hands, suggests the unintended—indeed unholy—similarities between the crescent and the cross.

"The Most Enlightened People under the Sun"

During the Tripolitan War, Washington Irving made use of the genre of Oriental letters in his early literary career to make satirical critiques of the place of cultural refinement in post-Revolutionary America. Published in twenty installments over the course of 1807–8, *Salmagundi, or the Whim-Whams and Opinions of Launcelot Langstaff, Esq. And Others* represents the collaboration of Irving, his brother William, and his brother-in-law, James Kirke Paulding. The work generally parodies the style of the Addisonian periodical essay in order to, as William Hedges noted long ago, "demolish the pretensions of [New York] city's polite society."[71] *Salmagundi*—a "hash," or hodge-podge, of social and political commentary—makes complex satirical use of various contemporaries through such figures as Launcelot Langstaff, Anthony Evergreen, Will Wizard, and Mustapha Rub-a-Dub Keli Khan, a Tripolitan captive on parole in New York. The literary precedents for the Mustapha letters include Lady Mary Wortley Montague's *Letters*, Montesquieu's *Persian Letters*, and Oliver Goldsmith's *The Citizen of the World*. The genre provides an outsider's perspective filled with innocent, deadpan observations, which easily expose the pretensions of civilized society. Indeed, its manipulation of point of view matches its thematic concerns with the complex and uneasy relations between civilization and barbarity. In this way, *Salmagundi* does not merely debunk cultural foibles but creatively antagonizes its audience's cultural assumptions.

This view of *Salmagundi* demands some reconsideration of Irving as a transatlantic literary figure. In the early national period, it was Irving who in *The Sketch-Book* (1819–20) attempted to broker cultural compromises between national aspirations and British tastes. Critics tend to represent Irving as either the genteel Anglophile (the un-American writer compared, say, to Melville), or the displaced romantic American wanderer, finding himself "adrift in the old world."[72] Either image makes Irving the representative example of the development of a national literature.[73] Below, I want to reconsider *Salmagundi* transatlantically—that is, to think about Irving's thematic concerns in light of antislavery's preoccupation with the cultural terms of enslavement. *Salmagundi* satirizes modern society by linking cosmopolitan and provincial mentalities as well as the categories of refinement and barbarity.

Even its style accomplishes this end. The Mustapha letters conflate Christian and Muslim discourses as a way of blurring cultural boundaries. One might even compare *Salmagundi* to one its major generic antecedents, Oliver Goldsmith's *The Citizen of the World:* in the first passage below, from Goldsmith, the Chinese narrator, Lien Chi Altangi, compares British and Oriental dramatic cultures; in the second passage, Irving's persona of Mustapha exposes the corruption of democratic politics.

> The English are as fond of seeing plays acted as the Chinese; but there is a vast difference in the manner of conducting them. We play our pieces in the open air, the English theirs under cover; we act by day-light, they by the blaze of torches. One of our plays continues eight or ten days successively; an English piece seldom takes up above four hours in the representation.[74]

> I was surprised to observe a bashaw, high in office, shaking a fellow by the hand, that looked rather more ragged, than a scare-crow, and inquiring with apparent solicitude concerning the health of his family; after which he slipped a little folded paper into his hand and turned away. I could not help applauding his humility in shaking the fellow's hand, and his benevolence in relieving his distresses. . . . My friend, however, soon undeceived me by saying that this was an elector, and the bashaw had merely given him the list of candidates, for whom he was to vote.[75]

Both samples obviously employ the foreign observer as a means for cultural analysis and, most often, cultural critique. Yet their rhetorical styles markedly differ. Goldsmith's persona works contrapuntal tensions within an overall rhetorical equilibrium. The semicolons are syntactic markers that maintain clear cultural distinctions. This is a comparative analysis. Its rhetorical balance, moreover, suggests the theme of cultural equivalence, since syntax literally and figuratively puts the two groups on even ground. This enables readers to see themselves in a larger context while keeping a safe enough distance from Oriental people and practice. Irving, however, destroys such a tidy comparative format. He merges the two cultures in this incident of the American "bashaw" engaged in modern-day electioneering. Irving's language collapses cultural boundaries, albeit humorously. Sometimes sardonic, sometimes innocent, this writerly voice intentionally (on Irving's part) undermines the categorical distinctions between American and Muslim (or "Mussulman") cultures. It happens everywhere: New York City's "stupendous mosques," "a small bashaw [dressed] in yellow and gold," the superior man who must, "like the idolatrous Egyptian," worship the "wallowing" mob, the "magi" of professional gamblers, and so forth. The effect is to violate that distance that Goldsmith preserves, to disrupt the immediate audience's cultural sensibility.

One wonders what actually distinguishes barbarous from enlightened nations, since, as Mustapha concludes, "in all nations, barbarous or enlightened, the mass of the people, the *mob,* must be slaves, or they will be tyrants" (p. 195). Critics of the early Irving recognize his antidemocratic, if not exactly Federalist (for he was a Burr Republican for a while) politics. Yet Irving's works may be read as well for their concerns for the foibles of aristocratic society. Certainly, his private writings often demonstrate the desire to repossess the very meaning of manners from the extremes of cultural over-refinement. During his early travels in Europe between 1804 and 1806, Irving's journal reveals all the features one might expect from a jejune sojourner in Europe: sublime and picturesque landscapes, the fascination with historical relics, and the frustrations of foreign travel. But Irving's fascination with the manifestations of culture throughout Europe is tempered by anxieties over both the violent legacy of the French Revolution and the depravity of aristocratic culture, as in this comment:

I confess my american notions of delicacy & propriety are not sufficiently conquered for me to view this shameless exposure of their persons without sentiments bordering on disgust. . . . As to the men they all profess much gallantry and libertinism and often accuse themselves of being far more extravagant in this respect than I am convinced they really are. The keeping of a Mistress is considered a matter of course & of consequence, nothing ill is thought of it. . . . When I first arrived at Bordeaux I understood hardly a word of the language, I was of course advised immediately to apply myself to *the study.* I told my advisers that I had taken a French master—"very good, very good," was the reply, "but you must take a French *mistress* also." An old gentleman of much respectability, to whom I was introduced gave me similar counsel. . . . As to the advice that has been so liberally bestowed upon me, I have been too headstrong to attend to it, and have endeavored to keep the morals I brought with me from america as untainted as possible

from foreign profligacy. . . . You have heard no doubt much of *french polite-*
ness and I'll assure you if politeness consists in bows and scrapes and compli-
ments and professions of friendship & rapture at seeing you and proffers of
service &c &c &c they are the most polite people under the sun.—But if politeness consists more in *actions than words & promises,* I must confess are very
deficient in it.[76]

Irving's fear of contracting syphilis exceeds the boundaries of metaphor. Indeed, the importance he invests in maintaining his American health puts
him on his guard against the Old World's moral and bodily pathogens. In
this case, the journal's persona comes close to Geoffrey Crayon's skittishness
about bodily contact. The prospect of sexual pleasure segues into the danger
of barbarity of aristocratic *politesse.* He glosses the larger message of *Salma-*
gundi, and his comment also resembles Tyler's satirical concerns. Both wish
to distinguish manners from mere politeness. The passage above accomplishes this by contrasting European social surfaces with the substance of
American morality.

Salmagundi argues that cosmopolitan New York has culturally over-
reached itself. Irving employs the genre's traditional tactics of using the persona of a cultural outsider to unsettle the stability of what his Mustapha
mockingly calls "'the most enlightened people under the sun'" (p. 262). The
cultural meditations the letters provide often turn on the matter of taste. In
Salmagundi XVI (15 October 1807), for example, the satire exposes the public dinner in honor of "great men." As Mustapha complains to his friend
Asem, instead of building monuments to the deceased, Americans gorge
themselves in honor of the living. Why honor the dead, they figure, when
the dead can't hear anyway? "The barbarous nations of antiquity immolated
human victims to the memory of their lamented dead, but the enlightened
Americans offer up whole hecatombs of geese and calves, and oceans of
wine in honoring the illustrious living; and the patriot has the felicity of
hearing from every quarter the vast exploits in gluttony and reveling that
have been celebrated to the glory of his name" (p. 262). In a rather Swiftian
move, reminiscent of "A Modest Proposal," Irving figures consumption itself
as the means by which this society devours itself.

Salmagundi XVIII's subject of female fashion locates this cultural problem
within a gender-specific arena of national manners. Like the contemporary
antislavery assault upon the tea table, the place where women of leisure
consumed West Indian "blood sugar," Irving assumes women's right—or

duty—of moral and cultural stewardship.[77] Accordingly, he has Mustapha debunk this ideal—American women are simply "beautiful barbarians" and "lovely savages" (pp. 284–285). Whereas Tyler deflates the social pretensions of backcountry rubes aping European manners (recall the folk dialect of the letter challenging Updike to a duel), Irving more openly plays games with the very category of civilization. "We have heard much of their painting themselves most hideously, and making use of bear's-grease in great profusion; but this, I solemnly assure thee, is a misrepresentation, civilization, no doubt, having gradually extirpated these nauseous practices" (p. 285). Through its deadpan voice, *Salmagundi* interrogates the assumptions behind historical progress, suggesting the moment where modernity bends backward, so to speak, where civilization becomes savagery, and where the foundations for stable cultural categories are all but lost.

The persona of Mustapha only amplifies these ambiguities. His inconsistencies, his capacity for both rational analysis and cultural myopia, heighten the satirical effects that are themselves founded on the thematic equivalence between refinement and barbarity. Even as Mustapha decries "the shameless and abandoned exposure" (p. 285) of New York's fashionable women, he is still a dope-smoking polygamist, pining for his "three-and-twenty wives" (p. 289), an epistolary observer whom Irving's audience surely would have found suspect, if not barbaric. *Salmagundi* thus reverses the rhetorical design of the American Barbary captivity narrative. Rather than staging a civilized narrator captive in a presumably savage place, it provides an inconsistently barbaric narrator captive in a society riding the fine line between politeness and barbarity. *Salmagundi* works so well satirically because it exposes the unreliability of those cultural categories upon which war and captivity literatures were founded. It also refuses to employ the British as a way of redeeming national manners—rather it brings the political trope of the "Savage Briton" home to roost. American barbarians differ little from "the barbarians of the British island" (pp. 292, 233). Asking readers to think simultaneously within and beyond national boundaries, *Salmagundi* refuses to reduce culture to politics and manners to the patriotic nation.

The literature of Barbary captivity literalizes the theme of cultural enslavement that pervades antislavery writing during this era. As Brissot de Warville argued, "slavery most infallibly debases at once, the master and the slave."[78] The argument derived largely from Montesquieu's emphasis upon cultural and moral enslavement in *L'Esprit des Lois* (1748), arguing that the master "contracts with his slave all sorts of bad habits, insensibly accustoms himself to want all moral virtues; becomes haughty, hasty, hard-hearted, passionate, voluptuous and cruel."[79] Jefferson recapitulated the argument in the famous (or infamous) Query XIV of *Notes on the State of Virginia* (1785). Yet the actual bodily captivity that Americans endured in North Africa functioned in this particular kind of antislavery literature as a cultural crisis. This literature dwells on the excesses of British and Muslim cultures while situating America somewhere safely between them. In *A Poem on the Happiness of America* (1790), David Humphreys articulated this fantasy of a "golden mean" of cultural refinement:

> No feudal ties the rising genius mar,
> Compel to servile toils, or drag to war;
> But, free, each youth his fav'rite course pursues,
> The plough paternal, or the sylvan muse.
> For here exists, once more, th'Arcadian scene,
> Those simple manners, and that golden mean:
> Here holds society in its middle stage,
> Between too rude and too refin'd an age;
> Far from that age, when not a gleam of light
> The dismal darkness cheer'd of gothic night,
> From brutal rudeness of that savage state—
> As from refinements which o'erwhelm the great,
> Those dissipations which their bliss annoy,
> And blast and poison each domestic joy.[80]

The interplay between bodily and cultural forms of enslavement becomes all the more important in the literature of the eighteenth-century Black Atlantic. Rhetorically, this often involves the complexity of the register for redemption. Remember that in *Slaves in Algiers* Rebecca's possession of Hassan's bills of exchange places her in the awkward position of having to redeem both these notes and her daughter Olivia's freedom. This image brings to mind the brutal irony of slavery, which reduces liberty and humanity to marketable commodities. It also places the white American slave in the closest possible resemblance during this era to those African slaves held in the United States and the West Indies.

CHAPTER 4

Liberty, Slavery, and Black Atlantic Autobiography

> Many of us are men of property, for the security of which, we have hitherto looked to the laws of our blessed state, but should this become a law, our property is jeopardized, since the same power which can expose to sale an unfortunate fellow creature, can wrest from him those estates, which years of honest industry have accumulated.
>
> —James Forten, *Letters From a Man of Colour on a Late Bill Before the Senate of Pennsylvania* (1813)

> What has not been recognized is how early and how significantly the poor and disadvantaged participated in writing their selves. . . . By writing themselves onto the public stage, they too were making a public claim to newly recognized rights.
>
> —Mechal Sobel, "The Revolution in Selves: Black and White Inner Aliens" (1997)

In examining the literary and cultural dynamics of the commercial jeremiad from a variety of sources and genres, I argued that Anglo-American antislavery literature directly considered the relations between commercial exchange and enlightened culture. In this chapter I maintain that historical focus on culture, looking specifically at the autobiographical writing of eighteenth-century black subjects—historical figures within what Paul Gilroy influentially has called the "Black Atlantic."[1]

I want to begin by considering the language of Benjamin Banneker, a free African American living in Maryland who was well known as an able mathematician, astronomer, and producer of almanacs. His famous letter to Secretary of State Thomas Jefferson was published in 1792, along with Jefferson's reply, and a short testimony to Banneker's character written by the Maryland politician James McHenry. As William L. Andrews has observed, the most interesting rhetorical feature of the letter is Banneker's strategic manipulation of persona.[2] Banneker begins humbly enough: "SIR: I am fully sensible of the greatness of that freedom which I take with you on the present occasion, a liberty which seemed to me scarcely allowable, when I reflected on that distinguished and dignified station in which you stand, and the most general prejudice and prepossession, which is so prevalent in the world against those of my complexion."[3]

But then his tone changes altogether. Making good use of the language of the *Declaration of Independence* (1776)—a common strategy in the antislavery literature of this period—Banneker turns Jefferson the famous author into Jefferson the chastened reader. This move exposes the dissonance between American principles and practice, which at once establishes Banneker's authority and opens the way to interrogating the *res* (or "race") *publica*.

> Sir, I freely and cheerfully acknowledge that I am of the African race, and in that color which is natural to them of the deepest dye; and it is under a sense of the most profound gratitude to the Supreme Ruler of the Universe that I now confess to you that I am not under that state of tyrannical thralldom and inhuman captivity to which many of my brethren are doomed, but that I have abundantly tasted of the fruition of those blessings, which proceed from that free and unequalled liberty with which you are favored; and which, I hope, you will willingly allow you have mercifully received from the immediate hand of that Being from whom proceedeth every good and perfect gift.[4]

Let us pause here over the ambiguity of Banneker's language. As he proclaims himself to be a free man, what is the meaning of the phrase "free and unequalled liberty"? Both Banneker and Jefferson would appear to enjoy its "blessings." Yet the phrase suggests the paradoxes of liberty and equality in the republic that Jefferson helped to author, himself against slavery yet a slave owner. If the "unequalled liberty" of the republic has no peer because of its origins in "the Supreme Ruler of the Universe," then the two men, theoretically, are equal.

Banneker surely knows this is not the case. So does Jefferson. But the rhetorical possibility of raising such a claim is important, for it highlights the contingent meanings of such words as "liberty" and "equality" that were empowering for eighteenth-century black writing. My argument maintains that the rise of liberal society was not necessarily inimical to the blacks' language of identity politics. In contrast, Gilroy argues that the "rational, scientific, and enlightened Euro-American thought" emerging in the eighteenth century functioned as the ideological source of modern "terror" for Black Atlantic writers. Indeed, the very construct of the Black Atlantic is meant to displace the modern categories of "race" and "nation" that subtly codify "the supposedly primitive outlook of prehistorical, cultureless, and bestial Africans."[5] Gilroy likely would read Banneker as an example of the "politics of fulfillment" as opposed to the "politics of transfiguration": "The politics of fulfillment is mostly content to play occidental rationality at its own game. It necessitates a hermeneutic orientation that can assimilate the semiotic, verbal, and textual. The politics of transfiguration strives in pursuit of the sublime, struggling to repeat the unrepeatable, to present the unpresentable."[6] Similarly, Saidiya Hartman has argued that "Liberalism, in general, and rights discourse in particular, assure entitlements and privileges as they enable and efface elemental forms of domination primarily because of the atomistic portrayal of social relations, the inability to address collective interests and needs, and the sanctioning of subordination and the free reign of prejudice in the construction of the social or the private."[7]

Historians tend to agree. Ira Berlin, for example, points out that "On the one hand, [white Americans] condemned newly freed slaves as dissolute wastrels whose unrestrained exuberance for freedom would reduce them to the penury they deserved. On the other hand, they mocked those who strove for respectability as feckless imposters whose ill-fitting periwigs and pretentious oratory would elicit the ridicule they deserved."[8] Post-Revolutionary New Englanders, as Joanne Pope Melish has argued, meant to contain African Americans during the era of gradual emancipation. This era generally left them in a social abyss somewhere between being "freed" and truly "free." New forms of social control "produced two overlapping discourses that rendered free people of color categorical rather than individual: abolitionist discourse, which identified them with slaves as a class of undifferentiated objects of compassion and charity; and master/employer discourse, which identified them with slaves, a class of undifferentiated objects of ownership and entitlement."[9]

I propose a more flexible relation between the formation of liberal culture and the formation of black autobiographical identities. The social-historical contexts for changes in the meanings of "liberty" and "rights" enrich the rhetorical possibilities for creative agency of black subjects, a fact that at once registers and unsettles the "color line."[10]

This is particularly intriguing for autobiographies that were not written but only related by black subjects. In this chapter I focus on two of them, *A Narrative of the Lord's Wonderful Dealings with John Marrant, a Black* (1785), and *A Narrative of the Life and Adventures of Venture, a Native of Africa* (1798). Because of the power dynamics informing the collaborative production of these early autobiographies, critics tend to view them suspiciously.[11] But, more recently, others have challenged traditional critiques of collaborative autobiography. As Robert Desrochers, Jr. has argued, "But in assuming that whites consciously and effectively silenced the voices of the first black narrators, scholars too often limit themselves in search of a 'true' black voice of irreconcilable and discernible difference."[12] The works of Marrant and Smith fit the category of Anglo-American antislavery writing as well as contemporary black writing like *The Interesting Narrative of the Life of Olaudah Equiano, or Gustavus Vassa, the African, Written by Himself* (1789). These collaborative autobiographies involved complex negotiations of language between black subjects and Anglo-American editors that neither erased nor fully liberated the rhetorical agency of black subjects.[13]

Distinctions of Rank and Condition

During the late eighteenth century, social and political movements in both British America and Europe put pressure upon traditional notions of the extent of individual liberties. As Gordon Wood has argued, the American Revolution helped to transform a monarchical society into a republican one, thereby providing the social and political conditions for the subsequent development of democratic life. Replacing monarchical systems of patronage and deference with republican bonds of benevolence and gratitude, the Revolution significantly softened traditional norms for patriarchal authority. "Throughout the eighteenth-century Anglo-American world, traditional authority was brought into question. Personal and social relations were not working properly. The social hierarchy seemed less natural, less ordained by God, and more man-made, more arbitrary. . . . Leaders lost some of their aura of mystery and sacredness. Subordinates and inferiors felt more independent, more free, than they had in the past."[14] Wood's concept of a "radical" Revolution does not, however, account for the relatively unchanged position of African Americans, Native Americans, and American women or take seriously the historical agency of these disenfranchised groups. My argument takes up this issue of agency in the context of language and identity.

The sentimentalization of social and political authority was commensurate with important changes that took place in the United States between the Revolution and the early antebellum period. As many important histori-cal studies of this era have shown, this period witnessed numerous develop-ments that we associate with modernity: the expansion of the economy, particularly in agricultural products; the beginnings of industrial capitalism; the increase in the population and the increasing demographic movements into different regions; and, finally, the growth of cities, particularly commer-cial ports along the eastern seacoast. These changes influenced public de-bates about political economy, which included the emergent view "extolling voluntarism, free will, and the harmony of unfettered economic agents in a web of free markets."[15]

The unsettling effects of such change inform David Brion Davis's influen-tial interpretation that antislavery was driven by fundamental concerns for social stability and labor discipline. "By the eighteenth century, however, profound social changes, particularly those connected with the rise of new classes and new economic interests in Britain and America, created an audi-ence hospitable to antislavery ideology."[16] Rejecting Marxist understandings of capitalist ideology, Davis summarizes the historical complexity of anti-slavery principles:

> The antislavery movement . . . reflected the needs and values of the emerg-
> ing capitalist order. . . . [It] appealed, of course, to the highest ideals of man.
> Yet the very effectiveness of ideals requires a certain blindness to their social
> power and social consequences. They must be taken as pure and transcen-
> dent, free of ambiguous implication. Thus for abolitionists it was unthink-
> able that an attack on a specific system of labor and domination might also
> validate other forms of oppression and test the boundaries of legitimate re-
> form. . . . Antislavery not only reflected the needs and tensions of a transi-
> tional social system, but provided a new conceptual and categorical frame-
> work that imposed its own "logic" on events. . . . In a more positive sense,
> [abolitionists] succeeded in making a sincere humanitarianism an integral
> part of class ideology, and thus of British culture.[17]

Notwithstanding the problematic notion of the "blindness" of abolitionism to its own interests, the argument situates antislavery politics within larger cultural questions about the nature of free labor and even freedom itself.

For early antislavery writers, these questions extended to the prospect of emancipated African slaves. Put another way, antislavery priorities about so-cial order and labor discipline define the rhetorical shape and ideological boundaries of black freedom. Before discussing their narratives, I want to situate Marrant and Smith in context of these contemporary discourses of Anglo-American antislavery. They help to focus the social project of early black writing.

One way Anglo-American antislavery managed widespread anxieties about free blacks was to emphasize the importance of such virtues as labor and industry. There is no little irony in observing that the very same virtues antislavery emphasized to establish the full humanity of Africans were used to illustrate the intimidating prospect of free Africans in the western hemisphere. Both Anthony Benezet and Thomas Clarkson, for example, insisted upon the capacity of Africans to labor industriously, although they admitted the climate and conditions in Africa had precluded its absolute necessity. "Africans, by proper encouragement, can be brought into *habits of labour.*"[18] When considering emancipation, Benezet pushed the argument to assuage contemporary fears about "free" blacks: "If, under proper regulations, liberty was proclaimed through the colonies, the Negroes, from dangerous, grudging, half-fed slaves, might become able, willing-minded laborers."[19] In a letter to Benezet, Granville Sharp praised plans for gradual emancipation in the Spanish colonies, which encouraged slaves to work in order to buy their freedom: "This is such encouragement to industry, that even the most indolent are tempted to exert themselves.—Men who have thus worked out their freedom are enured to the labor of the Country and are certainly the most useful subjects that a Colony can acquire."[20]

Notwithstanding, then, the connections between natural rights and African humanity, Anglo-American antislavery strictly construed black freedom to accord with traditional social hierarchies. This is apparent, for example, in the Scottish philosopher John Millar's argument against slavery in *The Origin of the Distinction of Ranks* (1771). Recognizing that the spirit of Christianity "softened the rigours" of slavery, Millar nevertheless emphasized that "it does not seem to have been the intention of Christianity to alter the civil rights of mankind, or to abolish those distinctions of rank which were already established. There is no precept of the gospel by which the authority of the master is in any respect restrained or limited." Such selective exegesis registers the larger cultural project in this era of associating Christianity with enlightened civilization while maintaining the legitimacy of hierarchical social structure.

The antislavery pulpit particularly manifested these concerns. Having witnessed slavery for decades in the British West Indies, James Ramsay railed against the brutality of the planters there, but affirmed the "natural inequality, or diversity, which prevails among men that fits them for society."[21] As he saw it, "social servitude" existed even in the "freest state." The dissenting minister Joseph Priestley similarly declared in an antislavery sermon, "At the same time we justly think that every man is a great and exalted being . . . we consider all distinctions among men as temporary, calculated for the ultimate benefit of all; and consequently that it is for the interest of the lower orders, as well as the highest, that such a subordination should exist."[22] Similarly, across the Atlantic Jedidiah Morse instructed an audience in Boston's African Meeting House, celebrating in 1808 the abolition of the slave trade that, "Distinctions of rank and condition in life are requisite to the perfection of the social state. There must be rulers and subjects, masters and servants, rich and poor. The human body is not perfect without all its members, some of which are more honourable than others; so it is with the body politic. There is nevertheless a kind of equality among the members; all are free."[23] Moreover, Morse shows a rhetorical self-consciousness about the dangerously ambiguous discourses of "freedom"—that is, he worries that some African Americans might make liberty "a cloak for licentiousness."[24] If slavery once debilitated African American morals, freedom might do so as well.[25]

What kind of freedom was meant? The interpretive range of such a question underlies the rhetorical self-consciousness that early black writings about liberty and slavery demonstrate. Before turning to Marrant's *Narrative*, I want to examine two notable examples of the enabling effects this period's semantic elasticity helped to create in early black writing. This feature makes the theme of liberty highly performative. In 1813, before the African Methodist Episcopal Church in New York, George Lawrence celebrated the anniversary of the abolition of the slave trade. After condemning the slave trade, Lawrence turns to subject of liberty:

> In all ages of the world . . . we behold mankind worshipping at the shrine of liberty, and willingly sacrificing their all in pursuit of that fair goddess. We behold the rational man walk undauntedly in the very jaws of death to retain his liberty; he surmounts all difficulties; wades through all dangers; i.e., industriously climbs the rough and craggy mount, and undauntedly leaps forth from its lofty and dangerous precipice if he but beholds the most distant gleams of liberty.[26]

The passage almost secularizes the Christian trope of salvation—indeed, the phrase "distant gleams of liberty" suggests ambiguous meanings for one's rise in (or above) the world. Its rhetorical power lies in its uncertainties. What kind of salvation does Lawrence mean? How far does the desire for liberty actually go? These same tensions and questions inform the eulogy that the African American minister Peter Williams gave a few years later for the famous maritime merchant Paul Cuffe. Like Venture Smith, Cuffe was a commercial success story in his day, a model for the self-made entrepreneur. As Williams noted, this "son of a poor African" succeeded "by his own indefatigable exertions" in "the pursuits of commerce."[27] Cuffe is "one who, from a state of poverty, ignorance, and obscurity, through a host of difficulties, and with an unsullied conscience, by the native energy of his mind, has elevated himself to wealth, to influence, to respectability, and honour."[28] The eulogy does not merely defend commercial behavior in light of aristocratic traditions of gentlemanly honor; it praises the kind of commercial ventures that afford an "unsullied conscience" and that, by implication, demarcate the boundaries of black entrepreneurial individualism. Cuffe, says Williams, refused to engage in the African slave trade. "O! that all Christian traders had been actuated by a similar spirit."[29]

Righteous Labor

The genre of black autobiography emerged during an era in which antislavery culture interpreted the crucial concepts of liberty and slavery in generally conservative ways. The context of antislavery culture highlights the thematic emphasis that John Marrant places upon "mastery" in the *Narrative*. Although the evidentiary record of Marrant's biography is thin, the *Narrative* recounts the story of a "free" black boy who very soon in life pushed at the boundaries of autonomy and identity. Marrant moved from New York with his mother to Florida, and then to Georgia, before he was sent at age eleven to live with his sister in Charleston. There he was meant to learn a respectable trade and make a life for himself. Smitten at the age of fourteen by the preaching of the famous minister George Whitefield, a prominent figure in much of early Black Atlantic writing, Marrant was converted to evangelical Methodism. He then wandered in the wilderness, evangelizing among the Cherokee, before returning to Charleston sometime in the early 1770s. Supposedly impressed into the British navy during the Revolutionary War, Marrant eventually ended up in London, where he embraced the Calvinistic Methodism of the Huntingdonian Connexion. (The Countess of Huntington was Whitefield's correspondent as well as Phillis Wheatley's literary patron.)

Later, Marrant was ordained a Methodist minister at the Huntingdonian chapel in Bath. Soon thereafter, the Huntingdonians sent him on an evangelical mission to Nova Scotia, where, as Marrant's *Journal* shows, he suffered from ill health, sectarian hostility from Wesleyan Methodists, and poor funding.[30] Marrant made his way to Boston where he preached to Prince Hall's African Masonic Lodge. He soon returned to London and died in 1790.

The *Narrative* was first published in 1785 as a Methodist spiritual autobiography, and, as its numerous reprintings attest, was a literary success. Indeed, the collaborative work that arises from the relation between Marrant and English minister William Aldridge represents him as a version of the archetypal Christian in *The Pilgrim's Progress*, who must lose his unconverted family in order to find himself. As Aldridge asks in the Preface, "Were the power, grace, and providence of God ever more eminently displayed, than in the conversion, success, and deliverances of John Marrant?"[31] The *Narrative* employs the conventions of this brand of Protestant conversion: the saint's emotional upheaval and debilitating guilt, the operative power of Whitefield's stentorian voice, the contrite sinner's physical illness, his spiritual itinerancy in the wilderness, and the typological identifications that include Paul, Daniel, the ancient Israelites, and Luke's account of the Prodigal Son.

No wonder, then, that critics emphasize the *Narrative*'s religious structure of "rebirth and resurrection."[32] Recent readings of Marrant recognize the social and political importance that Methodist-evangelical cultures lend to this structure. Nancy Ruttenberg has argued that "The revolutionary self of the Whitefieldian convert was distinguished first and foremost by the aggressive uncontainability of his or her speech, underwritten by the reconceptualization of the self as a pure conduit for the expression of God's will."[33] Notwithstanding the *Narrative*'s religious contexts and implications, its capacity to thematize multiple meanings of liberty both depends upon and far outstrips its evangelical design. Marrant rebels against social and political authority long before he meets Whitefield or undergoes conversion. The *Narrative* explores what it means to be free in eighteenth-century British America by emphasizing Marrant's social dependence in a milieu where the brutality of chattel slavery and indentured servitude often resembled one another.[34]

Structurally, the theme of self-mastery emerges through a crucial series of youthful rebellions meant to show the dynamics of personal independence.

The issue turns on the deeper one about control over one's labor. In its historical context, the *Narrative* actually reveals a high degree of self-consciousness about the necessity of property to independent identity. This is why Marrant's ensuing musical career means much more (or something in addition to) the spiritual autobiographical convention of first portraying the saint's descent into iniquity.[35] Music serves as the trope for both black voice and black labor.

> [A]s I was walking one day, I passed by a school, and heard music and dancing, which took my fancy very much, and I felt a strong inclination to learn the music. I went home, and informed my sister, that I had rather learn to play upon music than go to a trade. She told me she could do nothing in it, until she had acquainted my mother with my desire. [My mother] persuaded me much against it, but her persuasions were fruitless. Disobedience to God or man, being one of the first fruits of sin, grew out from me in early buds. Finding I was set upon it, and resolved to learn nothing else, she agreed to it, and went with me to speak to the man, and to settle upon the best terms with him she could. He insisted upon twenty pounds currency, which was paid, and I was engaged to stay with him eighteen months, and my mother to find me everything during that time. (p. 112)

In this scene, Marrant's resistance to the dependence of indentured servitude is commensurate with his resistance to parental authority. Indeed, his mother becomes one of Marrant's autobiographical foils, since she suffers from both spiritual malaise and economic ineptitude. The allusion, then, to Proverbs 10:16 ("The labour of the righteous tendeth to life; the fruit of the wicked to sin") maps out the path to salvation for autobiographical subject, editor, and implied Methodist reader. More obliquely, it suggests the worldly means to independence.

This is all the more significant in light of the changing social and religious contexts that inform the language of Marrant's *Narrative*. Joyce Appleby has argued that the disruptions to traditional "community-oriented societies" in mid-eighteenth-century colonial America made young men especially hypersensitive to the state of dependence: "To be dependent in a society of interdependence was quite a different thing from being dependent or fearing dependence in a society in which institutions no longer integrated people's lives into a satisfying social order."[36] If these changing social conditions begin to suggest the *Narrative*'s self-consciousness about personal independence, there were also important changes taking place at this time in British-

American Methodism that further explain the rhetoric used in the *Narrative* to express such uncertainty and desire. Historians recently have emphasized how the commercial and consumption revolutions of the eighteenth century significantly transformed evangelical religion in general and Methodism in particular. A number of factors—the expansion of evangelical print culture, greater activity in the transatlantic book trade, the increase of advertising within religious reading materials, the revolutionary changes in habits of consumption of commercial goods—both commercialized and popularized evangelical religion.[37] Religious hymnals, psalters, sermons, theological tracts, and spiritual narratives increasingly became popular consumer commodities. This process had, in turn, the political effect of producing in evangelical discourse the "intertwining of evangelical piety and lower-class claims to equal social consideration."[38]

The *Narrative* registers this conflation of religious piety and social aspiration through its diverse meanings of "liberty." Consider, for example, the Marrant/Aldridge account of the young sinner's waywardness:

> In the evenings after the scholars were dismissed, I used to resort to the bottom of our garden, where it was customary for some musicians to assemble to blow the French-horn. Here my improvement was so rapid, that in a twelve-month's time I became master both of the violin and of the French-horn, and was much respected by the Gentlemen and Ladies whose children attended the school, as also by my master. This opened to me a large door of vanity and vice, for I was invited to all the balls and assemblies that were held in the town, and met me with the general applause of the inhabitants. I was a stranger to want, being supplied with as much money as I had any occasion for. (p. 112)

The passage creates two seemingly opposite trajectories of the protagonist's economic emancipation and spiritual enslavement by emphasizing the dissonance between private and public conditions. If the text shows that Marrant is not yet the "new" man of Pauline conversion, it just as effectively, if more obliquely, dramatizes how a young African American is able to rescue his "labour" from indentured servitude to obtain virtual freedom. Now he has both money and public acclaim.

While the *Narrative* dramatizes the sinner's descent into iniquity, it also dramatizes the would-be apprentice's mastery of the labor market. The literary performance of collaborative autobiography lies in the relation of these two stories. Early on in the *Narrative*, Marrant struggles with various "masters" over the terms and value of his labor. These encounters have the effect of gradually destabilizing traditional master-apprentice arrangements. Music becomes the source of his newfound value and the medium of contested exchange. Marrant notes that he had become so valuable that "The time I had engaged to serve my master being expired, he persuaded me to stay with him, and offered me any thing, or any money, not to leave him. His intreaties proving ineffectual, I quitted his service, and visited my mother in the country; with her I staid two months, living without God or hope in the world, fishing and hunting on the sabbath-day" (p. 112). His second master—a carpenter—fares no better. "Accordingly I went, but every evening I was sent for to play on music, somewhere or another; and I often continued out very late, sometimes all night, so as to render me incapable of attending my master's business the next day, yet in this manner I served him a year and four months, and was much approved of by him" (pp. 112–113). Rhetorically, these muted declarations of independence rely on careful syntactic arrangement—the first sentence closes with the reminder of sinfulness, the second brackets the suggestion of rebellion with Marrant's feigned respect for hierarchical subordination.

The dual trajectories of the *Narrative* coalesce during Marrant's religious conversion. His spiritual awakening by George Whitefield occurs at the very moment where he again faces the prospect of enslavement to indentured servitude. As he casually notes, his second master "wrote a letter to my mother to come and have me bound, and whilst my mother was weighing the matter in her own mind, the gracious purposes of God, respecting a perishing sinner, were now to be disclosed" (p. 113). The young man's encounter with the "crazy man" Whitefield—the vocal medium of black salvation and the vocal model of black expression—occurs while Marrant balances precariously between the social conditions of liberty and dependence. His conversion prevents dual forms of enslavement.

The *Narrative*'s submerged theme of economic autonomy provides an important point of comparison with *The Interesting Narrative of Olaudah Equiano, or Gustavus Vassa, the African, Written by Himself* (1789). Whereas Marrant structures this theme within the framework of spiritual regeneration, the *Interesting Narrative* juxtaposes the virtue of Equiano's commercial identity with the barbarity of the African slave trade. Analysts of the *Interesting Narrative* have recently emphasized the important relations it maintains between Equiano's self-representation and the ideologies of modern liberal capitalism.[39] From its very outset, however, the autobiography suggests another kind of context for reading its major economic themes. It is addressed to the British Parliament as a "genuine Narrative" whose "chief design . . . is to excite in your august assemblies a sense of compassion for the miseries which the Slave-Trade has entailed on my unfortunate countrymen."[40] Many of his contemporaries viewed Equiano as a key player in abolitionist politics and recognized the role the *Interesting Narrative* played in bringing about Parliament's 1791 vote on the African slave trade[41] (the unsuccessful one that inspired Anna Barbauld's poem to William Wilberforce). The argument against slave trading in the *Interesting Narrative* establishes the ideological context for Equiano's commercial identity.

This is all the more intriguing in light of the fact that Equiano himself traded in slaves in order to free himself. Indeed, the rhetorical design of the *Interesting Narrative* turns on the crucial ambiguity of the very meaning of free trade itself—as both an economic and cultural activity. Equiano's narrative ingenuity attenuates his culpability in the slave trade; he is able to place himself *against* its larger evils. The language of the commercial jeremiad served him well. By manipulating, or even exchanging, the moral categories of trade in antislavery discourses, Equiano can, in turn, exchange the narrative image of himself as agent for victim of barbaric commerce.

The strategy works less by logical consistency than by emotive appeal and narrative indirection. From the moment that the young protagonist endures the Middle Passage,[42] the *Interesting Narrative* speaks a familiar, antislavery language. Consider, for example, that before he even crosses the Atlantic, Equiano reiterates the common antislavery argument for the relative mildness of African slavery compared to the kind perpetrated by Europeans (p. 38). Struck unconscious by the "horrors" of this barbaric traffic, he recovers:

> I asked [the African traders] if we were not to be eaten by those white men with horrible looks, red faces, and loose hair. They told me I was not; and one of the crew brought me a small portion of spiritous liquor in a wine glass; but, being afraid of him, I would not take it out of his hand. One of the blacks therefore took it from him and gave it to me, and I took a little down my palate, which, instead of reviving me, as they thought it would, threw me into the greatest consternation at the strange feeling it produced, having never tasted any such liquor before. (p. 39)

Scenes like this create irony arising from the juxtaposition of perspectives between experienced autobiographer and naïve protagonist. But the irony here unfolds on many levels, as Equiano rhetorically makes use of the symbolic potential of the slave trade. Its association here with spirits—and the passions of which they are simultaneously cause and effect—connects commerce to modes of cultural taste that are themselves premised on the juxtaposition of civilization and savagery.

The *Interesting Narrative*'s presentation of the Middle Passage continues to deploy the period's most resonant imagery of and arguments against slave trading: the slave's lament for the loss of home, the figure of savage European traders, "the loathsomeness of the stench" on board the slave ship, the association of "improvident avarice" with "pestilential" trade, and, finally, the contemplation of suicide, which, in turn, pressures the very categories of freedom and slavery. The chapter culminates powerfully with a description of the West Indian slave market that cannot help but recall the account of the "scramble" that Alexander Falconbridge offered in *An Account of the Slave Trade on the Coast of Africa* (1788). Equiano's is worth quoting at length:

> On a signal given, (as the beat of a drum) the buyers rush at once into the yard where the slaves are confined, and make choice of that parcel they like best. The noise and clamour with which this is attended, and the eagerness visible in the countenance of the buyers, serve not a little to increase the apprehensions of the terrified Africans, who may well be supposed to consider them as the ministers of that destruction to which they think themselves devoted. In this manner, without scruple, are relations and friends separated, most of them never to see each other again. . . . O, ye nominal Christians! Might not an African ask you, learned you this from your God, who says unto you, Do unto all men as you would men should do unto you? Is it not enough that we are torn from our country and friends to toil for your luxury and avarice? (p. 43)

In this frequently cited passage, the rising pitch of prophecy works largely through ventriloquy. That is, Equiano recycles what is, by 1789, an almost archetypal scene of savage trade. The passage does not merely contrast biblical precept (the allusion to Matthew 7.12) with human vice as a way of exposing false Christianity. Rather, it goes to the heart of what it means to be a Christian—the status, after all, of the African autobiographer who is now examining the terms through which one conducts commercial relations. The category of enlightened manners underlies the entire passage, enabling the conflation of race, civilization, and culture and putting the very idea of "civilized" culture into interrogation. Hence he finally dubs the slave trade "a new refinement in cruelty" (p. 43), a phrase that recalls Phillis Wheatley's submerged theme of "On Being Brought from Africa to America."

This shrewdly frames the sequence of Equiano's commercial transactions that structure so much of the *Interesting Narrative*. As virtually all readers recognize, these scenes depict the market-oriented protagonist as both the capitalist agent of his own liberation, who must turn himself from property into humanity, and the racial victim of swindling trade, who suffers from what is in effect the savage brutality of British West Indian merchants. Equiano recalls the birth of his commercial identity innocuously enough: "After I had been sailing for some time with this captain, at length I endeavored to try my luck and commence merchant" (p. 86). If such language faintly suggests the impersonal nature of the capitalist market, Equiano immediately undermines it by entering that market, as he notes, with both "small capital" and "trust" in God. He consistently balances in these crucial scenes the languages of the market and sentimental morality in ways that both resemble and are distinct from Marrant's. "In the midst of these thoughts I therefore looked up with prayers anxiously to God for my liberty; and at the same time I used every honest means, and endeavored all that was possible on my part to obtain it. In process of time I became master of a few pounds, and in a fair way of making more, which my friendly captain knew well" (p. 89).

For a good part of the *Interesting Narrative*, sentiment and commerce work symbiotically, to the point where these categories mutually enhance one another. This has potent narrative effects. The "ill usage" he receives from "Europeans" creates sympathy for the protagonist and, in turn, embellishes Equiano's own claims to civilized identity. "Indeed I was more than once obliged to look up to God on high, as I had advised the poor fishermen some time before" (p. 86). In this scene Equiano and a fellow slave lose their "ventures" to savage white traders: "They still therefore swore, and desired us to be gone, and even took sticks to beat us; while we, seeing they meant what they said, went off in the greatest confusion and despair. Thus, in the very minute of gaining more by three times than I ever did in my life before, was I deprived of every farthing I was worth" (p. 87). Speculative loss in commerce produces sympathy.

This is all the more ironic because abolitionists railed against the "barbaric traffic" as precisely this kind of speculative commerce arising from unregulated passions. Equiano is able to reverse this formula autobiographically by displacing such passions with the sympathy produced from the very loss of speculative profits. These scenes of commercial exchange become even more complex when Equiano acknowledges his involvement in slave trading. The protagonist presents himself as simultaneously the agent and victim of uncivilized commercial practices—and employs a particular language to distance his moral accountability.

> I used frequently to have different cargoes of new negroes in my care for sale; and it was almost a constant practice with our clerks, and other whites, to commit violent depredations on the chastity of the female slaves; and these I was, though with reluctance, obliged to submit to at all times, being unable to help them. When we have had some of the slaves on board my master's vessels to carry them to other islands, or to America, I have known our mates to commit these acts most shamefully, to the disgrace, not of Christians only, but of men. I have even known them to gratify their brutal passion with females not ten years old; and these abominations some of them practised to such scandalous excess, that one of our captains discharged the mate and others on that account. (p. 77)

In recalling such moments, the author hedges on the otherwise dominant theme of the importance of individual agency. Whereas Marrant locates himself simultaneously as subject and object, according to social and spiritual registers of agency, Equiano makes strategic retreats from commercial self-assertion in order to attenuate his guilt in slave trading. Key phrases ("with reluctance, obliged to submit to . . . being unable") suggest he is more victim than agent in barbaric traffic and thereby align him with antislavery readers as common spectators to the scene of suffering.

Put another way, the scene glosses the traffic in slaves through the cultural narrative against slave trading. If this is a deft, even duplicitous, move on Equiano's part, it is made possible largely through the trope of commercial and sexual violation. Both slave trade and rape itself express unregulated desire, specifically the lack of rational control over one's passions, a common theme in antislavery writings. Premised on the civilized balance of the faculties, the scene implicitly aligns not merely Equiano the autobiographer but also the autobiographical protagonist with those readers—those "men"—against savage white traders. As in the antislavery poetry I discussed earlier (Day's *Dying Negro,* for example, which Equiano quotes), the *Interesting Narrative* represents humanity somewhere between the categories of culture and race.

Captivity and Conversion

The commercial energies in these spiritual autobiographies raise further issues about genre. Like Equiano's, Marrant's *Narrative* interweaves commercial and spiritual narratives with the particular effect of creating layered
meanings of the trope of captivity. In Marrant's case this is particularly revealing, since most critics read the *Narrative* in light of the literary tradition
of Indian captivity. Indeed, its most memorable moments recount his journey into the South Carolinian wilderness and his captivity among the Cherokee there. Conventional readings of Indian captivity in the *Narrative* de-
pend upon the traditional view of the genre's moral and racial geography
juxtaposing civilized society with savage wilderness. The minister Aldridge,
for example, offers such a reading when he describes Marrant's crucial passage "between the wilderness and the cultivated country" (p. 111) as the
key to understanding the protagonist's spiritual journey as well as physical
one. But Marrant's itinerancy, supposedly propelled by irrepressible spiritual hunger, might also be read in social terms. For itinerancy was feared in
this era as the path to "social erosion": it "not only eroded the deferential
boundaries which subordinated 'private persons' to their magistrates and lay
persons to their ministers; it also challenged the distinctions of parenthood,
gender and race which eighteenth-century thinkers conceived of establishing a natural hierarchy of authority and status."[43]

The tension between wandering God-seeker and resourceful individual
sustains the enabling ambiguities of the *Narrative*. The very status of the protagonist is sometimes left in doubt. At the moment, for example, when
Marrant distances himself from the first Native American he encounters in
the wilderness, he notes: "Having heard me praising God before I came to
him, he enquired who I was talking to? I told him I was talking to my Lord
Jesus; he seemed surprized, and asked me where he was? For he did not see
him there. I told him he could not be seen with bodily eyes" (p. 116). Is this
the testament to the protagonist's expanding spiritual vision, or merely his
way of manipulating his captor—of turning him into his business partner?
For this is just what the two become. Together, they kill deer, dry their skins,
and after securing their wares, live by their wits in the wilderness:

> We collected a number of large bushes, and placed them nearly in a circular
> form, which uniting at the extremity, afforded us both a verdant covering,
> and a sufficient shelter from night dews. What moss we could gather was

strewed upon the ground, and this composed our bed. A fire was kindled in the front of our temporary lodging-room, and fed with fresh fuel all night, as we slept and watched by turns; and this was our defense from the dreadful animals, whose shining eyes and tremendous roar we often saw and heard during the night. (p. 117)

The association of the wilderness with self-realization involves some linguistic ingenuity. Put another way, the *Narrative*'s earlier theme of social insubordination expresses itself through the theme of linguistic mastery later on. As Sandra M. Gustafson has shown, the representation of Marrant's "captivity" contains culturally syncretic forms of eloquence.[44] The two crucial passages recounting Marrant's mastery of the Cherokee language also reflect back upon the earlier scenes, where he challenged the hierarchical structure of indentured servitude. They suggest, moreover, what inspired the literary production of the *Narrative* itself. On the verge of being tortured by his Cherokee captors, Marrant experiences the first of two miracles: "I prayed in English a considerable time, and about the middle of my prayer, the Lord impressed a strong desire upon my mind to turn into their language, and pray in their tongue. I did so, and with remarkable liberty, which wonderfully affected the people" (p. 118). Later, while on the verge of starvation and again threatened with death, Marrant miraculously heals the king's daughter and converts both king and people to the Word:

[T]he Lord appeared most lovely and glorious; the king himself was awakened, and the others set at liberty. A great change took place among the people; the king's house became God's house; the soldiers were ordered away, and the poor condemned prisoner had perfect liberty, and was treated like a prince. Now the Lord made all my enemies to become my great friends. I remained nine weeks in the king's palace, praising God all day and night: I was never out but three days all the time. I had assumed the habit of the country, and was dressed much like the king, and nothing was too good for me. The king would take off his golden ornaments, his chain and bracelets, like a child, if I objected to them, and lay them aside. Here I learned to speak their tongue in the highest stile. (p. 120)

Cast in the language of divine deliverance, these two scenes reveal the power of language for both protagonist and autobiographer alike. The typological identification with Daniel held captive in Nebuchadnezzar's court suggests as much the resourceful individualist as it does the persecuted martyr. As the ingenious individual, Marrant likens himself to a king and the Cherokee king to a child. Like the earlier conflicts over the terms of indentured servitude, this one ends in another successful negotiation of masters.

The rhetorical complexity of *The Narrative of the Lord's Wonderful Dealings with John Marrant* thus arises from the fact of collaboration in a historical moment in which the languages of "liberty" and "slavery" had density—and mutability. The ongoing negotiation between editor and subject both shapes and is shaped by the slipperiness of language. By playing upon the ambiguities of "liberty," the oral autobiographer Marrant fulfills both the expectations of evangelical Methodism overseeing the *Narrative*'s publication and the anti-authoritarian themes residing just below the narrative surface. This makes for potent ambiguities in language, such as the moment when Marrant becomes known as "the free Carpenter" (p. 123).

In a larger historical context, then, spiritual narratives such as Marrant's are part of a black literary and political tradition that crystallized during the American Revolutionary era. During the 1770s, African American slaves and free persons petitioned state legislatures, particularly in Massachusetts, for the freedom of enslaved blacks. As many have noted, these petitions usually turned on the argument pointing out the hypocrisy of a slave-holding republic. Thus African American Caesar Sarter testified that:

> As this is a time of great anxiety and distress among you . . . permit a poor, though *freeborn* African, who, in his youth, was trepanned into Slavery, and who has born the galling yoke of bondage for more than twenty years; though at last, by the blessing of God, has shaken it off, to tell you, and that from experience, that as *Slavery* is the greatest, and consequently most to be dreaded, of all temporal calamities: So its opposite, *Liberty*, is the greatest temporal good with which you can be blest![45]

Revolutionary-era black declamations of slavery such as Sarter's (or those by Felix, Belinda, and many others) put great pressure on republican language and principles. In light of its more expansive contexts and purposes, which include the transatlantic reach of evangelical Methodism, Marrant's story both deepens and broadens the rhetorical texture of this kind of Revolutionary black language. It speaks to the demands of evangelical religion while it subtly resists those very demands through language.

The scene of collaborative exchange broadens the context for the politics of literacy in early black autobiography. Henry Louis Gates has argued influentially for the central importance of the "trope of the talking book" as the chief means to contradict the Enlightenment belief in the impossibility of literary originality for blacks.[46] David Hume's "Of National Characters" is the most egregious example of this belief in savaging the poetry of the free Jamaican Francis Williams. "I am apt to suspect that the negroes and in general all other species of men (for there are four or five different kinds) to be naturally inferior to the whites. . . . In Jamaica, indeed, they talk of one negroe as a man of parts and learning; but it is likely he is admired for slender accomplishments, like a parrot who speaks a few words plainly."[47] If, as Gates argues, Marrant is the first black autobiographer to turn himself into an active interpreter of texts, this process involves oral performance as well. The *Narrative,* in other words, self-reflexively comments on its own oral and literary production. Marrant's manipulation of the "Indian tongue" (p. 117) "in the highest stile" (p. 120)—his miraculous mastery of a foreign language—signals his active role in the collaborative process of autobiography. The black subject creatively encounters Cherokee captors, English editor, and Anglo-American audiences alike. The originality of the language that those like Marrant "parrot" to such great effect lies in creative imitation, a process that involves oral and written communication and that functions according to the shared understanding—and misunderstanding—of the meanings of language.

Venture Capitalist

Before turning to Venture Smith's *Narrative,* I want to revisit Equiano's, for it begins to suggest the problem in early black autobiography of disentangling the categories of property and humanity. Both Marrant and Equiano are quite effective in avoiding the pitfall of equating the two as they parry arguments about African inferiority. There are moments in the *Interesting Narrative,* however, when Equiano succumbs to the polemical temptation of fighting proslavery thought on its own terms. An example:

> I have sometimes heard it asserted that a negro cannot earn his master the
> first cost; but nothing can be further from the truth. I suppose nine tenths of
> the mechanics throughout the West Indies are negro slaves; and I well
> know the coopers among them earn two dollars a day. . . . I have known
> many slaves whose masters would not take a thousand pounds current for
> them. But surely this assertion refutes itself; for, if it be true, why do the
> planters and merchants pay such a high price for slaves? And, above all,

why do those who make this assertion exclaim the most loudly against the abolition of the slave trade? So much are men blinded, and to such inconsistent arguments are they driven by mistaken interest! (p. 77)

Coming as it does immediately before the scene (cited above) of Equiano trading in slaves, this one further confounds the stable meaning of human value in the *Interesting Narrative*. To assail the "mistaken interest" of racial bias, Equiano argues for the productive capacity of African labor, so much so that the passage reduces African humanity to what African slaves can produce in the capitalist market. This engenders a terrible irony: the *value* of humanity becomes indistinct from capital, or property, in this case figured as the exemplary slave worth more than a thousand pounds.

This problem in early black autobiography raises issues about the liberal ideology and its influence on the late eighteenth-century slave narrative, specifically on liberalism's ability to reduce humanity to capital or property. As Eric Cheyfitz has put it, "In the West, property, in that tangled space where the physical and metaphysical mix, is the very mark of identity, of that which is identical to itself: what we typically call a 'self' or an 'individual,' indicating the absolute boundaries that are predicated on this entity."[48] The most influential philosophical context for property as the source of individual identity was of course John Locke's *Second Treatise on Government* (1688). When the Connecticut minister Samuel Sherwood, for example, lamented the loss of English liberty during the Revolutionary crisis, he declared, "Property is prior to all human laws, constitutions and charters. *God hath given the earth to the children of men.* Our fathers acquired property in this land, and were rightfully possessed of it, previous to their obtaining a royal charter."[49]

This ideological contiguity posed serious problems for antislavery reform, since, as Winthrop Jordan has noted, property rights actually weakened its moral leverage: "The absence of any clear disjunction between what are now called 'human' and 'property' rights formed a massive roadblock across the route to the abolition of slavery."[50] This partly explains the painful contortions that antislavery writers underwent to disentangle the two. For example, Anthony Benezet cited George Wallis's *System of the Principles of the Laws of Scotland* (1761) to argue that "Men and their liberty are *not in Commercio,* they are not saleable or purchaseable."[51] But such a distinction often foundered on traditional assumptions about private property rights. When the evangelical minister David Rice gave his antislavery pitch before the Kentucky Constitutional Convention in 1792, he declared: "To call our fellow-men, who have not forfeited, nor voluntarily resigned their liberty, our property, is a gross absurdity, a contradiction to common sense, and an indignity to human nature." In the very next breath, however, he expressed the core belief that property legitimized humanity (much in the same way Thomas Paine had done twenty nearly years before): "On the one hand, we see a man deprived of all property, and all capacity to possess property, of his own free agency . . . on the other, a man [a slave owner] deprived of eighty or a hundred pounds. Shall we hesitate a moment to determine, who is the greatest sufferer, and who is treated with greatest injustice?"[52]

The rhetorical mix of liberty, property, and humanity both empowers and undermines early Black Atlantic writing. Certainly, the prevalence of post-Lockean ideas in this writing helped to combat cultural stereotypes about the supposed lassitude and ease of Africans themselves. Ironically, this image, derived from the antislavery motif of the Edenic nature of West African societies (in Benezet, John Wesley, and others), meant to amplify the crimes of the African slave trade. The stereotype of African ease became especially toxic in proslavery apologia. When, in the 1770s, the former West Indian planter Richard Nisbet responded to Benjamin Rush's *An Address to the Inhabitants of the British Settlements in North America, upon Slave-Keeping,* he sardonically complained that Rush merely wanted to end West Indian slavery so that "that Africans might indulge their natural laziness in their own country."[53] Hence the defense of African "industry" became particularly necessary in Black Atlantic autobiography, even in those texts (like Equiano's) that deploy the Edenic trope of African innocence.

The dialogue, then, between Black Atlantic and Anglo-American antislavery writers was fundamentally about the very meaning of the virtue of black industry, an issue that contained within it serious social implications. As my epigraph from James Forten suggests, however, the defense of black virtue could stumble rhetorically upon the tangle of humanity and property. A free African American, Forten was a hero from the Revolutionary war, a well-known and prosperous businessman in Philadelphia, and an outspoken advocate of black American rights. *Letters From a Man of Color* (1813) assails the law before the Pennsylvania senate forbidding further black emigration into the state, which in effect would ensure the enslavement and deportation of miscreant black Pennsylvanians. To combat it, Forten cultivates the persona of the industrious American and ends up complaining that the law deprives African Americans of their humanity by taking away their property.

Daniel Coker, the minister of Baltimore's African Methodist Episcopal

Church, also encountered the stumbling block of equating humanity with property. Writing in the tradition of the antislavery dialogue, popularized in such works as Thomas Tryon's *Friendly Advice to the Gentlemen-Planters of the East and West Indies* (1684) and Samuel Hopkins's *A Dialogue on Slavery* (1776), Coker stages a conversation between a true Christian and an ambivalent southern slave owner. At a crucial moment, the former responds to the slave owner's complaint that taking away his slaves "would be equally unjust with dispossessing me of my horses, cattle or any other species of property": "Many years ago, men being deprived of their natural rights to freedom, and made slaves, were by law converted into property. . . . But the question is concerning the liberty of a man. The man himself claims it as his own property. He pleads, (and I think in truth) that it was originally his own; that he has never forfeited, nor alienated it; and therefore, by the common laws of justice and humanity, it is still his own."[54]

The notion of "propertied humanity" actually premises much of the important criticism about eighteenth-century black autobiography. As I suggested earlier, Houston Baker, Jr. notes that Equiano realizes and exploits the paradox whereby only acquiring property will transform him from chattel slave to free man. Similarly, discussions of Venture Smith focus on his mastery of the bourgeois success story.[55] So would he. Yet Smith's *Narrative* runs headlong into the central ideological problem of the reduction of humanity to property.

Born sometime in the late 1720s in the West African region of Gangara, Broteer Furro (Smith's original name) was the son of the local monarch. At about the age of eight, Furro was captured by slave traders and taken to Rhode Island, and thereafter spent most of his life in Long Island and eastern Connecticut until he died in 1805. A more openly secular account than Marrant's *Narrative* or Equiano's *Interesting Narrative*, Smith's also arose from the collaboration between black subject and white editor. Smith's was Elisha Niles, a Connecticut schoolteacher and antislavery advocate, who published it over a six-week period in a local newspaper, *The New London Bee*. Republished in 1835 and 1897, Smith's text was accompanied by "Traditions of Venture" that provide legendary (and perhaps sensationalized) accounts of his physical strength and capacity for work. Even the first edition's preface, written by Niles, models its African subject as a paragon of bourgeois virtue:

> The subject of the following pages, had he received only a common education, might have been a man of high respectability and usefulness; and had

his education been suited to his genius, he might have been an ornament and an honor to human nature. It may, perhaps, not be unpleasing to see the efforts of a great mind wholly uncultivated, enfeebled, and depressed by slavery, and struggling under every disadvantage—The reader may see here a Franklin and a Washington in a state of nature, or rather in a state of slavery. . . .

This narrative exhibits a pattern of honesty, prudence and industry, to people of his own colour; and perhaps some white people would not find themselves degraded by imitating such an example.[56]

Premised on the didactic function of autobiography, the preface signals the tricky status of exemplary black selfhood. Eighteenth-century Anglo-Americans were somewhat familiar with the aristocratic figure of the "noble African" like the fictional Oroonoko and his real counterparts, William Ansah Sessarakoo and Job Ben Solomon. But Smith, like Marrant and Equiano, occupies a socially more humble place from which to claim autobiographical representativeness, one that placed greater value on the virtues of labor and industry and that was perhaps more accessible to contemporary bourgeois readers. Rather than simply read Niles's hedging ("might," "perhaps") as latent racism, I think it suggests a more profound problem within the collaborative scene of writing: that of drawing "racial" boundaries for bourgeois ideology. In other words, Niles is struggling with the trope of the black Ben Franklin. Do the values of "respectability and usefulness," his Preface asks, erase the differences between Smith and his largely white audience? Does Smith live in a state of nature—or slavery? Does the epithet "native" for him suggest a state of nature associated with Africa? Or are Smith's "native ingenuity and good sense" representative of all Americans? (p. 369).

Notwithstanding its status as a collaborative project, the *Narrative* clearly presents what James Olney has called the autobiographical genre's "metaphor of self."[57] Its version of this "order-produced and order-producing" trope fulfills the virtue of bourgeois industry while avoiding (though pressing) the extreme limits of individual acquisitiveness. The *Narrative*'s ambiguous achievement is its transformation of Smith from object to subject in a capitalist slave economy, a transformation that ultimately returns him to the status of property, which he must, in turn, autobiographically engage.

Like Marrant's *Narrative*, Smith's is self-conscious about the role of language to this process. As Orlando Patterson has argued, the "social death" enacted by chattel slavery occurs first in naming: "The slave's former name died with his former self."[58] Smith's *Narrative* accordingly invests great thematic significance in the crucial moment when Broteer becomes Venture. "I was bought on board [the slave trading vessel] by one Robertson Mumford, steward of the said vessel, for four gallons of rum, and a piece of calico, and called VENTURE, on account of his having purchased me with his own private venture. Thus I came by my name" (p. 374). At this moment, then, the African "Broteer" becomes "Venture"—the object of a venturesome act of capitalist slave economy. This loss of name endangers the very nature of his identity. That is, Smith needs to reassert his full humanity by specifically reconstructing himself from within the operative categories of the slave economy. To enact the movement from object to subject, Smith collaboratively creates with Niles a persona cut from exemplary middle-class values.[59] But he does, like Marrant, autobiographically claim an individuated identity from the anonymity of slavery. Early on, Smith establishes the persona of the self-interested venturesome capitalist in this competitive social arena. Betrayed by an indentured servant named Heddy during their planned escape, he immediately shows the self-preservation necessary to survive: "I then thought it might afford some chance for my freedom, or at least a palliation for my running away, to return Heddy immediately to his master, and inform him that I was induced to go away by Heddy's address" (p. 377).

This ingenuity extends to the realms of language and representation. Like Marrant's mastery of the "Indian tongue," the protagonist Smith's manipulation of persona signals the self-consciousness with which the black autobiographer recognizes the forms of power that control chattel slavery and black writing alike. Indeed, the persona of his *Narrative* is premised on this realization: "This [money] I took out of the earth and tendered to my master, having previously engaged a free negro man to take his security for it, as I was property of my master, and could not safely take his obligation myself. . . . By cultivating this land with greatest diligence and economy, at times when my master did not require my labor, in two years I laid up ten pounds" (p. 380). While Smith tills his and others' land, makes wise investments, lends money at interest, and bargains his time and labor wisely, he successfully negotiates the hard, prosaic realities of the slave economy. The *Narrative*, like Marrant's, makes labor the foundation of freedom. In Lockean terms, Smith dramatizes making property his own by mixing his labor with the land. The claim that free labor signifies personal liberty means, for Smith, his ability to maintain an autonomous will. After his new master

Stanton puts him in shackles, he notes, "I continued to wear the chain peaceably for two or three days, when my master asked me with contemptuous hard names whether I had not better be freed from my chains and go to work. I answered him, No" (p. 378).

Rhetorical irony is important to the *Narrative*'s larger autobiographical design. Throughout this chapter I have been making an argument about black language—spoken rather than written—that derives from the Bakhtinian concepts of dialogism and heteroglossia, which emphasize the multivalent play of the single utterance (of "liberty") within a particular social moment. This makes the language of these related life stories creatively hybrid, as they suggest the delicate play of authorial control and editorial management. As Bakhtin further distinguishes forms of linguistic dialogism, they comes chiefly in two forms: one "intentional," in which one discourse unmasks the other, and one "organic," in which two cultural discourses unintentionally and unconsciously collide, mix, fuse, and ultimately enable the historical evolution of language.[60] In this light, Smith's *Narrative* ably manages competing religious and economic meanings of the language of redemption. "What was wanting in redeeming myself, my master agreed to wait on me for, until I could procure it for him. I still continued to work for Col. Smith" (p. 380). While modeling industrious black identity, the process of redemption tends to reduce that identity to monetary value:

> Being encouraged by the success which I had met in redeeming myself, I again solicited my master for a further chance of completing it. The chance for which I solicited him was that of going out to work the ensuing winter. He agreed to this on condition that I would give him one quarter of my earnings. . . . I returned to my master and gave him what I received of my six months' labor. This left only thirteen pounds eighteen shillings to make up the full sum of my redemption. My master liberated me, saying that I might pay what was behind if I could ever make it convenient, otherwise it would be well. The amount of money which I had paid my master towards redeeming my time, was seventy-one pounds two shillings. The reason of my master for asking such an unreasonable price, was, he said, to secure himself in case I should ever come to want. (pp. 380–381)

In light of an earlier scene in the *Narrative*, Smith's language here actually reveals satiric intentions. In the earlier scene, the young Smith justifies his defiance of his master's son by claiming that he is merely obeying his master's instructions. When the son becomes violently irate, Smith wryly summarizes the American slave's predicament by invoking Matthew 6.24: "This was to serve two masters" (p. 376). By alluding to Christ's injunction to distinguish between spiritual and secular authority, Smith is able to call attention to the moral bankruptcy of slaveholding Christianity—a staple of the slave narrative apparent in later famous slave narratives by Frederick Douglass, Harriet Jacobs, and others. Being a more openly secular account than Marrant's, Smith's *Narrative* simultaneously demystifies religious hypocrisy and sanctifies (through the religious connotations of "redemption") its protagonist's economic drive for freedom.

From the very moment that Smith calls attention to his transformation within the setting of the slave economy, the *Narrative* introduces the difficulty of separating property from humanity. This directly involves the value Smith places on the productive self. The historian Shane White has described the achievement of slaves such as Venture Smith who labored for their emancipation: "Success in such negotiations [of slaves with their masters] and an early release from slavery were partly the result of luck, but the process also favored the most industrious, tenacious, and skilled of the slaves."[61] This kind of assessment of black virtue should call our attention to the epistemological slippage accompanying self-emancipation. The necessity to demonstrate individuality in market culture actually translates into the need to possess property. Yet for a slave to own property that can free him is to become reduced to property in a post-Lockean culture. Succumbing to this epistemological trap, Smith makes even the most potentially intimate of familial relations a matter of profits and losses. Consider the account of his son's death:

> Solomon, my eldest son, being then in his seventeenth year, and all my hope and dependence for help, I hired him out to one Charles Church, of Rhode-Island, for one year, on consideration of his giving him twelve pounds and an opportunity of acquiring some learning. In the course of the year, Church fitted out a vessel for a whaling voyage, and being in want of hands to man her, he induced my son to go, with the promise of giving him, on his return, a pair of silver buckles, besides his wages. As soon as I heard of his going to sea, I immediately set out to go and prevent it if possible— But on my arrival at Church's, to my great grief, I could only see the vessel my son was in almost out of sight going to sea. My son died of the scurvy in this voyage, and Church has never yet paid me the least of his wages. In my son, besides the loss of his life, I lost equal to seventy-five pounds. (p. 382)

Strangely, despite its use of the antislavery trope of commercial seduction, the account of Solomon's demise is empty of sentimental appeal. Read, moreover, in light of the antislavery motif of the separated family, the passage surprisingly avoids the sentimental rhetoric that one would expect. Whatever sadness Smith feels arises chiefly from his material loss. Solomon's value is "equal to" the amount paid to "redeem" him; accordingly, sentimental family relations are buried in the subordinate clause beginning with "besides." Thus Solomon is virtually reduced to the value he possessed *as a slave*. Similarly, Smith abruptly interrupts his lament about his daughter Hannah's "lingering and painful" death with financial concerns—"The physician's bills for attending her during her illness amounted to forty pounds" (p. 383)—and then immediately returns to his ensuing business transactions.

The reduction of family relations to the status of things might be seen as a reincarnation, of sorts, of the U.S. Constitutional settlement of 1787–88. As virtually everyone recognizes, the Constitution institutionalizes the paradoxical ontological condition where slaves (or "such persons") stand simultaneously as human beings and chattel property. The most infamous theoretical formulation of this condition occurs in the *Federalist* #54, where James Madison rationalizes the Constitution's Three-Fifths Compromise, which made each slave account for three-fifths of a human being for purposes of taxation and representation. Madison argues here for "the mixt character of persons and property." In this context, then, Smith similarly reduces familial relations to the prosaic realities of the slave economy—they are, in effect, both persons and property. As he tries to convert himself from property into humanity—and out of the Madisonian paradox in the *Federalist*—he nonetheless encounters the inextricably ideological connection between property and humanity. He never fully narrates his life out of it. If antislavery writers like Benezet and Clarkson were able to use Scottish theory to argue against the commodification of human liberty, the black subjects of collaborative autobiography never enjoyed such abstract distance. Smith and others like him were forced to conduct antislavery polemics within—and through—the medium of personal identity.

To turn this dilemma into metacritical commentary about collaborative autobiography is the most striking achievement of Smith's *Narrative*. Rather than ultimately reject "his own success as a cultural identification," as Robert Ferguson has argued,[62] Smith exploits his cultural role by commenting on the performative potential that his status as "property" affords. Indeed,

he invests what Gilroy calls "the politics of fulfillment" with its own performative dimensions. When he threatens his master, William Hooker, for
example, Smith knows that by binding him Hooker would lower his market
value: "'If you will go by no other measures, I will tie you down in my
sleigh.' I replied to him, that if he carried me in that manner, no person
would purchase me, for it would be thought he had a murderer for sale. After this he tried no more, and said he would not have me as a gift" (p. 379).

Recognizing the uncertain distinction between humanity and property,
Smith masters the symbolic economy of slave trading. At crucial moments
he takes control of his body as a symbolic commodity and deploys its cultural function. At one point, for example, he schemes with a white man,
Hempsted Miner, to appear "discontented" during negotiations in order to
lower his market value and thereby retaliate against his master Stanton.
"[A]nd that in return he would give me a good chance to gain my freedom
when I came to live with him. I did as he requested me. Not long after,
Hempsted Miner purchased me of my master for fifty-six pounds lawful. He
took the chain and padlocks from off me immediately after" (p. 379). This
anecdote lends irony to Smith's lament that Stanton wished to sell him only
"to convert me into cash, and speculate with me as with other commodities"
(p. 379). For this is just what Smith does in the *Narrative*—he exploits the
speculative potential of his slave body. To convert himself from object to
subject, the black autobiographer, like the black venture capitalist working
his way to freedom, must master the ideological resources made available to
him. Like the slave body, the slave narrative performs itself publicly within
the context of such an exchange.

In 1957 the famous African-American novelist Richard Wright published
White Man, Listen!, a book of essays dedicated to the Caribbean politician, activist, and historian of the African slave trade, Eric Williams. In the essay
"The Literature of the Negro in the United States," Wright assessed the difference between Phillis Wheatley and her literary successors. The distinction
goes right to the heart of what Wright thought true black writing should be:

> Again, let me recall to you the concept I mentioned before. Phyllis [sic]
> Wheatley was at one with her culture. What a far cry this is from the Negro
> Seabees who staged a sit-down strike a few years ago on the Pacific Coast
> when the war against Japan was at its hardest! What makes for this dif-
> ference in loyalty? Are these three excerpts [by Dumas, Pushkin, and

Wheatley] I've read to you the writing of Negroes? No, not by present-day American standards. Then, what is a Negro? What is Negro writing?[63]

Wright's questions are critically resonant even today. The assumption that true black writing has a certain racial self-consciousness and political agency that Wheatley's (and Pushkin's) presumably lacked is important today because it registers contemporary critical assumptions about the literature of the eighteenth-century Black Atlantic writing. Over the last two decades critics have come to question the extent of cultural assimilation that Wright assumes in this writing. Yet the field is still shaped by the ongoing question of the degree to which writers like Wheatley, Equiano, John Marrant, and Venture Smith consent to dominant cultural and ideological norms.[64]

In this chapter I have interrogated the cultural and literary history of the early Black Atlantic by engaging in what William Andrews has called "creative hearing." From such reading of these early collaborative autobiographies I theorize a position for early black thought and writing that is simultaneously inside and outside Anglo-American culture. Such a reading further addresses the crucial issue of black agency—or even of black radicalism— that, for example, divides historians over the full meaning and consequences of the American Revolution. The work of Marrant and Smith allows us to articulate spaces for dissent without overstating the case for their autonomy.

CHAPTER 5

Yellow Fever and the Black Market

To explain the fever we need no boatloads of refugees, ragged and wracked with killing fevers, bringing death to our shores. We have bred the affliction within our breasts. Each solitary heart contains all the world's tribes, and its precarious dance echoes the drum's thunder. We are our ancestors and our children, neighbors and strangers to ourselves. Fever descends when the waters that connect us are clogged with filth. When our seas are garbage.

—John Edgar Wideman, "Fever" (1989)

Previous chapters have focused in various ways on the commercial and cultural pathology of the slave trade. Slave trading figured, in other words, as a particular kind of disease that undermined social health. Now, inverting the theme, this chapter examines the literature of disease as cultural criticism that takes up much the same issues the abolitionists discussed. The writings arising from Philadelphia's yellow fever epidemic in 1793 (and several epidemics thereafter) fundamentally concerned themselves with the economics of citizenship during moments of social crisis. Our focus therefore shifts from enslaved to free African Americans and from international commerce to the domestic labor market.

Eighteenth-century discourses drew a direct association between trade and disease. For example, during the infamous South Sea Bubble, in which thousands of English stockholders were ruined by the company's reckless speculation, an early number of *Cato's Letters* (1720) likened its "fatal effects" to the plague in Marseilles. "The terrible circumstances of our French neighbours, under the plague in some places, expecting it in others, and dreading it in all, is a loud warning to take all expedients and possible precautions against such a formidable calamity. We have already had, and still have, a contagion of another sort, more universal, and less merciful than that at

Marseilles."[1] Antislavery poetry employed similar rhetorical strategies, referring to slave trading as "the breath of Pestilence," "pestilence's silent tread," "unseen contagion," a "foul plague," "pestilential fury," or a "soft luxurious plague."[2] This rhetoric of commercial pathology often figured the slave trade as yellow fever. In the Introduction to *The Penitential Tyrant* (1805), the ex-Antiguan planter Thomas Branagan, who was then living in Philadelphia and writing vigorously for the antislavery movement, proclaimed: "When I consider the revival of the slave trade in the American republic in a political, theological or philosophical point of view, I must come to this conclusion, that it is to the body politic what the yellow fever is to an individual. Every slave ship that arrives in Charleston is to our nation what the Grecian's wooden horse was to Troy—the fate of St. Domingo will abundantly demonstrate this hypothesis."[3]

The trope blurs the boundary between metaphor and reality. Contemporary medical theories, which emphasized the closely related forms of physical, moral, and psychological health, facilitated the rhetorical power of "disease." Consider, for example, the Scottish poet James Grahame's *Africa Delivered; or The Slave Trade Abolished* (1809), a work that recounts the plague that destroys a slave ship headed for the West Indies. The poem impugns the "brutal traffickers" engaged in the slave trade, questions the European claim to civilization ("Against the savage tenants of the wild / More savage men yet were there unknown"),[4] and turns its sights on the pathology of British culture:

> And is it for a system such as this,
> That Britain sends devoted legions forth,
> The victims not of warfare but disease!
> What is the clashing steel, or cannon's roar,
> Death's toys and baubles! what the thundering surge,
> Compared to pestilence's silent tread,
> That like the angel sent through Pharaoh's land
> (O would Britannia read the lesson right)
> The bondman's dwelling passes o'er untouched!
>> What hecatombs of human beings die
> Upon thy altar, Commerce! Ages hence
> Thy bloody superstition will arouse
> The horror of mankind, as now the rites
> Almost incredible of Saturn's shrine,

At which the infant died to expiate
The parent's guilt.[5]

The diseased slave ship symbolizes the cultural inversion of trade as enlightened and sociable exchange. Both the description of the foundering ship, and the engraving that accompanies it (see Figure 4), represent this pathology as a form of inertia:

> Dearth next approaches, handmaid of disease,
> With slow but certain step: the measured draught
> Of water is dealt out with cautious hand;
> For now the sails hang wavering in the breeze;
> The lambent waves rise gently to the prow;
> His bulk the following sluth-hound of the deep
> Rolls, gamboling, and shows his vault-like gorge;
> And every signs foretells a lasting calm.
>   Fainting, the breeze dies gradually away,
> Till not a breath is felt; the vessel lies
> Moveless, as if encased in Arctic ice,
> While fierce with perpendicular rays, the sun
> Withers up life, and from within thirst burns unquenched.[6]

Instead of fostering civilized social relations, the slave trade destroys them; it reduces commerce, in its sense as both economic and cultural exchange, to stasis, pestilence, and death. The image of the sharks "gamboling" about the ship raises a larger question about the relation between human nature and the natural order, one that is expressed as well in the curious—indeed unnatural—yoking together of extreme heat and cold.

The ability of corrupt commerce to do more than metaphorize disease—to actually engender it—suggests the cultural stakes of the many writings about yellow fever in Philadelphia during the 1790s.[7] Before pursuing the subject as a literary and cultural event, I want to sketch out a few basic facts about the episode. First, the 1793 epidemic was the beginning of a series of yellow fever epidemics that struck the city during the 1790s. If not the worst epidemic in American history, it was nevertheless a horrific episode and a major medical crisis, killing off about 5,000 of the city's inhabitants, or roughly ten percent of its total population, and causing another 15,000 to flee the city. Not surprisingly, the epidemic brought on a widespread social

Figure 4. Untitled photograph from *Poems on the Abolition of the Slave Trade, written by James Montgomery, James Grahame, and E. Benger* (London, 1809).

crisis as well. From August until October, when the frosts ridded the city of
the mosquitoes that actually were transmitting the disease (a fact that science did not discover until the work of Walter Reed at the beginning of the
twentieth century), the epidemic ruined families, paralyzed social and political institutions, and bitterly divided the medical community over the nature
and treatment of the disease.[8]

The social crisis placed the city's African Americans in a particularly difficult position that subsequently led to a series of important public exchanges about their behavior during the epidemic. If the requests by civic
leaders to the city's black population to help nurse the sick and bury the
dead increased their visibility, they only highlighted the absolute hypocrisy
of asking (or begging) people to whom citizenship had been denied to act as
ideal citizens. Indeed, one piece appearing in early September in the city's
leading commercial periodical, *Dunlap's Daily American Advertiser*, claimed
that "a noble opportunity" now presented itself to the city's African Americans "of manifesting their gratitude" to those citizens, who had placed them
"in point of civil and religious privileges, upon a footing with themselves."[9]
Such language, at best outlandish and at worst duplicitous, appears again in
the hopelessly awkward letter that the city's famous physician Benjamin
Rush wrote to the African American minister Richard Allen as the epidemic
worsened. Embarrassed at the shortage of Anglo-American volunteers,
Rush turned to African Americans for help, reminding Allen that all the aid
he could muster would be "pleasing to the light of that God who will [re-
ward] every act of kindness done to creatures whom he calls his brethren."[10]
Both newspaper and letter raise the troubling question about the status of
African Americans in post-Revolutionary America—that is, what *were* the
moral obligations of the politically disenfranchised to the politically empow-
ered?

The question erupted in the public exchange between the publisher
Mathew Carey and the African American leaders Absalom Jones and Richard Allen. Although Jones and Allen, along with the recently formed Free
African Society, heeded Rush's request for volunteers, Carey's major publication about the episode, *A Short Account of the Malignant Fever Lately Prevalent
in Philadelphia* (1793), unfairly accused the city's blacks of theft, negligence,
and extortion. Understandably stung by these accusations, especially in light
of the two hundred African Americans who died from the disease, Jones and
Allen responded by writing *A Narrative of the Proceedings of the Black People,
During the Late Awful Calamity in Philadelphia* (1794). The pamphlet defends

the behavior of African Americans and assails Carey for cowardice and self-promotion.

Present-day scholars are understandably intrigued by the public war of words. There are few apologists for the racial aspersions that Carey offers in this "dramatic narrative of community destruction and regeneration."[11] Rather, most of the writers vehemently defend Philadelphia's African Americans, emphasizing, for example, the "spirit of Christian love" they demonstrated during the crisis.[12] The historian Gary B. Nash has argued that Jones and Allen saw the epidemic "as a God-sent opportunity to prove their courage and worth and to show that they could drive anger and bitterness from their hearts. Perhaps they could dissolve white racism by demonstrating that in their capabilities, civic virtue, and Christian humanitarianism they were not inferior, but in fact superior, to those who regarded former slaves as a degraded, hopelessly backward people."[13] Julia Stern also admires "the dramatic show of fellow feeling these African Americans extend to their white brethren": "In their tract, [Allen and Jones] discuss the problem of African American social invisibility, the way in which blacks are excluded from the community's imagination of sympathy."[14]

Although focus on this episode serves to unmask previously invisible social history, it all but reduces Philadelphia's black population in 1793 to the values of sympathy and benevolence. It elides the historical fact that African Americans, like Anglo-Americans, worked for real wages and regarded their own interests. The comments only invert the ethical opposition that Carey tried to maintain between Anglo- and African Americans without actually interrogating the premises for the racial hierarchy itself. I too recognize that Philadelphia's African Americans *did* provide substantial help to the city of Philadelphia. But I intend to reconsider sentimental black citizenship by placing the cultural value of sentiment *itself* in context of its historical relations to emergent capitalist ideologies favoring the impersonality of market forces. Just as the literature against the African slave trade tried to separate virtuous from vicious commercial relations, the literature of yellow fever—itself embedded in larger issues of commerce and West Indian slavery—tried to distinguish between sentimental and capitalist modes of social relations during a particular historical crisis. But the crisis reveals the period's entanglement of sympathy and the market.[15] The complex relations between the two underlie the writings of Anglo- and African Americans alike, both of which rhetorically devolved upon the uncertain meanings of "labor," "value," and "interest." The result of such an analysis of the writings of

Carey and Jones and Allen is to bring them into a closer and perhaps unexpected ideological proximity.

Economic Bodies

When yellow fever struck Philadelphia in the summer of 1793, it disrupted the commercial life of the most modern city in early America. By the 1790s, it was certainly the wealthiest American city, and, as the commercial and political capital of the republic, Philadelphia was the site of the new Federal government, the home of the American Philosophical Society and the prestigious College of Physicians, and, in effect, the center of the American Enlightenment. Yet modernization in Philadelphia came at a cost, particularly the urban blight that had developed there, the increasing polarity between rich and poor, the expansion of credit, the increase in speculative venture capitalism, and the unpredictable quality of the city's free labor market.[16] Moreover, its population in the 1790s was expanding rapidly, as significant numbers of émigrés and fugitives escaping revolutions in France and Saint Domingue migrated to Philadelphia. This influx exacerbated existing problems by further driving up the costs of property and rentals. The city's unprecedented demands for consumer goods and displays of luxury and extravagance only highlighted the growing polarization of social classes.

Commentators on the yellow fever crisis were forced to take a hard look at the "health" of this urban and commercial society—that is, Philadelphia served as the model for considering recent transformations in social and economic life. Recent historians of modern capitalism have argued that the development of the open market in labor tends to produce anxious questions about the nature of social relations in general: "The commercialization of social relations, especially the creation of a market in labor-power, forced a rethinking of social responsibility, ideological hegemony, and the nature of human identity."[17] John Ashworth, for example, claims that such a process describes the "paradox of freedom" facing post-Revolutionary American society: "The spread of the market meant that a growing part of human life was subject to the force of individual self-interest. But a society in which the pursuit of self-interest is universal is a society that is about to collapse."[18]

Even if such a statement is hyperbolic, it does capture the anxieties about the "natural" laws of the market that arose during Philadelphia's yellow fever epidemic. The "racial" war between Mathew Carey and Absalom Jones and Richard Allen was about the conduct of the city's African Americans during the crisis—particularly their behavior as workers who nursed the sick and transported the dead. The conflict involved competing understandings of the labor market during a period of social crisis. Carey foisted his fears about market forces of supply and demand onto the city's African American population. The debate over African Americans and their labor was part of a larger cultural narrative about the nature of labor in a capitalist system.

To clarify the positions of Carey and Jones and Allen, it will be useful to examine the literatures of yellow fever that directly addressed the deeply connected issues of cultural, psychological, and bodily health. Contemporary analysts believed that the epidemic was symptomatic of commercial "diseases" currently plaguing Philadelphia. These writings thus didactically aimed to recuperate urban health by restoring equilibrium to mind and body, the individual and society, and economic and social relations.[19] Consider, for example, one of the short histories written in response to one of the later epidemics that struck Philadelphia in 1798:

> Citizens over-reaching their capitals, the general failure of land speculation, the depredations committed upon our commerce, together with the general stagnation of trade in almost every department, has of late been followed by an increased number of bankruptcies, that at least equal any period since the revolution. Such a combination of untoward circumstances could hardly fail of producing numberless distresses. But evils of a more serious nature followed: The malignant scourge of mankind, the Yellow Fever, again appeared in the city, marking its path with unprecedented horror and devastation. . . . Philadelphia was this year again doomed to experience a repetition of these baneful consequences, in a degree far beyond any former period, when mediocrity of circumstances enabled citizens, by a timely flight, to escape from a premature death.[20]

The "stagnation of trade" resulted from constraints on the American export-trade during this era of European wars, and the yellow fever epidemic became significantly worse as a result of this commercial decline. Intriguingly, however, the passage also expresses anxiety about commercial excess. (After all, "untoward" can mean either "unfavorable" or "unruly or reckless.") Philadelphia's citizens dangerously overextend their credit, speculate wildly, and exceed their means. The paradox here is that the city's economy is at once booming and declining, too fast and too slow, a condition that can be resolved only through a "mediocrity of circumstances."

This fantasy of economic balance begins to suggest how writing about disease operates on multiple levels. The literature of yellow fever generally expresses what David Brion Davis has called the problem for early Americans of the "perishability of Revolutionary time": "there was, inevitably, a widening chasm of time between the transcendent moment of rebirth—when the 'Word of Liberty' created the nation—and the recurring rediscoveries of America's unredeemed sin."[21] Seeing yellow fever as the just retribution for the national sin (of slavery), most cultural critics of the epidemic took the opportunity to advise contemporary Philadelphians of the need to regulate themselves in many different ways—socially, psychologically, commercially, and so forth. The dominant motif in this literature of balance arises from this need. This was expressed in terms of an ideal economy that avoided the extremes of languid depression and hyperactivity. For example, one poetic representation of the city's absence of commercial life during the epidemic captures this desire:

> The shops were shut, and business at a stand;
> The Plague, 'twas thought, would desolate the land!
> The People, pent as in a lonesome den,
> Sell not their goods unto their countrymen;
> The vessels too lay loaded by the shore,
> For want of hands the num'rous goods to store.[22]

But if the loss of commercial activity here means a loss of civilized exchange, other writings about yellow fever just as vigorously questioned the very nature of commercial "civilization." Philadelphia's ministers, for example, used the epidemic as the occasion to proclaim divine displeasure with modern forms of luxury and idle entertainment, such as the fare offered by the Chestnut Street Theater or Rickett's Circus. These, as one German divine put it, created a "kind of dissipation" that obliterated "in [the people's] hearts all taste for what is serious and useful."[23] In other words, the writings about the epidemic, like antislavery literature, engendered a narrative about the nature of culture, specifically, the pitfalls of cultural refinement.

This argument emerged much earlier in eighteenth-century Britain. Daniel Defoe's historical novel about the 1665 bubonic plague in London, *A Journal of the Plague Year* (1722), similarly represented the breakdown of civilized society. Its anonymous narrator, H. F., remarks that, "Tears and lamentations were seen almost in every house, especially in the first part of the visitation; for towards the latter end men's hearts were hardened, and death was so always before their eyes, that they did not so much concern themselves for the loss of their friends, expecting that themselves should be summoned the next hour."[24] Defoe's narrative of the loss of human sympathy, exemplified by the tavern revelers who mock the city's suffering citizens, ultimately gives way to the theme of civic charity. While the novel's narrator is no more certain than is Philadelphia's clergy about the people's prospects for moral regeneration, he does manage to praise both the city government and private citizens for their charitable acts: "Certain it is, the greater part of the poor, or families who formerly lived by their labour, or by retail trade, lived now on charity; and had there not been prodigious sums of money given by charitable, well-minded Christians for the support of such, the city poor could never have subsisted."[25]

Public comments in response to Philadelphia's bouts of epidemics similarly tried to reaffirm humanitarian values, but they notably failed to make their case. For example, the Philadelphia physician William Currie cited a passage from John Fenno's *United States Gazette,* in order to make a sentimental appeal for city funding for a new hospital:

> Let us recall the case of the unfortunate man home to our own bosoms—diseased, friendless, and disconsolate—situated in a strange country, where he knew not the countenance of a single human being, incapable of providing for himself, and unable from illness to leave the city, willing to take refuge in an infected hospital, and I am sure there is no man who is not absolutely callous to the voice of misery, and dead to every thing which bears the stamp of humanity, who will not approve of some plan being fallen on for the comfortable accommodation of such of his suffering fellow-men.[26]

Like Rush's letter to Richard Allen, Currie's recycled comment extends the universal scope of sympathy ("the unfortunate man," "suffering fellow-men") to the crucial point where distinctions between citizens and noncitizens begin to evaporate. Yet this expanding field of sympathetic attention founders on the uncertain faith in American citizens themselves. As a trope for the power of sympathy, the "stamp of humanity" suggests that it may be only a representational sign.

The cultural failure of sympathy—itself a kind of disease—took on national proportions. If, as David Waldstreicher claims, early national celebrations of Independence Day ritualized the ideology of sentimental citizenship, the social crisis of epidemic certainly deflated it.[27] For instance, the satire "A Dialogue Between a Citizen of Philadelphia and a Jersey Farmer," which appeared in Philip Freneau's *National Gazette,* lampooned the lack of sympathy that New Jersey (and the rest of the eastern United States) showed those Philadelphians who left the city in fear. Probably written by Freneau himself, the piece has the rube Farmer reject the suffering fugitive Citizen: "You are a moving mass of putridity, corruption, plague, poison, and putrefecation."[28] This rather morbid allegory of national alienation actually reverses the urban/rural moral geography of works like Crevecoeur's *Letters from an American Farmer* (1782) or Jefferson's *Notes on the State of Virginia* (1785). The Citizen's final admonition appeals to human values beyond those of national citizenship.

> *The common duties of humanity between man and man,* should have as much weight with a rational creature as *the great duty of self-preservation itself;* and be equally observed. Cowards shrink from danger: the brave, when necessary, meet it with fortitude: and, trust me, you will find, in at least ninety instances out of a hundred, that cowards perish through the very effects of their fears, while the firm escape and enjoy a comfortable length of existence.[29]

The denunciation places pressure on the category of citizenship itself. Sentimental virtue extends the field of national attention to the point where the distinction between citizens and non-citizens begins to blur. Political identification within the United States (recalling the national motto "E Pluribus Unum") spills into the more far-reaching forms of humanitarianism (or the "duties of humanity"). What are the ties that bind New Jersey farmer and fugitive Philadelphian? Who makes up the sympathetic nation?

Climate, Contagion, and National Health

The medical rhetoric of the "Dialogue" begins to suggest the importance of contemporary medical theories to cultural debates about the health of the early U.S. environment. Early American medicine derived largely from British theories, which were rooted in writings of Newton and Locke on sensation and perceptions. Broadly speaking, eighteenth-century medical thinking on both sides of the Atlantic generally maintained that physical, psychological, and moral forms of health were intricately and reciprocally related to one another. The natural environment affected mind and body alike: physical sensations could produce psychological effects, and psychological change could produce physical bodily symptoms. The extent to which such thinking became popularized in the late eighteenth century is

apparent, for example, in Benjamin Rush's "A Moral and Physical Thermometer," which appeared in numerous early American periodicals, including *The Columbian Magazine* and Isaiah Thomas's *Massachusetts Magazine*
(see Figure 5). With exacting, clinical precision, Rush registers the direct cor-
respondences theoretically existing among habits of consumption, state of
mind, and moral well-being. This psychological scheme, like contemporary
representations of the slave trade, associates disease with distilled spirits and
requires self-regulation of both mind and body.

The two reigning (and often haphazardly overlapping) eighteenth-century conceptions of bodily health emphasized balance. In the earlier part of
the century, the well-established theory of the body's humors shaped both
learned and popular views of physical and emotional health. The body's four
humors controlled internal health and appearance (including racial appearance) and were subject to changes in the environment.[30] As much as
humoral theory upheld the ideal of a balanced constitution, a more modern
medical thinking that was premised on the circulation of bodily fluids even
more rigorously theorized the proper balance of arterial flow. Propounded
most influentially by the Scottish physicians William Cullen and John
Brown, the theory of "solidism" claimed, as one medical historian has put
it, "that illness represents pathological imbalances in the irritability of the
body's tissues as manifested by the tone, the innate strength and elasticity, of
the solid fibrous components of blood vessels and nerves. . . . That is, the
body was healthy when blood and 'nerve fluids' could circulate freely."[31]
Modeled on the larger ideal of balance, the concept of "free" circulation envisioned the easy flow of bodily fluids that avoided dangerous extremes.

Circulation, moreover, connects the worlds of the body and the commercial economy. The foundations for such a connection derive in part from
Montesquieu's belief that the environment—including the commercial environment and the nature and exchange of commercial goods—affects the
health of both the individual and the nation. This extended easily to a commercial empire. As one analyst has observed, "Scientific advances, such as
[William] Harvey's discovery of the circulation of blood, seemed to reinforce, and even to suggest improvements upon these theories. An empire,
conceived of as a body, relied upon the circulation of goods but also of persons for its continued existence."[32] As we have seen, popular writing about
the yellow fever epidemic urged regulation of the commercial economy;
medical writing also called for a similar kind of regulation. Indeed, economic
and physical domains did not merely parallel but metaphorized one another,

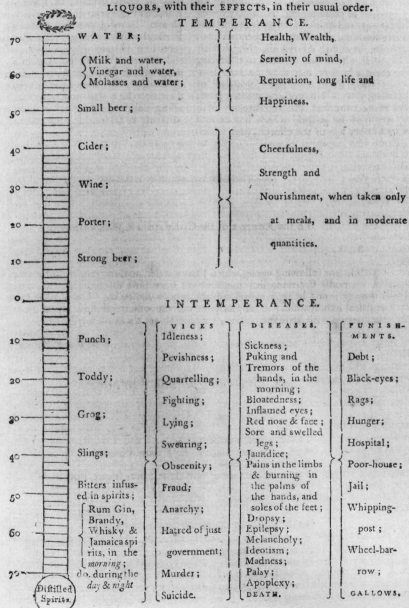

Figure 5. Benjamin Rush, "A Moral and Physical Thermometer."
From *The Columbian Magazine* (Philadelphia, 1789).

functioning as conceptual templates with which to theorize balance, circulation, and the proper state of health. As Roy Porter has summarized, "Medical materialism . . . conceived the pulsating body as a through-put economy whose efficient functioning depended upon generous input and unimpeded outflow. But how was this need for positive stimulus to be squared with age-old doctrines—both medical and moral—of temperance, moderation and the golden mean? Might not energizing the system precipitate pathological excess?"[33]

These questions underlie much of the writing about yellow fever during the 1790s. The "pathological excess" of both individual behavior and aggregate economy, moreover, was represented largely in terms of the nature of the "passions." Most commentators about the medical and social crisis regarded the passions as both cause and effect of the epidemic. Benjamin Rush, for example, cited the problem of "indirect debility" as one of the disease's principal causes: he believed that excessive fears or appetites stimulated the body's natural contagion into activity, thereby triggering the disease. One of the most influential books on the causes and treatments of common maladies, William Buchan's *Domestic Medicine,* similarly argued that the 1793 epidemic "suffered all the varieties produced by the age, constitution, and state of atmosphere, season of the year, together with a number of other causes; such as fear, grief, and despondency, which powerfully operated on the mind."[34] This goes far in explaining why during the crisis public health officials in Philadelphia urged citizens to maintain a balanced mind. Dr. Jean Deveze, a French émigré from Saint Domingue and the physician overseeing the makeshift hospital at Bush Hill, urged: "The particular means which regard individuals only, consist in some precautions. The most necessary is to fortify the mind, and resist as much as possible the fears naturally inspired by epidemics. This emotion of the soul disorders the mind, effaces reason . . . which renders the body more liable to disease."[35]

The bitter divisions that broke out within Philadelphia's College of Physicians reveal deep anxieties about the health of both national environment and international commerce. The medical controversy principally involved Benjamin Rush and William Currie, who were the leading advocates of "climatist" and "contagionist" positions respectively. The differences between Rush and Currie concerned the causes of and remedies for yellow fever. Was the disease the result of problems in the local environment, or was it imported to the United States and transmitted by personal contact with afflicted victims? Rush was the chief advocate of climatist theory, and ar-

gued that toxic "putrefecations" and "effluvia" were in effect poisoning local Philadelphians. The infected atmosphere, he believed, originally came
from the piles of rotten coffee that that the ship *Amelia*, from Saint
Domingue, had dumped on Ball's Wharf near Arch Street.[36]

Contagionist thinking had roots in eighteenth-century British medical
theory about the nature of plagues and epidemics. Responding to the plague
that beset the city of Marseilles in 1720, the famous English physician Richard Mead warned London's inhabitants about the danger of commercial relations with those southern and tropical climates where the disease supposedly originated. "It is very remarkable," Mead argued, "that the several
countries of Europe have always suffered more or less in this way, according
as they have a greater or lesser commerce with Africa, or with those parts of
the east that have traded there."[37] His *Short Discourse on the Pestilential Contagion* (1720) established the contagionist position, so that commerce in effect
became the means by which nations became infected with epidemics. "The
Plague is a real poison, which, being bred in the southern parts of the world,
is carried by commerce into other countries, particularly into Turkey, where
it maintains itself by a kind of circulation from persons to goods."[38] If British
savants like Mead envisioned the danger of trading with sub-Saharan Africa,
American ones like Currie looked more immediately to the West Indies.
Influenced by the writings of Dr. John Lining, who observed the epidemic
that struck Charleston, South Carolina, in the 1740s, Currie and others
speculated that yellow fever was imported to Philadelphia via either commercial goods from the West Indies, or, perhaps even more dangerously,
brought by the refugees of St. Domingue who were escaping the violent revolution there.[39]

"Contagionists," as one historian summarizes, "would prevent fever by
quarantining incoming vessels from sickly regions; climatists would purify
the city and society itself by sanitary measures."[40] In fact, both camps were
addressing the *same* cultural problem of how to maintain (or recover) the
health of the commercial city. After all, both sides urged the regulation of
commerce and consumption. In this context, the African slave trade significantly impeded the project of cultural and commercial purification. Benjamin Rush (who himself owned a slave) connects the yellow fever crisis
with the antislavery movement. In his antislavery writings from the 1770s
Rush represented the slave trade as a disease: "When we look back and esti-
mate the numbers which have been sacrificed by this Trade . . . we would
wish to forget the obligations we owe to Justice, Humanity, Religion, and to

the British name. What War, or *Pestilence* ever made such Havock with the human species?"[41]

Hence Rush's later assertion that the epidemic began with a pile of rotten *coffee* dumped on a wharf is all the more intriguing. Why, amidst all the city's heaping piles of raw sewage, vermin, floating animal carcasses, and other putrid material, did Rush fixate upon an imported consumer good from the slave-holding West Indies? As we have seen, antislavery culture was steeped in larger issues about the nature of consumer goods and the ethics of consumption. The questions it raised about consumption included such "luxury" items as coffee, tea, and sugar.[42] As the source of almost half of the world's coffee and sugar, Saint Domingue was often mentioned in antislavery writings, and the thousands of white refugees fleeing the revolution there, many of whom forced their African slaves to come along, certainly brought it to the attention of Philadelphians and others in the 1790s. In this context, the rotting coffee on the Philadelphia waterfront possessed resonant symbolic meanings. Like the "blood sugar" that British antislavery poets castigated, rotting coffee was associated with West Indian slavery, and in Rush's imagination became another kind of "poisonous" commodity infecting the commercial port of Philadelphia.

Despite the hostile differences of opinion within Philadelphia's medical community, Rush's view of contamination actually parallels Currie's own. As the leading contagionist, or importationist, Currie helped to initiate the College of Physicians' call for "the quarantine and purification of vessels"[43] during the 1790s, a move that ought to prevent further epidemics by purifying American commerce. Currie blamed the city's otherwise lucrative West Indian trade for the contamination of the American environment:

> A few days after the middle of July several vessels from Cape Francois arrived at the port of Philadelphia, crowded with passengers and goods of various descriptions; and about the same time, or a few days later, a French private called the *Sans-culotte*, from Nantes but last from the West Indies, which brought in the ship *Flora* of Glasgow, captured on her passage.
>
> The disease made its appearance the beginning of August, first in the lodging of Mr. Denny, in the neighbourhood of the wharves where two vessels which had landed sickly passengers and the *Sans-culotte* lay.[44]

This position significantly resembles the antislavery position of preserving "free" trade by regulating it. Lucrative as it might be—and proslavery writers like Richard Nisbet certainly emphasized its financial benefits—the trade between the United States and the West Indies, Currie believed, undermined "the true interest of the country." If the United States maintained it, "foreign commerce would shun our dangerous ports, and the vessels of our merchants would be subjected to the inconvenience and vexation of a tedious and expensive quarantine in foreign ports."[45]

What was the best means of securing the health of the United States? What were the potential effects of the modern commercial environment on the American body and mind? These questions were important because they addressed the larger problem of purifying the American environment in an era characterized by debates over the health of West Indian commerce in general and the slave trade in particular. Indeed, the enduring presence of the slave trade, which the U.S. Constitution protected for twenty years, hampered the imaginary purification of national health. Put another way, the yellow fever epidemic actualizes the figure of diseased commerce associated with the African slave trade, a figure that itself outstrips the bounds of metaphor. Consider, for example, the advertisement that appeared in Charleston, South Carolina, in 1769, for the sale of newly imported African slaves (see Figure 6). The advertisement directly connects the slave trade with infection and, in this way, glosses the yellow fever epidemics that during the eighteenth century struck British American seaports like Charleston and Philadelphia. The advertisement assures potential buyers of the health of slave trading. These slaves, these imported goods, are in no way infected with the case of smallpox that broke out the *Countess of Sussex*. By claiming the restoration of health, however, the advertisement opens up the likelihood that such outbreaks are common enough and recur often. Pushed to the point where bodily and cultural diseases converge, it suggests, for the antislavery imagination, that all slave traders are infected.

The Black Market

The yellow fever crisis thus sharpened the question of both the nature and prospect of national health. The deeper question embedded in this one concerned who "naturally" belonged in the nation itself—who, in other words, maintained national health, or, alternatively, injured it. This issue underlies Mathew Carey's *Short Account* as well as the African American response by Absalom Jones and Richard Allen, *Narrative of the Proceedings*. The public exchange about who behaved well or badly, and therefore who could make legitimate claims to citizenship, focused on the ability to demonstrate public feeling in context of the medical and social crisis. Carey's *Short Account* ex-

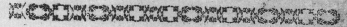

CHARLESTOWN, *April* 27, 1769.

TO BE SOLD,

On WEDNESDAY the Tenth Day of
MAY *next*,

A CHOICE CARGO OF

Two Hundred & Fifty

NEGROES:

ARRIVED in the Ship
COUNTESS of SUSSEX, THOMAS DAVIES,
Maſter, directly from GAMBIA, by

JOHN CHAPMAN, & Co.

⁂ *THIS is the Veſſel that had the Small-Pox
on Board at the Time of her Arrival the* 31ſt *of
March laſt : Every neceſſary Precaution hath ſince
been taken to cleanſe both Ship and Cargo thoroughly,
ſo that thoſe who may be inclined to purchaſe need not
be under the leaſt Apprehenſion of Danger from Infection.*

The NEGROES *are allowed to be the likelieſt Parcel
that have been imported this Seaſon.*

1769

Figure 6. Broadside advertising the sale of slaves, Charleston, 1769.

presses the contagionist position on the nature of disease; though troubled by the behavior of Anglo-American citizens during the crisis, it ultimately makes African Americans, however unintentionally, an external threat to the body politic. Like the period's medical literature, which alienated the slave-holding West Indies, Carey alienates Philadelphia's African Americans in order to restore the viability of Anglo-American citizenship.

The *Short Account* represents the yellow fever epidemic as a crisis whose significance lies on many levels: moral, cultural, political, commercial, and even metaphysical. That contemporaries read Carey in light of the problem of national health is apparent, for example, in a review of it that appeared in 1793 in Isaiah Thomas's *Massachusetts Magazine*. It begins with the *Short Account*'s crucial first chapter:

> The author of this sensible and well written pamphlet, begins the account which he has published, with some prefatory observations of a moral nature, and these, in a more especial manner, are highly worthy the attention of every friend to the happiness of America; for the luxury, dissipation and extravagance, which are treated of, as but too prevalent in Philadelphia, have also erected the Hydra head of ruin in other States: and the once virtuous New Englanders are at present no less devoted to the Goddess of Pleasure, than their Southern Sisters. Similar follies merit similar chastisement. The eventual consequences need not be predicted.[46]

Not only does the reviewer read Carey as a meditation on national health, but he also aligns slavery's cultural malaise with the "luxury, dissipation, and extravagance" besetting the northeast. The trope of the hydra, moreover, recalls the "many-headed Hydra" that Thomas Clarkson and others used to represent the African slave trade and all the cultural evils accompanying it.[47] New England and its "Southern Sisters" should be different—and yet they are not.

The *Short Account* frames this cultural crisis in terms of economic conditions, though Carey appears unable to decide upon the nature of the market forces that appear to be consuming the city of Philadelphia, forces that evidently have overstimulated social and individual bodies alike.[48] The *Short Account* immediately announces the cultural stakes of yellow fever by pointing out that other writers have portrayed "the manners of the people in an unfavourable light."[49] Trying to uphold the benevolence of the city's residents, Carey describes the crisis as a deviation from mores, one in which "all the 'mild charities of social life' were suppressed by regard for self—as to stamp eternal infamy on a nation for all the atrocities perpetuated in times of civil broils, when all the 'angry passions' are roused into dreadful and ferocious activity" (p. viii).

Throughout, Carey has difficulty separating social affections from noxious passions. The distinction is important because it underlies the one between healthy and diseased forms of commercial capitalism. The difficulty he has policing this thematic boundary partly derives from Carey's early financial struggles as an aspiring printer in Philadelphia.[50] The son of an Irish baker, Carey emigrated to America in 1784 and soon established himself as an aggressive editor and publisher of newspapers and magazines such as the *Pennsylvania Evening Herald,* the *Columbian Magazine,* and the *American Museum.* His reputation as an entrepreneurial innovator in the printing trade is justly deserved. He outmaneuvered competitors in Philadelphia's newspaper industry; he tried to nationalize the market for "local" magazines like the *American Museum;* he successfully employed networks of factors and agents (like Mason Locke Weems) to market his publications in cities as well as in more remote markets; he had an eye for best sellers like Rowson's *Charlotte Temple,* which he published (the first to do so in America) in 1794; he dropped out of the Philadelphia Company of Printers and Booksellers in 1796 to fulfill his individual ambitions; and he was the first to market the Bible in America as a commodity for popular consumption.[51]

But at the time of the epidemic, Carey was struggling financially; indeed, he was deep in debt. One might even see the publication of the *Short Account* (as his African American critics later did) as a commercial venture capitalizing upon the short-term market for the literature of disease. Carey was certainly conscious of this, and responded soon afterwards by casting the project in terms of the "duty that I owed the city . . . and indeed the United States generally, to give a candid and full statement of affairs as they really stood, without bias or partiality."[52] Later on, he claimed that he also intended to encourage creditors to indulge their debtors in the plague-stricken city. In light of Carey's marketing strategies for the work, however, these rationales ring hollow. His characteristic business acumen served him well in this early venture: for example, he published the first edition on 14 November 1793 without first securing subscription orders because of his confidence in the work's market appeal.[53] Its "speedy sale" (p. vii) led to a second edition that appeared on 23 November; by January of 1794, the *Short Account* went through two more editions, an impressive publishing venture that extended well beyond the local reading public. Yet Carey's success with the

Short Account did not end all of his financial struggles. His autobiography reveals (albeit retrospectively) the sense of relief he evidently felt by the enforced suspension of the city's financial activities. "I was for the first time for ten years, wholly free from the cares of business—had no money to borrow—no notes to pay—and my mind was fully occupied by the duties to which I devoted myself."[54]

This biographical background may explain Carey's frame for the crisis. "Before I enter on the consideration of this disorder, it may not be improper to offer a few introductory remarks on the situation of Philadelphia previous to its commencement, which will reflect light on some of the circumstances mentioned in the course of the narrative" (p. 9). The "situation" puts the epidemic in context, explains its causes, links bodily and cultural disease. The booming economy becomes the central figure for the city's pathological condition:

> New houses, in almost every street, built in a very neat, elegant stile, adorned, at the same time that they enlarged the city. Its population was extending fast. House rent had risen to a most extravagant height; it was in many cases double, and in some treble what it had been a year or two before; and, as is generally the case, when a city is thriving, it went far beyond the real increase of trade. The number of applicants for houses, exceeding the number of houses to be let, one bid over another; and affairs were in such a situation, that many people, though they had a tolerable run of business, could hardly do more than clear their rents, and were, literally, toiling for their landlords alone. Luxury, the usual and perhaps inevitable concomitant of prosperity, was gaining ground in a manner very alarming to those who considered how far the virtue, the liberty, and the happiness of a nation depend on their temperance and sober manners. Men had been for some time in the habit of regulating their expenses by prospects formed in sanguine hours, when every probability was caught at as a certainty, not by their actual profits, or income. The number of coaches, coachees, chairs, &c. lately set up by men in the middle rank of life, is hardly credible. (pp. 10–11)

While castigating commercial excess, Carey touches on various forms of regulation: moral, cultural, psychological, and commercial. Like the individual citizen whose derangement makes him susceptible to yellow fever, Carey's Philadelphia has lost its reason. Just as the human body needs regulation, so too does the economic body. To this end, the free capitalist market is sustained by unregulated passions associated now with imaginatively rampant speculation.

But the *Short Account* makes such claims ambivalently. Carey seems to be unable to imagine republican morality outside commercial capitalism. His writing is not so much a reactionary corrective to capitalist enterprise and free markets as it is an ongoing (Cullenian) deliberation upon the necessary level of stimulation that the American citizen and the American economy need. His complaint about escalating rental prices in the city is compromised by his belief that the middling classes lacked only the necessary capital ("actual profits, or income") to sustain their investments in luxury items. Hedging on the very premises of moral (that is, regulated) capitalism, Carey cannot decide whether or not luxury is *in itself* poisonous to republican health. To manage his ambivalence he resorts to the rather contrived persona of an elite commentator who is above these vices. The aspiring printer is supposedly suspicious of speculative projects—those like the *Short Account* itself.

The *Short Account* expresses a similar ambivalent anxiety about overstimulated and depressed economies. If Carey laments the excessive speculation that was occurring on the eve of the epidemic—"But how fleeting are all human views!"(p. 13)—he becomes equally concerned for the "stagnation of business" (p. 65) that occurs afterwards. Certainly, the economic depression becomes prominent: "Business then became extremely dull. Mechanics and artists were unemployed; and the streets wore the appearance of gloom and melancholy" (p. 21). Even his earlier publication about the epidemic strained to maintain optimism about the present state of commerce and society: "Business is not entirely at a stand. Many stores are still open; and even now not more than half our houses are deserted."[55] In time, however, false hope gave way to recognizing a crisis that, as in Freneau, took on national proportions:

For these prefatory observations, I hope I shall be pardoned. . . . At first view, it would appear that Philadelphia alone felt the scourge; but its effects have spread in almost every direction through a great portion of the union. Many parts of Jersey, Delaware, Maryland, Virginia, North and South Carolina, and Georgia, exclusive of the back settlements of Pennsylvania, drew their supplies, if not wholly, at least principally, from Philadelphia, which was of course the mart whither they sent their produce. Cut off from this quarter, their merchants have had to seek out other markets, which being unprepared for such an increased demand, their supplies have been imperfect; and owing to the briskness of the sales, the prices have been, naturally enough, very considerably enhanced. . . . Business, therefore, has languished in many parts of the union; and it is probable, that, considering the matter merely in a commercial point of light, the shock caused by the fever, has been felt to the southern extremity of the United States.[56]

The "commercial point of light" concluding the opening chapter signals the context for the social and cultural crisis that will ensue. Yet the analysis reveals paradoxical conditions. On the one hand, the epidemic brings on economic stagnation; on the other, economic inflation. The phrase "naturally enough" is more important than it initially might appear. It suggests Carey's need to master the natural laws of the economy, to know them fully, to make the "invisible hand" of the market completely visible. The problem, however, is that the economy, like the suffering victim of yellow fever, is diseased. Just as Currie's afflicted patient suffers intermittent fits of "restlessness" and "debility," the afflicted economy experiences uncontrollable spasms of excess and constriction. How long will it persist in this way? How does one regulate it? And, if this condition occurs naturally in the economy, what does this say about the "natural" laws of the market?

Carey turns away from this unsettling prospect toward the power of sympathy. In the *Short Account* sentiment functions as the chief means of regulating society and economy—to bring them balance. This suggests an important resemblance between contemporary writings about disease and those about the slave trade. Both imbue commercial capitalism with sentimental values in order to purify it, to restore its healthy constitution. Once again, there are parallels between individual and economic bodies. Like Benjamin Rush's proposed regimen of bleeding and purging to cure victims of yellow fever, Carey's ideal of sentimental citizenship purges a sickly society of its toxic agents in order to revitalize it. To accomplish this, the *Short Account* turns to those financial institutions that manage credit, and it strains to find a viable alternative to capitalist principles of self-interest. Carey praised the Bank of North America for refusing to squeeze its debtors mercilessly during a time of special need: "It ought to be mentioned, that on the payment of these sums, the directors generally declined accepting interest for the use of them."[57] The *Short Account* also features "Notes" at the bottom of many pages that prominently display didactic commentaries on civic behavior. In one of them Carey remarks: "It is with great pleasure, I embrace this opportunity of declaring, that the very liberal conduct of the bank of the United States, at this trying season, was the means of saving many a deserving and industrious man from ruin. No similar institution was ever conducted on a more favourable, and, at the same time, prudent plan" (p. 12). Likewise, he goes on to praise the bank's decision on 15 October 1793 to renew discounted notes for struggling merchants and, later, its second loan of $5,000—without interest—to fund the hospital at Bush Hill. The "extraordinary liberality" of altruistic bankers contrasts with the "hardened hearts" of unforgiving landlords, who "know no compassion, and who will have 'the pound of flesh—the penalty of the bond'" (p. 88).

The allusion to Shylock is consistent with Carey's overall suspicion of the cold logic of unregulated, laissez-faire capitalism. His emphasis on the value of feeling within the larger structures of capitalism lends further rhetorical complexity to the work as a whole. These competing registers of value are particularly significant as they affect the work's treatment of labor value. For example, the *Short Account,* like so many accounts of the epidemic, idealizes two members of the Committee, Peter Helm and the famous merchant Stephen Girard, for their heroic efforts in running the makeshift hospital at Bush Hill. "Uninfluenced by any reflexions of this kind, without any possible inducement but the purest motives of humanity, they came forward, and offered themselves as the forlorn hope of the committee" (p. 60). Emphasizing the important exchange of gratitude for benevolence, Carey states, "I trust that the gratitude of their fellow citizens will remain as long as the memory of their beneficent conduct, which I hope will not die with the present generation" (p. 60). Girard's status as a shipping magnate, land speculator, financier, and one of Philadelphia's wealthiest citizens only enhances his civic benevolence.[58] Exceeding wealth contributes to his sentimental value instead of undercutting it, as though the selflessness of the rich and famous were particularly special because the time they provide is so potentially valuable. Carey finally transfers this value from a capitalist register to a sentimental one, claiming that, "Of these men it may be fairly said, that their services are *above all price.*"[59]

The *Short Account*'s attempt to separate the value of labor from market forces depends upon the uninterrupted supply of volunteer labor. But during the yellow fever crisis a shortage of volunteers crucially led to the recruitment of African Americans. As most readers recognize, the *Short Account* dramatizes the rapid disintegration of social affections caused by "the extraordinary public panic, and the great law of self-preservation, the dominion of which extends over the whole animated world" (p. 31). The panic notably infects familial relations as well—indeed the family both symbolizes and precipitates the civic crisis in Philadelphia and the nation. Carey recounts how mothers, fathers, and children become estranged from one another, fleeing neighborhoods or even the city proper, abandoning stricken family members to fend for themselves. This is the horror of isolation, the essence of the social tragedy of yellow fever. Carey finds no place in the social fold for the city's African Americans: "Many men of affluent fortunes, who have given employment and sustenance to hundreds every day in the year, have been abandoned to the care of a Negro, after their wives, children, friends, clerks, and servants, had fled away, and left them to their fate" (p. 31). The city's blacks are there but not really there, excluded from the republican dynamic of benevolence and gratitude.

Such a denial, however, repeatedly must return to the problematic issue of supply. Not unlike Defoe's work, the *Short Account* admits the rather barbaric treatment of the sick and the dead. Whereas Defoe emphasizes the supposedly unnatural cruelty of women toward those who are suffering, Carey focuses on the behavior of the lower classes, composed partly of African Americans. Constantly wavering between gothic anecdotes about the abuse of those who were ill and intermittent assurances that "most of them happened in the first stage of the public panic" (p. 34), Carey shows a city in which humanitarian behavior is all but gone. One anecdote, for example, recounts the incident of an ill "servant girl" who "could find no person to receive her" (p. 33). "One of the guardians of the poor provided a cart, and took her to the alms house, into which she was refused admittance. She was brought back, and the guardian offered five dollars to procure her a single night's lodging, but in vain" (p. 33). When Bush Hill's heroic administrators initially inspect the hospital, they see "a great human slaughter house": "A profligate, abandoned set of nurses and attendants (hardly any of good character could at that time be procured) rioted on the provisions and comforts, prepared for the sick, who (unless at the hours when the doctors attended) were left almost entirely destitute of every assistance" (p. 61).

But this emphasis upon social standing only mystifies the reality of the capitalist labor market. "If one believes," as one commentator about liberalism has put it, "that in a free market competitive trade among individuals serves to prevent selfish passions from becoming destructive, it follows that man's common social destination will take care of itself."[60] The *Short Account* shows how this mechanism fails. Indeed, in Philadelphia in 1793, neither sympathy nor self-interest supplies the city with an adequate number of laborers to handle the crisis. As Carey acknowledges, "High wages were offered for nurses for these poor people—but none could be procured" (p. 24).

Many critics blame the *Short Account*'s hostility to African Americans on racism alone. But several facts about Carey, particularly as an editor and publisher, complicate such an argument. Without overstating the case, Carey was in fact an opponent of slavery and the slave trade. In comparison with contemporary American periodicals, his *American Museum* (1787–1792) included a tremendous amount of antislavery materials, including Philip Freneau's "The Island-Field Negro," the complete version of James McHenry's letter about Benjamin Banneker, Belinda's famous petition for her freedom sent to the Massachusetts General Court in 1783, and a serialized translation of Joseph Laval's "The Negro Equaled by Few Europeans."[61] Even after his public dispute with Jones and Allen, he joined the Pennsylvania Abolition Society in 1797. This does not completely absolve the *Short Account* of racial hostility, but it creates enough of an ambiguous context for Carey himself to stop asking whether he is a racist and start asking how and why he represents African Americans the way he does.[62]

The *Short Account* alienates African Americans by "blackening" the capitalist labor market. It obfuscates the failure of Anglo-American benevolence in 1793 by attributing the unfeeling volatility of market forces to African Americans alone:

> At an early stage of the disorder, the elders of the African church met, and offered their services to the mayor, to procure nurses for the sick, and to assist in burying the dead. Their offers were accepted; and Absalom Jones and Richard Allen undertook the former department, that of furnishing nurses, and William Gray, the latter—the interment of the dead. The great demand for nurses afforded an opportunity for imposition, which was eagerly seized by some of the vilest of the blacks. They extorted two, three, four, and even five dollars a night for such attendance, as would have been well paid by a single dollar. Some of them were even detected in plundering the houses of the sick. But it is wrong to cast a censure on the whole for this sort of conduct, as many people have done. The services of Jones, Allen, and Gray, and others of their colour, have been very great, and demand public gratitude. (pp. 76–77)

Carey's rhetoric serves to cover up the failure of Anglo-American benevolence. In response to Rush's desperate plea for help, unmentioned here, it is the city's African-American leadership that provides the impetus for the plan. The passive voice of the first clause in the second sentence further removes that desperation from visibility. In place of Anglo-American demand for labor Carey places its African-American supply. But his credibility stumbles. That is, the reasonable price of "a single dollar" already has become inflated, and it, too, fails to produce a sufficient supply of Anglo-American labor. Five dollars per night fails as well.

Carey then faces the possibility that that real benevolence of African Americans exceeds those of white citizens. The revisions he made to the third edition (published on 30 November 1793), and before Jones and Allen actually responded to him in print, significantly change the context for the passage cited above. He moves to undermine the evidence for the humanitarian capacities of those who are not citizens, and thus revisits the issue that informs Benjamin Rush's letter to the city's black leaders. In the third and fourth editions of the *Short Account*, Carey frames the above passage with an important discussion of the city's widespread beliefs in black immunity to yellow fever:

> When the yellow fever prevailed in South Carolina, the Negroes, according to that accurate observer, Dr. [John] Lining, were wholly free from it. "There is something very singular in the constitution of the Negroes," says he, "which renders them not liable to this fever; for though many of them were as much exposed as the nurses to this infection; yet I never knew one instance of this fever among them, though they are equally subject with the white people to the bilious fever." The same idea prevailed for a considerable time in Philadelphia; but it was erroneous. They did not escape the disorder; however, the number of them that were seized with it, was not great; and, as I am informed by an eminent doctor, "it yielded to the power of medicine in them more easily than in the whites." The error that prevailed on this subject had a very salutary effect; for, at an early period of the disorder, hardly any white nurses could be procured; and had the negroes been equally terrified, the sufferings of the sick, great as they actually were, would have been exceedingly aggravated. At this period alluded to, the elders of the African church met, and offered their assistance to the mayor, to procure nurses for the sick, and aid in burying the dead. (4th ed., pp. 62–63)

Why, in this edition, did Carey expand this section and reposition this passage, moving it to its new place where it precedes the *Short Account*'s discussion of African-American labor? The "very salutary effect" of popular misconceptions about the yellow fever benefits those Anglo-American citizens suffering from the disease. The passage also emphasizes that blacks, like whites, are not immune to the irrational fears accompanying the epidemic. Should medical theory have maintained otherwise, Carey suggests, neither black leaders nor their followers would have stepped forward benevolently to aid the city. This spoils the image of their civic reputation. It also lets the city's political leaders (through their ignorance) off the hook. Finally, within the work's sentimental economy, the profits of the "sufferings of the sick" more than compensate for the costs of black mortality.

Pilferers and Privateers

A Narrative of the Proceedings of the Black People (1794) includes a text that clarifies the role African Americans played during the yellow fever epidemic, exonerates them of Carey's charges, and also addresses the overall plight of the enslaved. About sixteen pages in length, it is followed by a series of appendices. They include a reprinted letter by Jones and Allen to Mayor Clarkson accounting for the beds they buried with the dead, which acquits the caretakers of theft; Clarkson's reply, which serves as a "certificate of approbation" of the city's blacks; "An Address to Those who Keep Slaves, and Approve of the Practice," which condemns slavery in largely religious terms; "To the People of Colour," a spiritual meditation offering "affectionate sympathy" to those blacks who were still legally enslaved, as well as cautionary advice about the virtues of forgiveness and charity to those who were newly free; and, finally, "A Short Address to the Friends of Him who Hath no Helper," which announces their "inexpressible gratitude" to those white Americans (like Rush) who participated in the politics of antislavery.[63] The pamphlet concludes with a pious lyric poem of five stanzas, probably composed by Allen, calling for both individual and national regeneration to avoid divine judgment.

By emphasizing spiritual values in a metaphysical context, the appended material shrewdly covers the yellow fever narrative's more politically volatile engagement with the subjects of African American citizenship and of labor value during a time of social crisis. Notwithstanding their personal record of striving for civil and political rights for the city's disfranchised African Americans, Richard Allen and Absalom Jones realized the advantages of keeping on good terms with their Anglo-American patrons and friends. Hence the *Narrative* operates on multiple levels, asserting full equality yet deflecting that claim, politicizing their present situation and deferring justice to divine afterlife. Generally, however, the *Narrative* pushes, no less skillfully than the life writings of John Marrant and Venture Smith, at the legitimate boundaries of black liberty in early America. Understandably enraged at Carey, whom others praised as "that indefatigable man and meritorious author,"[64] Jones and Allen nevertheless sublimated their anger in order to maintain the moral high ground upon which black citizenship ideally was located.

The *Narrative*'s opening establishes that the behavior of black laborers during the epidemic is the crux of its argument with Carey. "In consequence of a partial representation of the conduct of the people who were employed to nurse the sick, in the late calamitous state of the city of Philadelphia, we are solicited, by a number of those who feel themselves injured thereby, and by the advice of several respectable citizens, to step forward and declare facts as they really were" (p. 3). Even if the *Narrative* seeks legitimacy by resorting to Anglo-American authority, the work challenges the *Short Account* by inserting itself in American republic of letters. Like the slave narrative, this genre claims a place for African American writing through the value of experience. As Jones and Allen put it, "we had it more fully and generally in our power, to know and observe the conduct and behaviour of those that were so employed" (p. 3). By explaining themselves in this way, they suggest as well that the value of both the *Narrative* and African American labor derive from the same source:

> Early in September, a solicitation appeared in the public papers, to the people of colour to come forward and assist the distressed, perishing, and neglected sick; with a kind of assurance, that people of our colour were not liable to take the infection. Upon which we and a few others met and consulted how to act on so truly alarming and melancholy an occasion. After some conversation, we found a freedom to go forth, confiding in him who can preserve in the midst of burning fiery furnace, sensible that it was our duty to do all the good we could to our suffering fellow mortals. . . .
>
> Soon after, the mortality increasing, the difficulty of getting a corpse taken away, was such, that few were willing to do it, when offered great rewards. The black people were looked to. We then offered our services in the public papers, by advertising that we would remove the dead and procure nurses. Our services were the production of real sensibility;—we sought not fee nor reward, until the increase of the disorder rendered our labor so arduous that we were not adequate to the service we had assumed. (pp. 3–4)

Consider the sequence. First, the civilized exchange of public letters takes place; then African-American leaders deliberate rationally, even prudently, on the immediate crisis and their awkward position in relation to it; finally, the overflow of Christian "real sensibility" takes over, dictating their subsequent decision and course of action. This has further ramifications for how to read their *Narrative* in context of the republican world of print, for, just as the above advertisement responds to "public papers," the *Narrative* responds to the *Short Account*. If the process cannot help but render new social prominence to Jones and Allen, the awkwardly passive construction—that Philadelphia blacks "were looked to"—puts them in the safe position of merely responding to the city's (desperate) request. Yet mention of the request itself calls attention to the necessity of black laborers in the absence of white ones, and thus already tweaks Carey's nose.

In the immediate aftermath of the yellow fever epidemic, others agreed on the "real sensibility" that Jones and Allen had demonstrated.[65] In December of 1793, for example, *The Massachusetts Magazine* published the "Eulogium in Honour of Absalom Jones and Richard Allen, two of the Elders of the African Church, who furnished Nurses to the Sick, during the late pestilential Fever in Philadelphia."

> Brethren of Man and friends to human kind,
>   Made of that blood which flow'd in Adam's veins!
>   A muse, who ever spurn'd at adulation strains;
> Who rates not colour, but th'immortal mind,
> With transport guides the death redeeming plume;
> Nor leaves your names a victim to the tomb.
>
> 'Twas yours amid that life destructive hour,
> When terror's monarch rode in pomp of pow'r,
> And swept a nation to the silent grave;
> His two edged sword with fortitude to brave;
> Nor did ye heed the pallid courser's rage,
> Who trampled youth in dust, and trod on age.
>
> Brethren of Man, and friends of fairer clay!
> Your godlike zeal in Death's triumphant day
>   Benignant Angels saw—they lent a smile,
> 'Twas temper'd with the dew of sympathy divine;
>   And whilst they kenned your more than mortal toil,
>   To both, they cried, "the praise of doing well be thine."[66]

Granted, the hyperbolic language tends to romanticize the role of the city's African Americans during the crisis. Although the poem is unsigned, it seems likely that it was the work of an Anglo-American writer (or writers), since it significantly elides the entire issue of African American citizenship. It defuses the political potential of "real sensibility"—the fact that citizenship lies fundamentally in the affective feeling for the body politic—by recasting sentimental virtue into a metaphysical context.

This helps to further situate the *Narrative*'s historical emergence. For Jones and Allen were responding to both gratuitous praise and Carey's aspersions. These two polar extremes of Anglo-American writing about "blackness" set out rhetorical and ideological boundaries for Jones and Allen. Thus their advertisement requesting the aid of black Philadelphians suggests that feeling is indeed political—that, in other words, "real sensibility" qualifies them for political inclusion:

> As it is a time of great distress in this city, many people of the Black colour, under a grateful remembrance of the favours received from the white inhabitants, have agreed to assist them as far as their power for nursing of the sick, and burial of the dead; application made for either of the above purposes to Absalom Jones, living in South Third Street, a little below Stamper's alley, No. 165, or to Richard Allen, in Spruce Street between Fourth and Fifth Streets, No. 150, who have a knowledge of the nurses, and keep horses and carriages for taking the dead to the burial ground.
>
> Absalom Jones
> Richard Allen[67]

In a matter-of-fact tone, the "people of the Black colour" show gratitude in exchange for Anglo-American benevolence, a fact that in effect inserts the African American presence in the sentimental civic culture of the post-Revolutionary United States.

The advertisement, however, challenges the social hierarchy upon which that exchange is founded. Both Carey and Jones and Allen had to engage the social tensions that were becoming more visible during the yellow fever crisis. The historian Ira Berlin has argued that during the post-Revolutionary era, African American urban societies identified differences between "respectables" and "newcomers": "The most successful black leaders, such as Richard Allen or Prince Hall, managed to unite these diverse elements of African-American society."[68] Whereas Carey condemned the selfishness of poor urban whites, Jones and Allen defended the moral integrity of poor ur-

ban blacks. The *Narrative* defends its constituents by contrasting their motives with the self-interest of Anglo-Americans. "We can with certainty, assure the public that we have seen more humanity, more real sensibility from
the poor blacks than from the poor whites" (p. 9). This central argument
counters the one Carey made, which resorted to bogus medical theories
about the immunity of blacks to yellow fever. One anecdote puts it this way:

> An elderly lady, Mrs. Malony, was given into the care of a white woman,
> she died, we were called to remove the corpse, when we came, the woman
> was laying so drunk that she did not know what we were doing, but we
> knew that she had one of Mrs. Malony's rings on her finger, and another in
> her pocket. . . .
>
> It is unpleasant to point out the bad and unfeeling conduct of any colour,
> yet the defence we have undertaken obliges us to remark, that although
> "hardly any of good character at that time could be procured," yet only two
> black women were at that time in the [Bush Hill] hospital, and they were
> retained and the others discharged, when it was reduced to order and good
> government. (p. 8)

By interrogating the origins of "character," Jones and Allen play on the ambiguities of "the bad and unfeeling conduct of any color." For while this
phrase implies a sort of racial equivalence wherein all groups of "color" contain their meaner sorts, it also suggests the very real shortcomings of Anglo-
American citizenship during the epidemic.

The *Narrative* further challenges Carey's handling of racial and social categories, specifically the opposition he draws between virtuous blacks such as
Jones and Allen and the unregenerate black masses. "By naming us," Jones
and Allen note, "[Carey] leaves these others, in the hazardous state of being
classed with those who are called the 'vilest'" (p. 11). One of the rhetorical
means by which they undercut his lumping people into a mass is to treat
black laborers individually, to record their identities. Hence their anecdotal
list of specific acts of black heroism. The "poor colored man" Sampson,
Sarah Bass, Mary Scott, Caesar Cranchal—they not only legitimate the *Narrative* through historical detail but also help to construct a sentimental aesthetic made apparent by the exchange of sympathy between private individuals across racial boundaries. This occurs even over the bodies of the dead:

> A woman of our colour nursed Richard Mason and son, when they died,
> Richard's widow, considering the risk the poor woman had run, and from

observing the fears that sometimes rested on her mind, expected she would have demanded something considerable, but upon asking what she demanded, her reply was half a dollar per day. Mrs. Mason, intimated it was not sufficient for her attendance, she replied it was enough for what she had done, and would take no more. Mrs. Mason's feelings were such, that she settled an annuity of six pounds a year, on her, for life. Her name is Mary Scott. (p. 10)

As in Carey's *Short Account,* the significance of these negotiations is premised on the ideal difference between the just price regulated by humane feeling and the inflated wage arising from the laws of supply and demand. But in this case an African American women is the moral steward of the sentimental economy. Since Mrs. Mason is the final arbiter of wages, the labor economy of services and wages devolves upon demand instead of supply.

The *Narrative* is much more of a "parallel text" to the *Short Account* than critics have begun to imagine.[69] Like the *Short Account,* it has difficulty rigorously theorizing value in terms of humanitarian feeling. That is, it cannot prevent itself from becoming rhetorically and thematically entangled in the ideologies of profit, interest, and the natural mechanisms of the capitalist market. Both the *Narrative* and the *Short Account,* moreover, reconstruct sentimental benevolence in terms of the capitalist labor market. For instance, in the story of Mary Scott, the virtue of African American feeling actually produces financial gain; she secures her own interests, in other words, by publicly renouncing them. A more provocative example of the inextricable relations between sentimental and market economies occurs in the elaborate chart Jones and Allen include that accounts for African American expenditures. Whereas Carey sentimentalizes the economic circulation of credit in plague-ridden Philadelphia, Jones and Allen sentimentalize the debts they accrue:

We do assure the public, that *all* the money we have received for burying, and for coffins which we ourselves purchased and procured, has not defrayed the expense of wages which we had to pay to those whom we employed to assist us. The following statement is accurately made:

CASH RECEIVED

The whole amount of Cash we received for burying
The dead, and for burying beds, is,   L. 233 10 4

CASH PAID

For coffins, for which we have received nothing	L. 33 0 0
For the hire of five men, 3 of them 70 days Each, and the other two, 63 days each, at 22~6 per day	L. 378 0 0
	411 0 0
Debts due us, for which we expect but little	L. 110 0 0
From this statement, for the truth of which we solemnly vouch, it is evident, and we sensibly feel the operation of the fact, that we are out of pocket,	L. 177 9 8

Besides the costs of hearses, the maintenance of our families for 70 days, (being the period of our labours) and the support of the five hired men, during the respective times of their being employed; which expences, together with sundry gifts we occasionally made to poor families, might reasonably and properly be introduced, to shew our actual situation with regard to profit—but it is enough to exhibit to the public, from the above specified items, of *Cash paid, and Cash received,* without taking into view the other expences, that, by the employment we were engaged in, we lost L. 177 9 8. But, if the other expences, which we have actually paid, are added to that sum, how much then may we not say we have suffered! We leave the public to judge. (pp. 5–6)

The reason for the inclusion of such a meticulous account is obvious enough. By putting the "books" on display, the writers let the numbers speak for themselves. However, this public account is even more interesting as a complex cultural register, one that reveals more than it intends to. The account itself crucially frames the benevolence of blacks as a matter of financial losses. Repeatedly editorializing upon these losses—"for which we received nothing," "for which we expect but little"—Jones and Allen prove their benevolence only by quantifying it. Their resentment for expenditures for which they will not be compensated is barely repressible. As the argument concludes, they note that, "From this statement, for the truth of which we solemnly vouch, it is evident, and we sensibly feel the operation of the fact, that we are out of pocket" (p. 6). What is the relation between sentimental claims to citizenship and being "out of pocket?" Like Equiano's losses at the hands of savage West Indian traders, the financial losses accrued by Jones and Allen secure their status as both the subject and object of benevolence.

The ideological contiguity between sentiment and self-interest characterizes as well their exoneration of African Americans. According to Phillip Lapsansky, "Carey's charges of extortion and theft were most damaging, and Jones and Allen noted it was whites who drove up the prices, outbidding each other for the services of black nurses—the same simple forces of supply and demand that Carey noted had driven Philadelphia rents steadily upward, though he never described landlords as 'the vilest.'"[70] But this misses the key problem that, during a time of social crisis, the cultural legitimacy of the capitalist market gave Jones and Allen only a toehold on the moral high ground. They faced the crucial narrative challenge of acknowledging but not embracing the market's control of wages, and of, illogically, investing white Philadelphians with control of that market. To this end they deflect Carey's charges of exploitation by again emphasizing the demand side of the labor market. Recall, for instance, that they argue: "At first we made no charge, but left it to those we served in removing their dead, to give what they thought fit—we set no price until the reward was fixed by those we had served. After paying the people we had to assist us, our compensation was much less than many will believe" (p. 5). Later on, they revisit this argument by recounting the city's curious attempt to get them to intervene in market forces themselves:

[Mayor Clarkson] . . . sent for us, and requested we would use our influence, to lessen the wages of the nurses, but on informing him the cause, i.e., that of the people over-bidding one another, it was concluded unnecessary to attempt any thing on that head; therefore it was left to the people concerned. That there were some few black people guilty of plundering the distressed, we acknowledge; but in that they only are pointed out, and made mention of, we esteem partial and injurious; we know as many whites who were guilty of it; but this is looked over, while the blacks are held up to censure—Is it a greater crime for a black to pilfer, than for a white to privateer?

We wish not to offend; but when an unprovoked attempt is made to make us blacker than we are, it becomes less necessary to be over cautious on that account; therefore we shall take the liberty to tell of the conduct of some of the whites. (pp. 7–8)

The passage alleviates the burden of controlling the market forces that inflate wages in time of desperate need. It rather implausibly places African

Americans outside the mechanisms of supply and demand. The language, however, slips for a moment, and belies the passage's improbabilities. The subject "the people," for example, suggests the more realistic scenario that prices and wages arise from the complex and ongoing negotiations between both parties contracting business. Debunking Carey's association of blackness with the uncontrollable laws of the market, Jones and Allen simultaneously offer the brilliant insight to the cultural functions of language, which can alternatively attenuate or exacerbate the assignment of guilt. They point out the equivalence between "pilfering" and "privateering," and observe how in this case language serves to attenuate Anglo-American guilt while excluding African Americans from the arena of citizenship.

The equivalence between pilferers and privateers only further blurs the other boundaries separating these two groups. This is the *Narrative*'s major flaw. While demonstrating the unmatched benevolence of African Americans, it also tries to establish the equivalence between Anglo- and African Americans, an equivalence that is problematically predicated on economic self-interest. The *Narrative*, in other words, makes the predictable argument about human similarities, but chiefly by emphasizing capitalist desire. Some parts of the *Narrative* catalogue instances of black benevolence to obtain political leverage. In a sense, those sections sabotage their purpose by instead revealing how and Anglo- and African Americans are equally imperfect— overstimulated, so to speak, with passionate desires.

Sometimes the dual registers appear almost simultaneously: "When the people of color had the sickness and died, we were imposed upon, and told it was not with the prevailing sickness, until it became too notorious to be denied, then we were told some few died but not many. Thus were our services *extorted at the peril of our lives.* Yet you accuse us of extorting *a little money from you*" (p. 13). Premised on the politics of the color line (us/you), the complaint gains ethical weight from the imperilment of black labor. Yet the *Narrative* equally wants to show that such base motivations may be one way of thinking about the common humanity of black and white groups:

> It was natural for people in low circumstances to accept a voluntary, bounteous reward; especially under the loathsomeness of many of the sick, when nature shuddered at the thought of infection, and the task assigned was aggravated by lunacy, and being left much alone with them. Had Mr. Carey been solicited to such an undertaking, for hire, *Query,* "what would he have demanded?" (p. 7)

The discomfort Jones and Allen feel toward inflated wages results in their recourse to "reward," which cannot fail to recall Carey's fallacious use of the just price. Its "voluntary" quality affirms human agency in the market-driven economy; its "bounteous" quality belies the inevitable inflation that Philadelphia has been experiencing. To explain this process and salvage the public image of African Americans, the authors resort to the Smithian idea of prudence as an enlightened, not diseased, form of self-interest. But this solution nearly collapses when they cannot refrain from mocking Carey's self-righteousness. For the obvious difference they draw between Carey (who leaves town) and black laborers (who stay) leads immediately to their recognition of the fundamental desires that constitute our being. Whites and blacks are the same. What would Carey have charged the sick, the dying? Wouldn't he have acted prudently? Wouldn't anyone?

Even though Carey claimed initially that the *Narrative of the Proceedings of the Black People* was "undeserving of notice,"[71] he did respond to it by making an important revision to the fourth edition of the *Short Account*. Irked by the *Narrative*, he nevertheless felt compelled to qualify his earlier claims. So he added a brief footnote to the infamous passage about the city's blacks: "The extortion here mentioned, was very far from being confined to the negroes: many of the white nurses behaved with equal rapacity."[72] This terse admission does not compensate for the more damaging excision Carey performed in the fourth edition. The third edition of the *Short Account*, published before the *Narrative* appeared, concludes the newly organized chapter about the black labor crisis as follows: "On examining the books of the hospital at Bush Hill, it appears that there were above fifteen blacks received there, of whom three fourths died. There may have been more, as the examination was made very cursorily."[73] But the fourth edition drops this final sentence altogether. It gets back at Jones and Allen by eliding the reality of widespread black mortality, which would have embellished the image of African-American sacrifice. Instead, silence.

The hostility between Mathew Carey and Philadelphia's African American community continued well into the spring. The exchange between the two is less interesting for its traded barbs than for its exposition of the cultural meanings of print in post-Revolutionary America. Months after the yellow fever epidemic abated, an African American writer (or writers) under the pseudonym "Argus" repeated the accusation that Carey published the *Short Account* in order to capitalize on the social and medical crisis. His infuriated

response initially staked the *Short Account* on the "duty that I owed the city
. . . and indeed the United States generally, to give a candid and full statement of affairs as they really stood, without bias or impartiality."[74] Such self-
exoneration, however, which renounces even "the smallest view to profit,"
ultimately fails to depersonalize authorship in the name of objectivity. It immediately slides into the explicit acknowledgment of both the marketability
of print and the entrepreneurial nature of publishing. Accused of fleeing the
city and not performing his civic duty on the Committee, Carey resisted
Argus's claim that he should rightfully share the profits with the Committee
members: "As to the idea of partnership in the printing, it never entered my
mind. And sure I am, had a loss occurred, as does most commonly by the
publication of pamphlets, that I should have had to bear it unassisted."[75] His
response might be read as a historical touchstone for critical controversies
today, involving such figures as Michael Warner and Grantland Rice, over
the very nature of print itself.[76] Was print culturally figured as the depersonalized expression of the *res publica?* Or was it just another liberal commodity
circulating amidst a world of goods? Like the exchange between himself and
Jones and Allen, Carey's ambiguous response belies the difficulty early na-
tionals had articulating the virtue of benevolence in a world driven increasingly by market relations.

Like the yellow fever victims, the economy of Philadelphia demonstrated
"lunacy" and imbalance. Disease operated on multiple registers—bodily,
psychological, social, and economic—and affected Anglo- and African
Americans alike. It is the literature of yellow fever, then, that raises problematic racial oppositions during this particular historical moment. Two
leading members of Philadelphia's African American community offered an
effective rebuttal against unjust charges; their claim to benevolent citizenship highlights not only the power of their political voice but the commonal-
ity of values in making such a claim. Anglo-Americans like Mathew Carey
and African Americans like Absalom Jones and Richard Allen connect in
unexpected ways—indeed, in ways they did not fully comprehend. The entire episode and the public writings that arose from it demand creative reading of the racial literature of the early republic. They demand a more complex cultural geography than the one polarizing the center and margins of
power.

Epilogue

How did early antislavery literature influence the abolitionist imagination? That is an important question, though much too extensive to take up here; someone else may wish to address it in a future study. Even a cursory reading, however, of American antislavery writing of the antebellum era reveals its self-consciousness about the political origins of modern antislavery movements. Eighteenth-century writings and activism provided abolitionists with abundant statistical data and effective rhetorical strategies. It also gave them a pantheon of heroic "founders" to encourage their own efforts. American abolitionists hailed, for example, the British antislavery activist Thomas Clarkson as something of a saint. They read and cited Clarkson's *An Essay on the Slavery and Commerce of the Human Species* (1786), and *The History of the Rise, Progress, and Accomplishment of the Abolition of the African Slave Trade by the British Parliament* (1808), as foundational texts. The same was true for Fox, Pitt, Sharp, and Wilberforce. American abolitionists revered their British origins.

The politics of historical authority worked ambiguously, however. On the one hand, some abolitionists, Lydia Maria Child, for instance, cited British and European antislavery writers in order to substantiate her radical claims about race and slavery. Child's *An Appeal in Favor of that Class of Americans Called Africans* (1833) directly quoted figures like Clarkson and the Abbé Gregoire as moral and political authorities. For Child, as well as many other abolitionists, reference to British and European antislavery authorities was consistent with the abolitionist critique of the hypocrisy of American political ideals, specifically the dissonance between the political language of liberty and the historical reality of American slavery. (They had not read Edmund Morgan!) This transnational perspective, moreover, paralleled the motif of the journey to Great Britain, where, as writers of slave narratives such as Frederick Douglass, Harriet Jacobs, and William Wells Brown discovered, African Americans found greater freedom than they had in the United States.

On the other hand, abolitionist writings often cited antislavery sources from the American Revolutionary era. They revered the abolition of the slave trade in 1774 by the Continental Congress, and used it to contrast the moral weakness of the U.S. Congress, especially during the years of the gag rule against slavery legislation. Abolitionists also quoted at length from Jefferson's *Declaration of Independence* (1776) and *Notes on the State of Virginia* (1785), as a way of gaining valuable catch phrases and pithy epithets while providing patriotic cover for themselves. These sources of moral and historical authority, however, were themselves double-edged. They threw into bold relief the moral gap between Revolutionary ideals and early national realities. Whereas Abraham Lincoln later used the Jeffersonian moment of the *Declaration* in the "Gettysburg Address" (1863) to elide the sticky problem of the slave-holding Constitution, abolitionists like William Lloyd Garrison and Wendell Phillips had put Jeffersonian principles (as opposed to practice) in the service of fully exposing the U.S. Constitution as a "covenant with death."

The connection between eighteenth-century and antebellum antislavery also provides important glimpses into British-American print culture and the transatlantic history of the book. In the 1830s and 1840s, American antislavery writers culled from such famous British antislavery poems as "The Dying Negro" and "The Negro's Complaint." In this fashion, they situated themselves in both literary and political histories. Writers like Thomas Day and especially William Cowper afforded both political and literary status. Recall, for instance, that perhaps the most compelling image of Harriet Jacobs's *Incidents in the Life of a Slave Girl* (1861), "the loophole of retreat," is an allusion to Cowper's poem *The Task* (1785). These poets had such cachet among American abolitionists because they were already familiar to American reading publics. Works like "The Negro's Complaint" were reprinted widely in American magazines, sometimes completely, sometimes partially, and sometimes even deliberately bowdlerized, with only the poem's title to catch the eye of the perusing reader. By the 1830s, British antislavery poetry was already part of American literary culture, and the abolitionists marshaled it for their own political purposes.

Abolitionists also used well-known eighteenth-century antislavery writers as marketing tools in an expanding book market in the antebellum period. Lydia Maria Child's *Anti-Slavery Catechism* (1839) makes another historical connection between the two eras by including the popular satirical sketch about the slave Tom and the stolen corkscrew, which, as we have seen, Mathew Carey published in *The American Museum*. But her book also, interestingly, includes an advertisement for Phillis Wheatley's *Poems on Various Subjects, Religious and Moral* on its back cover. Child's publisher advertised it as one of the "available titles of interest." Samuel May's *A Discourse on the Slavery in the United States* (1832) similarly advertised "Books Recommended," which included works by Clarkson, Gregoire, southern antislavery advocates, British books about West Indian slavery, and Samuel Stanhope Smith's famous *Essay on the Causes of the Variety of Complexion and Figure in the Human Species* (1787). These advertisements begin to suggest a transatlantic, abolitionist book market that included reprintings of key eighteenth-century works.

After 1808, antislavery movements naturally redirected their energies from the slave trade to chattel slavery. As one abolitionist wrote in the 1830s, "Daily experience testifies that the abolition of slavery, is at the present day, what the abolition of the slave trade was in Clarkson's time, a test of character."[1] Acknowledging such a change, however, locates only the broad strokes of historical movements. We should not ignore the abundant details that early antislavery writing provided about the horrors of plantation crimes, as in Freneau's "To Sir Toby" or William Dickson's *Letters on Slavery*. Nor should we ignore the outrage antislavery writing continued to express over such issues as the smuggling of African slaves and the gross hypocrisy of the domestic slave trade, particularly in Washington, D.C. As May complained, "My own eyes have seen, within a few miles of our Capitol, a drove of colored men and women pinioned and chained, and led or driven along like cattle to be sold in Georgia."[2]

The savage slave trader continued to function iconically in the abolitionist imagination. The figure still had rhetorical and emotional effect. This marks an important site of rhetorical continuity between eighteenth- and nineteenth-century antislavery writing. Slave traders were "skulking kidnappers and pirates," as David Lee Child put it in 1834, "enemies of the human race."[3] As southern apologists criticized the severity of the northern industrial economy, northern abolitionists (many of them urban and industrial reformers as well) responded in kind by employing the well-established trope of the slave trade. It helped to secure regional claims to "civilization." In her *Appeal*, for example, Lydia Child commented that "Since the time when Clarkson, Wilberforce, and Fox made the horrors of the slave trade understood, the slave captain, or slave jockey is spontaneously and almost universally regarded with dislike and horror. Even in the slave-holding states it is deemed disreputable to associate with a professed slave-trader, though few would think it any harm to bargain with him."[4] The most famous antislavery novel of all, *Uncle Tom's Cabin* (1852), is premised on such a rejection. Indeed, the novel flows from the fountainhead of the domestic slave trade. At the outset, Harriet Beecher Stowe dramatizes the moral dilemma of the otherwise decent Mr. Shelby, who is, in context of slave capitalism, the de facto slave of the ill-mannered slave trader Haley. The scene establishes the ethical terms of the slave capitalist "system" that is emptied of sentimental values; it precipitates the plot of Eliza's flight and redemption, and establishes the conditions for Senator Bird's sentimental conversion; and thereby facilitates the archetypal image of motherhood dominating the novel.

President Lincoln supposedly greeted Harriet Beecher Stowe, in a rather patronizing way, as the "little lady" whose book started the "big war." But his rhetorical use of the slave trader resembled hers—and perhaps even borrowed from it. In 1854, for example, Lincoln, a rising politician who was on the verge of joining the Republican Party, gave one of his most important speeches of his career against the Kansas-Nebraska Act. In attacking the doctrine of popular sovereignty embraced by his chief political opponent, Stephen Douglas, Lincoln argued that the nation's dangerous increase in its African American population was due to the South's smuggling of African slaves. He reminded southerners that "In 1820 you joined the north, almost unanimously, in declaring the African slave trade piracy, and in annexing to it the punishment of death." Lincoln continued: "Again, you have amongst you, a sneaking individual, of the class of native tyrants, known as the 'SLAVE-DEALER.' He watches your necessities, and crawls up to buy your slave, at a speculating price. If you cannot help it, you sell to him; but if you can help it, you drive him from your door. You despise him utterly. Your children must not play with his; they may rollick freely with the little Negroes, but not with the 'slave dealers' children."[5]

Antebellum abolitionists did not isolate the figure of the slave trader. One could argue that they drew on expansive and longstanding ideas associated with slave trading, and then deployed them strategically. This feature of the abolitionist imagination further connects such disparate antislavery figures as Clarkson and Child. Her *Appeal* did not simply cull evidence from Clarkson; it shared many of the same assumptions about enlightened culture, commerce, and historical progress. Child complains, for example, that Europeans—who themselves were once in a "state of barbarism" before print and commerce civilized them—were destroying the prospects of African civilization by continuing to smuggle slaves. "While commerce has carried books and maps to other portions of the globe, she has sent kidnappers with guns and cutlasses into Africa. We have not preached the Gospel of peace to her princes; we have incited them to make war upon each other, to fill our markets with slaves."[6]

One might even consider the development of sectionalism in light of the legacy of early antislavery movements. Northern antislavery activists countered southern comfort in its gentility by seizing upon traditional antislavery imagery of barbarity. Future scholarly work might consider, for example, how the earlier Federalist attempt to foist the problem of slavery onto the West Indies, as a way of taking the heat off their southern political allies, eventually gave way by the 1820s to the dominant focus on the southern plantation and southern slave auction. What rhetorical and symbolic transfers accompanied this political change? Why did well-established representations of West Indian barbarity slide so easily into antislavery critiques of the American south? How, on the level of language, did these regions historically reflect one another?

An example: Ralph Waldo Emerson. Though slow to embrace the antislavery movement, Emerson's rhetorical powers did not fail him when he finally did. His address on "West Indian Emancipation," given in Waltham in 1845, makes the immediate correlation between the West Indies and the American South. In light of earlier criticism of West Indian slave-holding that came from the British metropole, Emerson's assessment sounds uncannily familiar. "Elevate, enlighten, civilize the semi-barbarous nations of South Carolina, Georgia, Alabama—take away from their debauched society the Bowie-knife, the rum-bowl, the dice-box, and the stews—take out the brute, and infuse a drop of civility and generosity, and you touch those selfish lords with thought and gentleness."[7] Substitute "Barbados" or "Jamaica" for "South Carolina, Georgia, Alabama," and such a critique could come from Clarkson himself. Emerson's metonymic catalogue of vice is precisely the one with which writers like Richard Ligon, Bryan Edwards, and Edward Long earlier contended as they tried to secure the status of British identity on the outer reaches of the empire.

One can push this idea a step further. Emerson's language highlights his

New England consciousness, and in this way resembles that of radical abolitionists like William Lloyd Garrison, with whom a genteel figure like Emerson had very little in common. This begins to show how certain regional characteristics span the wide political spectrum of "antislavery" during the antebellum era. Seen in light of earlier metropolitan representations of the Empire's provincial colonies, the scorn that New England antislavery advocates expressed for the South resembles that of the "center" critiquing the cultural "margins." For writers like Emerson and Garrison did not merely envision New England as a region within a nation. They "metropolitanized" that region, making Boston the focal point—what Oliver Wendell Holmes called the "hub"—of national civilization vis-à-vis the supposedly barbaric provinces of the American South.

The subject of the slave trade continued to shape the rhetorical contours of antebellum sectionalism. Proslavery writing drew on the plantation mythology (in such works as *Swallow Barn* and *The Planter's Northern Bride*), which in turn invoked pastoral and agrarian ideologies to reject northern industrial capitalism. For moral leverage, northern antislavery writers countered by redeploying longstanding ideas about the horrors of barbaric traffic. Relatively early in his antislavery activity, Emerson's "Letter to the Kidnapping Committee" explained his reasons for declining the invitation to speak at an upcoming antislavery event meant to protest the return of a fugitive slave. But Emerson did manage to state just what was facing Massachusetts in the debate over slavery—it was a matter of preserving civilized commercial relations. "The question you now propose," he told Samuel Gridley Howe, "is a good test of the honesty and manliness of our commerce."[8] Calling upon "the mercantile body" to resist making Boston "a slave-port," Emerson told him, "It is high time our bad wealth came to an end." Such a statement might have come from Coleridge himself, or from Ann Yearsley, as they contemplated commercial ports like Bristol and Liverpool.

For all of the rhetorical and ideological continuities between eighteenth-century antislavery and antebellum abolitionism, the arguments against "barbaric traffic" became increasingly more difficult to sustain in an era characterized by the development of liberal capitalism. Moral arguments against slavery increasingly found their moral norms outside the categories of commercial and industrial capitalism, instead of within them. How, after all, could one look to the increasingly aggressive, self-interested, and impersonal structures of market capitalism as a "Christian" or "enlightened" alternative to the "barbarity" of slavery or the slave trade? Abolitionists continued to attack the domestic slave trade, but their assumptions about commercial and cultural forms of exchange—that trade should not take place outside moral and enlightened commitments—appeared increasingly anachronistic. The density and complexity of the meaning of "commerce" had lost its cultural hold. Nineteenth-century antislavery movements continued to criticize the cultural depravity of slave-holding societies, but their focus on the loss of enlightened manners actually separated this crucial category from the impersonal exchanges of the mass marketplace. In retrospect, eighteenth-century antislavery writing was enabled by, even founded upon, the ambiguities of private and public behavior, which characterized the activity of trade. Whereas Thomas Clarkson and Samuel Hopkins could imagine reform from within the category of commercial capitalism—the translation of "barbaric" into "Christian" commerce—later writers like Garrison and Stowe could see reform taking place only from within the home or the individual soul. Commercial capitalism and slave capitalism became increasingly difficult to disentangle. In *Uncle Tom's Cabin*, both are barbaric.

NOTES

INDEX

Notes

Introduction

1. The piece first appeared in the *Columbian Magazine; or Monthly Miscellany* (Philadelphia: Sedden, Spotswood, Cist and Trenchard, 1787), pp. 235–238. It was later included in Benjamin Rush, *Essays, Literary, Moral, and Philosophical* (Philadelphia: Thomas and Samuel F. Bradford, 1798).
2. Rush, *Essays,* pp. 315–316.
3. Ibid., p. 320.
4. Eric Williams, *Capitalism and Slavery* (Chapel Hill: University of North Carolina Press, 1944; rep. 1994), p. 136. For historical overview of the African slave trade, see Herbert S. Klein, *The Atlantic Slave Trade* (Cambridge: Cambridge University Press, 1999).
5. Thomas Bender, "Introduction," *The Antislavery Debate: Capitalism and Abolitionism as a Problem in Historical Interpretation,* ed. Thomas Bender (Berkeley: University of California Press, 1992), p. 2. Revisions of the Williams thesis emphasize that Britain was actually profiting from the African slave trade during the 1780s, when abolitionist reform was gaining momentum. See, for example, Roger Anstey, *The Atlantic Slave Trade and British Abolition, 1760–1810* (London: Macmillan, 1975), and Seymour Drescher, *Econocide: British Slavery in the Era of Abolition* (Pittsburgh, 1977).
6. See David Brion Davis, *The Problem of Slavery in the Age of Revolution, 1770–1823* (Ithaca: Cornell University Press, 1975), p. 467.
7. Over the years, Davis has emphasized that his argument was a materialist but not a Marxist one—he was trying to avoid, as he put it, the "cynical reductionism" of the Williams thesis. Not only was he confining the argument to British antislavery, but he also was trying to avoid sweeping arguments about ideology and class interests: "Certainly I advanced no general theory of abolitionism per se as an instrument of hegemonic control." Rather, Davis emphasizes that the "mode of consciousness" behind antislavery movements was itself "elastic" and irreducible to a singular idea or social type. See Davis, "Capitalism, Abolitionism, and Hegemony," in *British Capitalism and Caribbean Slav-*

ery: The Legacy of Eric Williams, eds. Barbara Solon and Stanley Engerman (Cambridge: Cambridge University Press, 1982), pp. 209–210, 212–213, and Davis, *Slavery and Human Progress* (New York: Oxford University Press, 1984). See esp. pp. 109–110. Though its focus is later than mine is, that book's concept of civilization and barbarity certainly informs my understanding of the cultural stakes of the African slave trade.

8. The debates among Davis, Thomas Haskell, and John Ashworth are fully drawn in Bender, *The Antislavery Debate.* Haskell reconceptualizes the issue of bourgeois cultural hegemony by arguing that the capitalist market creates widening contexts for individual attention and decision-making. This new "cognitive style" made bourgeois society newly aware of distant peoples and places, which thus explains the conditions for its antislavery sympathy. Ashworth, too, departs from Davis' belief in bourgeois self-deception. Assuming that market values are wholly self-interested, he sees the rising capitalist ranks as resorting to the ideals of home, feeling, and moral conscience in order to combat the acutely impersonal forces of capitalist society. Below, I am less concerned with the *intentions* of antislavery reformers than with the language they used to install the principles of "free" trade. Rather than viewing sentiment as somehow a façade for capitalist ideology, I see it as a central part of this era's commercial culture. For an important historical interpretation of the working-class appeal of antislavery, see Seymour Drescher, *Capitalism and Antislavery: British Mobilization in Comparative Perspective* (New York: Oxford University Press, 1987).

9. Ira Berlin, *Many Thousands Gone: The First Two Centuries of Slavery in North America* (Cambridge, Mass.: Harvard University Press, 1998), p. 4. See also Peter Kolchin, *American Slavery, 1619–1877* (New York: Hill and Wang, 1993), p. 67.

10. David Porter relies on laissez-faire ideology of eighteenth-century commerce in "A Peculiar but Uninteresting Nation: China and the Discourse of Commerce in Eighteenth-Century England," *Eighteenth-Century Studies* 33 (1999–2000), p. 185.

11. *American Museum* (Philadelphia: Mathew Carey, 1789), p. 429.

12. *The Case of Our Fellow-Creatures, the Oppressed Africans* (London: James Phillips, 1784), p. 5.

13. *An Oration on the Abolition of the Slave Trade; Delivered at the African Church in the City of New-York, January 1, 1808* (New York: Samuel Wood, 1808), pp. 11–12.

14. See Swan, *A Dissuasion to Great Britain and the Colonies, from the Slave Trade to Africa* (Boston: E. Russell, 1772), pp. xii–xiii, 25; Malachy Postlethwayt, *The Universal Dictionary of Trade and Commerce: With Large Additions and Improvements, Adapting the Same to the Present State of British Affairs in America, Since the Last Treaty of Peace Made in the Year 1763* (London: W. Strahan, 1774), n.p.; Samuel Bradburn, *An Address to the People Called Methodists; Concerning the Criminality of Encouraging Slavery* (London: M. Gurney, 1792), p. 3; Samuel Hopkins, "The Slave Trade and Slavery," in *Timely Articles on Slavery* (Boston: Congregational Board of Publication, 1854), pp. 613, 615; John Newton, *Thoughts Upon the Af-*

rican Slave Trade (London: J. Buckland, 1788), p. 98; Levi Hart, *Liberty Described and Recommended* (Hartford: Eben, Watson, 1775), p. v; Anthony Benezet, *Some Historical Account of Guinea, its Situation, Produce, and the General Disposition of its Inhabitants* (London: James Phillips, 1788), pp. xiv–xv; James Dana, *A Discourse on the African Slave Trade,* in *Political Sermons of the American Founding Era,* ed. Ellis Sandoz (Indianapolis: Liberty, 1990), p. 1047; John Parrish, *Remarks on the Slavery of the Black People* (Philadelphia: Kimber, Conrad, and Co., 1806), p. 21; Abbé Raynal, *The Philosophical and Political History of the Settlements and Trade of the Europeans in the East and West Indies* (London: W. Strahan and T. Cadell, 1783), vol. 5, p. 140; Elhanan Winchester, *The Reigning Abominations, Especially the Slave Trade, Considered as Causes of Lamentation* (London: H. Trapp, 1788), p. 15.

15. Davis makes this argument about the foundation of the English Society for Effecting the Abolition of the Slave Trade. This would avoid alienating public anxiety about the sudden prospect of free blacks. See Davis, *The Problem of Slavery in the Age of Revolution,* pp. 404–417. For a recent view that emphasizes the early movements' attempt to end chattel slavery, see Christopher L. Brown's "Empire Without Slaves: British Concepts of Emancipation in the Age of the American Revolution," *William and Mary Quarterly* 3rd ser. 56 (April 1999), pp. 273–306.

16. The relation among "manners," "politeness," and "benevolence" was complex and much debated in eighteenth-century culture. For example, the Scottish philosopher and antislavery writer James Beattie insisted upon the distinction between "morals and manners. The former depended upon internal dispositions, the latter on outward and visible accomplishments." See Beattie, *Elements of Moral Science* (Edinburgh: T. Caddell and William Creech, 1793), p. 3.

17. This movement "from the civic to the civil" eventually "replaced the *polis* by politeness, the *oikos* by the economy." See J. G. A. Pocock, "Cambridge Paradigms and Scotch Philosophers: A Study of the Relations Between Civic Humanist and the Civil Jurisprudential Interpretation of Eighteenth-Century Social Thought," *in Wealth and Virtue: The Shaping of the Political Economy in the Scottish Enlightenment,* eds. Istvan Hont and Michael Ignatieff (Cambridge: Cambridge University Press, 1983), pp. 240, 242. As Pocock explains, "Virtue was redefined . . . with the aid of a concept of 'manners.' As the individual moved from the farmer-warrior world of ancient citizenship or Gothic *libertas,* he entered an increasingly transactional universe of 'commerce and the arts'—the latter term signifying both the productive and audio-visual skills—in which his relationships and interactions with other human beings, and with their products, became increasingly complex and various, modifying and developing more and more aspects of his personality." See also, "Virtues, Rights and Manners: A Model for Historians of Political Thought," in Pocock, *Virtue, Commerce, History: Essays on Political Thought and History* (Cambridge: Cambridge University Press, 1985), pp. 48–49. Cf. James Tully's assessment in *An Approach to Political Philosophy: Locke in Contexts* (Cambridge: Cambridge University Press, 1993),

p. 94. For civil jurisprudential philosophy's relation to the Scottish Enlightenment, see Richard Teichgraeber III, *"Free Trade" and Moral Philosophy: Rethinking the Sources of Adam Smith's Wealth of Nations* (Durham: Duke University Press, 1986).

18. Pocock, *Barbarism and Religion, Volume Two: Narratives of Civil Government* (Cambridge: Cambridge University Press, 1999), pp. 19–20.

19. My argument about the meaning of "free" trade in this era is consistent with David Armitage's observation that during the 1720s and 1730s the first British empire was idealized as "Protestant, commercial, maritime, and free." See Armitage, *The Ideological Origins of the British Empire* (Cambridge: Cambridge University Press, 2000), pp. 173–174.

20. The political scientist Knud Haakonsen summarizes the theoretical problem of American Revolutionary historical studies: The synthesis between liberalism and republicanism "still assumes that it makes sense to talk of liberalism in this context, and that whatever else this might have been about, it was also concerned with natural rights. But liberalism is a nineteenth-century construct that is best kept out of these discussions, and the Scottish philosophy that influenced Americans was only concerned with rights within the natural-law and duty framework." See Haakonsen, "From Natural Law to the Rights of Man: a European Perspective on American Debates," in *A Culture of Rights: The Bill of Rights in Philosophy, Politics and Law—1791 and 1991*, eds. Michael J. Lacey and Knud Haakonsen (Cambridge: Cambridge University Press, 1991), p. 46. For a similar approach, see Orlando Patterson, "Freedom, Slavery and the Modern Construction of Rights," *in Historical Change and Human Rights*, ed. Oliver Hutton (New York: Basic Books, 1995), esp. pp. 141–142, 158–159.

21. The seminal work for this field is of course Norbert Elias, *The Civilizing Process*, trans. Edward Jephcott (Oxford: Blackwell, 1994). Recent important studies on cultural refinement include Richard Bushman, *The Refinement of America: Persons, Houses, Cities* (New York: 1992); David Shields, *Civil Tongues and Polite Letters in British America* (Chapel Hill: University of North Carolina Press, 1997); John Kasson, *Rudeness and Civility: Manners in Nineteenth-Century Urban America* (New York: Hill and Wang, 1990); and Lawrence Klein, *Shaftesbury and the Culture of Politeness* (Cambridge: Cambridge University Press, 1994).

22. See Klein, *Shaftesbury and the Culture of Politeness*. Cf. Quentin Skinner: "With the extension of the manners of the court to the bourgeoisie in the early eighteenth century, the virtues of the independent country gentleman began to look irrelevant and even inimical to a polite and commercial age." Skinner, *Liberty Before Liberalism* (Cambridge: Cambridge University Press, 1998), p. 97.

23. "While trading was fueled by the pursuit of gain, the actual practice of trade was sufficiently social to demand a good deal of social form." Lawrence Klein, "Politeness for Plebes: Consumption and Social Identity in Early Eighteenth-Century England," in *The Consumption of Culture, 1600–1800: Image, Object, Text*, eds. Ann Bermingham and John Brewer (London: Routledge, 1995), p. 372.

24. *The Tatler*, Saturday, May 28, 1709.

25. See "Extracts from Bishop Newton" in the *Boston Weekly Magazine* (25 June 1803), vol. 1, p. 146.
26. *American Magazine* (New York: Samuel Loudon, 1787), p. 561.
27. During the Revolutionary era, for example, Americans justified embargo movements against the importation and consumption of British goods by emphasizing the danger of cultural contamination—that is, imported goods were said to endanger the purity of American "republican" values. In Britain, as Kathleen Wilson argues, cultural critics vilified the effects of British affinities for French fashion and luxuries. See Wilson, *The Sense of the People: Politics, Culture and Imperialism in England, 1715–1785* (New York: Cambridge University Press, 1995), p. 202.
28. As Stuart Hall has argued, recent Marxist criticism re-appraises these traditional categories, and allows for the fact that ideology is socially contingent, fractured and diverse. Since language is always "multi-accentual" the ideological field is always one of "intersecting accents." What Hall calls a "Marxism without guarantees" resists the concept of correspondence between economics and ideological hegemony, and instead recognizes the diversity and multiplicity of social practices and ways of thinking during any historical moment. See Hall, "The Problem of Ideology: Marxism Without Guarantees," in *Stuart Hall: Critical Dialogues in Cultural Studies,* eds. David Morley and Kuan-Hsing Chen (London: Routledge, 1996), pp. 25–45. See also Raymond Williams, *Marxism and Literature* (Oxford: Oxford University Press, 1977), pp. 55–71.
29. T. H. Breen, "Subjecthood and Citizenship: The Context of James Otis' Radical Critique of John Locke," *New England Quarterly* 81 (1998), p. 389. For book-length studies premised on such assumptions, see, for example, J. E. Crowley, *"This Sheba, Self": The Conceptualization of Economic Life in Eighteenth-Century America* (Baltimore: Johns Hopkins University Press, 1974) and Barry Alan Shain, *The Myth of American Individualism: The Protestant Origins of American Political Thought* (Princeton: Princeton University Press, 1994).
30. Thomas Horne, "Bourgeois Virtue: Property and Moral Philosophy in America, 1750–1800," *History of Political Thought* 4 (1983), p. 319.
31. See James T. Kloppenberg, *The Virtues of Liberalism* (New York: Oxford University Press, 1998), p. 26. Kloppenberg distinguishes the notion of individual "autonomy" as opposed to unrestrained "freedom." He comments further that, "This concept of benevolence, flowing from the springs of natural law that fed Locke's liberalism as well as various streams of Protestantism in America, thus played a large part in Smith's philosophy as it did in those versions of Scottish common sense that figured more directly in eighteenth-century American thought," pp. 26–27. For similar reconsideration of Locke, see Tully, *An Approach to Political Philosophy,* pp. 71–79, and Ian Shapiro, *The Evolution of Rights in Liberal Theory* (Cambridge: Cambridge University Press, 1986), pp. 80, 98. For the Scottish Enlightenment's ambivalence to commercial capitalism, see John Dwyer, *Virtuous Discourse: Sensibility and Community in Late Eighteenth-Century Scotland* (Edinburgh: John Donald, 1987).

32. Srinivas Avaramuden, *Tropicopolitans: Colonialism and Agency, 1688–1804* (Durham: Duke University Press, 1999); Laura Brown, *Ends of Empire: Women and Ideology in Early Eighteenth-Century English Literature* (Ithaca: Cornell University Press, 1993); Markman Ellis, *The Politics of Sensibility: Race, Gender and Commerce in the Sentimental Novel* (Cambridge: Cambridge University Press, 1996); Suvir Kaul, *Poems of Nation, Anthems of Empire: English Verse in the Long Eighteenth Century* (Charlottesville: University of Virginia Press, 2000); Charlotte Sussman, *Consuming Anxieties: Consumer Protest, Gender, and British Slavery, 1713–1833* (Stanford: Stanford University Press, 2000); Helen Thomas, *Romanticism and Slave Narratives: Transatlantic Testimonies* (Cambridge: Cambridge University Press, 2000); and Roxann Wheeler, *The Complexion of Race: Categories of Difference in Eighteenth-Century British Culture* (Philadelphia: University of Pennsylvania Press, 2000).

33. For colonial settler claims to British identity and political rights, see Jack P. Greene, "The American Revolution," *American Historical Review* 105 (2000), 93–102.

34. See Shields, *Civil Tongues and Polite Letters*; Leonard Tennenhouse, *The Importance of Feeling English: American Literature and the English Diaspora, 1750–1850* (Princeton University Press, forthcoming); *A History of the Book in America: Volume One: The Colonial Book in the Atlantic World,* eds. Hugh Amory and David D. Hall (Cambridge: Cambridge University Press, 2000); *Possible Pasts: Becoming Colonial in Early America,* ed. Robert Blair St. George (Ithaca: Cornell University Press, 2001); and *Finding Colonial Americas: Essays in Honor of J. A. Leo Lemay,* eds. Carla Mulford and David S. Shields (Newark: University of Delaware Press, 2001).

35. Edward Said, *Culture and Imperialism* (New York: Vintage, 1994), p. 317. On the complex and reciprocal influences of metropolitan and colonial cultures see Aravamudan, *Tropicopolitans*.

36. Peter Hulme recently has critiqued narrow definitions of colonialism and postcoloniality (including Said's) that confine their application to nineteenth- and twentieth-century forms of imperialism: "[This argument's] basis is the point that the wars of independence were not primarily fought by people who were colonized against the people who had colonized them. This point is undoubtedly true, but the real question is, Why take that model of colonizer and colonized as providing the sole definition of colonialism and decide that because America does not fit the model you cannot talk about decolonization, colonial discourse, or postcolonial theory? If distinctions are going to be made— and they should be—then there are plenty of important distinctions that do not simply remove America from the colonial map." He emphasizes that colonization involves the subjugation of land as well as people and that we can conceive of Latin American nations and the US as simultaneously colonial (in their violence against indigenous populations) and postcolonial (in their new-found status of independence). See "Postcolonial Theory and Early America: An Approach to the Caribbean," in Blair St. George, *Possible Pasts*, p. 37.

37. This includes Benezet, William Dillwyn, James Phillips, and key members of the anti-slave trade movement during the 1780s such as Samuel Hoare, John Lloyd, and Joseph Woods. See Judith Jennings, *The Business of Abolishing the British Slave Trade, 1783–1807* (London: Frank Cass, 1997).

38. See Davis, *Problem of Slavery in the Age of Revolution; Unchained Voices: An Anthology of Black Authors in the English Speaking World of the Eighteenth Century*, ed. Vincent Carretta (Lexington: University of Kentucky Press, 1997); and Joan Baum, *Mind-Forg'd Manacles: Slavery and the English Romantic Poets* (North Haven, Conn.: Archon, 1994), pp. 13–14.

39. See Wheeler, *Complexion of Race;* and Nicholas Hudson, "From 'Nation' to 'Race': The Origins of Racial Classification in Eighteenth-Century Thought," *Eighteenth Century Studies* 29 (1996), pp. 247–264.

40. Barbara J. Fields, "Ideology and Race in American History," in *Region, Race, and Reconstruction: Essays in Honor of C. Vann Woodward*, eds. J. Morgan Kousser and James M. McPherson (New York: Oxford University Press, 1982), p. 144. See also Alden T. Vaughan, "The Origins Debate: Slavery and Racism in Seventeenth-Century Virginia," *Virginia Magazine of History and Biography* 97 (1989), pp. 311–354.

41. Monogenist theory emphasized the importance of environmental influences on visible human differences. As Smith argued, for example, contra Hume, Kames, and Jefferson, "Our experience verifies the power of climate on the complexion. . . . Every sensible difference, in the degree of the cause, will create a visible change in the human body." See Samuel Stanhope Smith, *An Essay on the Causes of the Variety of Complexion and Figure in the Human Species* (London: John Stockdale, 1789), pp. 10–11. The debates themselves are catalogued in *Race and the Enlightenment: A Reader*, ed. Emmanuel Chukwudi Eze (Oxford: Blackwell, 1997).

42. My argument differs from the one that makes racism the effect of modern liberal capitalism. See Immanuel Wallerstein, for example, "The Ideological Tensions of Capitalism: Universalism versus Racism and Sexism," in Wallerstein and Etienne Balibar, *Race, Nation, Class: Ambiguous Identities* (London: Verso, 1991), p. 33.

1. The Commercial Jeremiad

1. Thomas Jefferson, *A Summary View of the Rights of British America*, intro. Thomas Abernathy (New York: Scholars Facsimiles, 1943), pp. 13, 17.

2. The idea of "free" trade was of course highly contextual. As I show below, British antislavery writing often attacked the slave trade as a corrupt monopoly protected by British regulations. Yet British participants in the slave trade just as easily appropriated the language of free trade to serve their own interests. David Shields has noted how Britain's Free Company of Merchants trading in Africa held the motto, "Free Trade by Act of Parliament." See Shields, *Oracles of Empire: Poetry, Politics, and Commerce in British America, 1690–1750* (Chicago: Uni-

versity of Chicago Press, 1990), p. 77. For London's protection of the West Indian sugar trade, see Andrew Jackson O'Shaughnessy, *An Empire Divided: The American Revolution and the British Caribbean* (Philadelphia: University of Pennsylvania Press, 2000), pp. 58–62.

3. *The Federalist Papers,* ed. Clinton Rossiter (New York: Penguin, 1961), p. 266. Antifederalists actually used much the same language to assail the slave trade and the Constitution's support of it. George Mason, for one, denounced "this nefarious traffic" that had "the most pernicious effect on manners." See Paul Finkelman, "Slavery and the Constitutional Convention: Making a Covenant with Death," *in Beyond Confederation: Origins of the Constitution and American National Identity,* eds. Richard Beeman, Stephen Botein, and Edward Carter (Chapel Hill: University of North Carolina Press, 1987), p. 215. As Finkelman also notes, the issues of the federal regulation of commerce, the slave trade, and the fugitive slave law were closely related in the political negotiations that took place in Philadelphia in 1787.

4. This epithet is consistent with Linda Colley's argument that, after their defeat in the American Revolutionary war, many Britons "now sought to explain what appeared an almost inexplicable defeat at the hands of colonists by reference to their own failings in the sight of God. They had been corrupt and presumptuous . . . and they had been duly punished. In this mood, the slave trade, so obviously questionable in moral terms, and so productive of worldly profit and luxury, seemed far more of a liability." See Colley, *Britons: Forging the Nation, 1707–1837* (New Haven: Yale University Press, 1992), p. 353.

5. I would distinguish my argument here from Sacvan Bercovitch's view of the role of the jeremiad in American culture: "The concept of American revolution transformed self-reliance into a function not only of the common good but of the redemption of mankind. In virtually every area of life, the jeremiad became the official ritual form of continuing revolution. Mediating between religion and ideology, the jeremiad gave contract the sanctity of covenant, free enterprise the halo of grace, progress the assurance of the chiliad, and nationalism the grandeur of typology." Rather than codifying national mythology, the jeremiad, as I argue, should be read in the larger cultural context of transatlanticism. Seen in this context, the important similarities between British and American antislavery discourses divest the jeremiad of strictly Puritan origins and challenge its role as the medium of national self-affirmation. I argue below that it legitimates commerce not by divine sanction but by much more precarious assertions of historical progress. See Bercovitch, *The American Jeremiad* (Madison: University of Wisconsin Press, 1978), p. 141.

6. T. H. Breen, "Narrative of Commercial Life: Consumption, Ideology, and Community on the Eve of the American Revolution," *William and Mary Quarterly* 3rd ser. 50 (1993), p. 484. See also Breen's "'Baubles of Britain': The American and Consumer Revolutions of the Eighteenth Century," *Past and Present* 119 (1988), pp. 73–104.

7. Albert O. Hirschman misses the point when he argues that the slave trade un-

dermined cultural assumptions about the refining effects of commerce: "The term thus carried into its 'commercial' career an overload of meaning that denoted politeness, polished manners, and socially useful behavior in general. Even so, the persistent use of the term *le doux commerce* strikes us as a strange aberration for an age when the slave trade was at its peak and when trade in general was still a hazardous, adventurous, and often violent business." For it was *exactly* this ideological incongruity that antislavery writing exploited, and produced such metaphors as robbery, piracy, and prostitution—all illicit forms of commerce—as a means of distinguishing virtuous from vicious trade. See Hirschman, *The Passions and the Interests: Political Arguments for Capitalism Before Its Triumph* (Princeton: Princeton University Press, 1977), p. 62.

8. Breen, "Narrative of Commercial Life," p. 447.

9. George Keith, "An Exhortation and Caution to Friends Concerning Buying or Keeping of Negroes" (1693), in *Am I Not a Man and a Brother: The Antislavery Crusade in Revolutionary America, 1688–1788,* ed. Roger Bruns (New York: Chelsea House, 1977), p. 7.

10. Bruns, *Man and a Brother,* p. 20.

11. Ibid., p. 11.

12. For this famous debate, see David Brion Davis, *The Problem of Slavery in Western Culture* (Ithaca: Cornell University Press, 1966), pp. 341–348, and Albert J. Von Frank, "John Saffin: Slavery and Racism in Colonial Massachusetts," *Early American Literature* 29 (1994), pp. 254–272.

13. John Dunton, *The Athenian Oracle: Being an Entire Collection of All the Valuable Questions in the Athenian Mercuries,* vol 1 (London: Andrew Bell, 1704), p. 545. For Sewall's possible relation with Dunton, see Davis, *Problem of Slavery in Western Culture,* pp. 346–348. The essay begins with the query: "Whether Trading for Negros, i.e., Carrying them out of their own Country into perpetual Slavery, be in itself unlawful, and especially contrary to the great Law of Christianity?"

14. David Brion Davis, *The Problem of Slavery in the Age of Revolution, 1770–1823* (Ithaca: Cornell University Press, 1975), pp. 306–309.

15. "Samuel Hopkins to Moses Brown, Newport, October 22, 1787," in *A Necessary Evil?: Slavery and the Debate Over the Constitution,* ed. John P. Kaminski (Madison: Madison House, 1995), p. 73.

16. See Warner Mifflin, *A Serious Expostulation with the Members of the House of Representatives of the United States* (Philadelphia, 1793), p. 15.

17. Thomas Branagan, *Political and Theological Disquisitions on the Signs of the Times* (Trenton: Printed for the Author, 1807), pp. 15–16.

18. Branagan, *Disquisitions,* pp. 20–21.

19. Elhanan Winchester, *The Reigning Abominations, Especially the Slave Trade, Considered as Causes of Lamentation; Being the Substance of a Discourse Delivered at Fairfax County, Virginia, December 30, 1774* (London: H. Trapp, 1788), p. 16.

20. Samuel Cooke, *A Sermon Preached at Cambridge in the Audience of His Honor Thomas Hutchinson, esq.; Lieutenant Governor and Commander in Chief; the Honour-*

able His Majesty's Council, and the House of Representatives, of the Province of Massa-chusetts-Bay in New England, May 30th, 1770. Being the Anniversary for the Election of His Majesty's Council for the Said Province (Boston: Edes and Gill, 1770), p. 42.

21. Cooke, *Sermon*, p. 41.

22. *The Case of Our Fellow Creatures, the Oppressed Africans, Respectfully Recommended to the Serious Consideration of the Legislature of Great-Britain, by the People Called Quakers* (London: James Phillips, 1784), p. 5.

23. Historians recognize the importance of Quaker antislavery movements, though they disagree over the motivations generating them. For debates over the humanitarian and tribalistic strains of Quakerism, see Jack Marietta, *The Reformation of American Quakerism, 1748–1783* (Philadelphia: University of Pennsylvania Press, 1984); Jean Soderlund, *Quakers and Slavery: A Divided Spirit* (Princeton: Princeton University Press, 1985); and Barry Levy, *Quakers and the American Family* (New York: Oxford University Press, 1988).

24. John Hepburn, *The American Defense of the Christian Golden Rule* (1715), in Bruns, *Man and a Brother*, p. 18.

25. William Dillwyn, "Brief Considerations on Slavery and the Expediency of its Abolition with some Hints on the Means Whereby it may be Gradually Effected" (1773), in Bruns, *Man and a Brother*, p. 272.

26. This ambiguity informs, for example, Benezet's exhortation following a description of the slave auction: "Reader, if the Impressions of Grace, or even the common Feelings of Humanity are not suppressed in thy Heart, by the Love of Gain, compare what thou hast read with the Equity, the Sympathy, the Tenderness and affectionate Love, which is the Life of Christianity." See Anthony Benezet, *A Short Account of That Part of Africa, Inhabited by Negroes* (London: W. Baker and J. W. Galabin, 1788), pp. 29–30.

27. Montesquieu, *The Spirit of the Laws*, eds. Anne M. Cohler, Basia Carolyn Miller, and Harold Samuel Stone (Cambridge: Cambridge University Press, 1989), p. 338.

28. For example, Montesquieu attacked the role of Jewish merchants in early modern England: "Commerce passed to a nation then covered with infamy, and soon it was no longer distinguished from the most horrible usuries, from monopolies, from the levy of subsidies, and from all the dishonest means of acquiring silver." See *Spirit of the Laws*, p. 388. While he realized that the "commerce of luxury," which characterizes monarchial societies, was plagued by despotic abuses, he also believed that the "economic commerce" of republics easily slid into luxury and corruption. For his ambivalent view of commerce, see Richard B. Sher, "From Troglodytes to Americans: Montesquieu and the Scottish Enlightenment on Liberty, Virtue, and Commerce," in *Republicanism, Liberty, and Commercial Society, 1649–1776*, ed. David Wooton (Stanford: Stanford University Press, 1994), pp. 368–404.

29. Anand Chitnis, *The Scottish Enlightenment: A Social History* (London: Croom Helm, 1976), p. 96.

30. *Cato's Letters: or, Essays on Liberty, Civil and Religious, and Other Important Subjects*, vol 1., ed. Ronald Hamowy (Indianapolis: Liberty, 1995), pp. 442–443.

31. Terry Mulcaire, "Public Credit; or the Feminization of Virtue in the Market-place," *PMLA* 114 (1999), pp. 1034, 1035. Mulcaire challenges the Pocockian opposition between virtue and commerce as well as the masculine paradigm of liberal individualism. For an alternative reading of the gendered significance of the commercial literature surrounding the South Sea Bubble, which notes its misogynistic features, see Catherine Ingrassia, *Authorship, Commerce, and Gender in Early Eighteenth-Century England: A Culture of Paper Credit* (Cambridge: Cambridge University Press, 1998), pp. 17–39.

32. "So that, if we expect to carry on the Trade to *Africa* upon the Foot of a free and open Trade . . . to as great advantage as *France* does, the [Royal African] Company must have some Equivalent for the Privilege they have parted with, and the *French* Company possess." Malachy Postlethwayt, *The African Slave Trade, the Great Pillar and Support of the British Plantation Trade in America* (London: J. Robinson, 1745), p. 9. David Brion Davis argues that Postlethwayt's changing outlook reflected the slave trade's economic decline. See Davis, *Problem of Slavery in Western Culture*, p. 161. My interest is less in Postlethwayt's intentions than in the cultural and rhetorical expression of this change.

33. Peter N. Miller, *Defining the Common Good: Empire, Religion and Philosophy in Eighteenth-Century Britain* (Cambridge: Cambridge University Press, 1994), p. 154.

34. Malachy Postlethwayt, *The Universal Dictionary of Trade and Commerce: With Large Additions and Improvements, Adapting the Same to the Present State of British Affairs in America, Since the Last Treaty of Paris Made in the Year 1763* (London: W. Strahan, 1774), 4th edition, unpaginated.

35. *Universal Dictionary.* The quotation comes from the entry "English African Company."

36. Richard Nisbet, *Slavery not Forbidden by Scripture. Or a Defence of the West-India Planters, From the Aspersions Thrown out Against Them, by the Author of the Pamphlet, Entitled, "An Address to the Inhabitants of the British Settlements in America upon Slave-Keeping* (Philadelphia, 1773), p. ii.

37. Nisbet, *Slavery not Forbidden by Scripture*, p. 25.

38. During the Revolutionary crisis, James Otis wrote: "No better reason can be given for enslaving those of any color than such as Baron Montesquieu has humorously given as the foundation of that cruel slavery over the poor Ethiopians, which threatens one day to reduce both Europe and America to the ignorance and barbarity of the darkest ages." Otis, *The Rights of the British Colonies Asserted and Proved* (1764), in *Pamphlets of the American Revolution, 1750–1776*, ed. Bernard Bailyn (Cambridge, Mass.: Harvard University Press, 1965), pp. 439–440. Book 15 of *The Spirit of the Laws* offers a mock apologia for slavery that proslavery advocates actually used; the work's environmentalist approach to forms of government provided fodder for the proslavery argument that slavery "naturally" existed in particular climates and conditions. For Montesquieu and slavery, see Davis, *The Problem of Slavery in Western Culture*, pp. 394–410.

39. The piece was printed in Anthony Benezet's *A Short Account of that Part of Africa Inhabited by Negroes* (Philadelphia, 1762; London: W. Baker and J. W. Galabin, 1768), p. 57.

40. As a clergyman, Ramsay actually spent decades living in St. Christopher's (now St. Kitts), where he witnessed slavery first-hand. See James Ramsay, *An Essay on the Treatment and Conversion of the African Slaves in the British Sugar Colonies* (London: James Phillips, 1784), p. 127.

41. William Wilberforce, *A Letter on the Abolition of the Slave Trade; Addressed to the Freeholders and Other Inhabitants of Yorkshire* (London: T. Caddell, 1807), p. 339. In 1787 Rhode Island's law against slave trade similarly proclaimed that, "Whereas the trade to Africa for slaves, and the transportation and selling of them into other countries, are inconsistent with justice and the principles of humanity, as well as the laws of nature, and that more enlightened and civilized sense of freedom which has late prevailed." See *Constitution of a Society for Abolishing the Slave-Trade with Several Acts of the Legislatures of the State of Massachusetts, Connecticut, and Rhode Island for that Purpose* (Providence: John Carter, 1789).

42. Winthrop Jordan's critique of antislavery's "half-intended emotionalism" and "partial titillation of human sympathizing" exemplifies this view. See Jordan, *White Over Black: American Attitudes Toward the Negro, 1550–1812* (Chapel Hill: University of North Carolina Press, 1968), pp. 365–372.

43. David Cooper, *A Mite Cast into the Treasury: or, Observation on Slave-Keeping* (Philadelphia, 1772), pp. 8, 15.

44. James Dana, *The African Slave Trade*, in *Political Sermons of the American Founding Era, 1730–1805*, ed. Ellis Sandoz (Indianapolis: Liberty Press, 1991), p. 1034.

45. John Brewer, "'The Most Polite Age and the Most Vicious': Attitudes Towards Culture as a Commodity, 1660–1800," in *The Consumption of Culture*, eds. Brewer and Ann Bermingham (London: Routledge, 1995), pp. 345, 350.

46. James Swan, *A Disuasion to Great-Britain and the Colonies, from the Slave Trade to Africa* (Boston: E. Russell, 1772), pp. xii, 33.

47. William Belsham, *An Essay on the African Slave Trade* (Philadelphia: Daniel Humphreys, 1790), p. 8.

48. Alexander Falconbridge, *An Account of the Slave Trade on the Coast of Africa* (London: J. Phillips, 1788), p. 34.

49. David S. Shields, *Oracles of Empire: Poetry, Politics, and Commerce in British America, 1690–1750* (Chicago: University of Chicago Press, 1990), p. 175.

50. Wilberforce, *Letter on the Abolition of the Slave Trade*, pp. 85–86.

51. Ibid., p. 86.

52. For example, see Cathy N. Davidson, *Revolution and the Word: The Rise of the Novel in America* (New York: Oxford University Press, 1986); Julia Stern, *The Plight of Feeling: Sympathy and Dissent in the Early American Novel* (Chicago: University of Chicago Press, 1997); and Elizabeth Barnes, *States of Sympathy: Seduction and Democracy in the American Novel* (New York: Columbia University Press, 1997).

53. I would preface the following discussion with the caveat that contemporary historiography about the African slave trade offers a more complex account of the relation between European and African traders, particularly the leverage

that the latter group often exerted over the commercial traffic in African slaves. See, for example, Herbert S. Klein, *The Atlantic Slave Trade* (Cambridge: Cambridge University Press, 1999), esp. pp. 103–129.

54. John Atkins, *A Voyage to Guinea, Brasil, and the West-Indies; in His Majesty's Ships the Swallow and Weymouth* (London: Ward and Chandler, 1737), pp. 168–169.

55. Thomas Clarkson, *An Essay on the Slavery and Commerce of the Human Species, Particularly the African* (London: J. Phillips, 1786), p. 44.

56. George M. Fredrickson, *The Black Image in the White Mind: The Debate on Afro-American Character and Destiny* (New York: Harper and Row, 1971).

57. Peter Williams, *An Oration on the Abolition of the Slave Trade; Delivered at the African Church in the City of New-York, January 1st, 1808* (New York: Samuel Wood, 1808), pp. 12–13.

58. Ibid., pp. 13, 15.

59. The discourses of seduction in antislavery writing and the novel converge, for example, in the work of Susanna Rowson. In one of her sentimentally didactic works in the tradition of Lawrence Sterne, entitled *The Inquisitor* (1794), Rowson's narrator self-consciously imagines the scene of slave-trading while encountering an African slave:

    "She [Fancy] held up to my mind's eye, a man born in good inheritance, and surrounded with all the comforts, all the blessings, he desired—but he was a Negro.

    He was sitting in his little hut, his jetty companion by his side; one infant at her breast, two others prattling at her knee; she looked, she felt happy. . . . Some Europeans enter—they deck his beloved children with baubles—they tie beads round the arms of his wife—and ornament her jetty locks with glittering toys— He is charmed with their courtesy—He walks with them to the sea side, and takes his boy, his eldest darling, with him—they invite him on board the vessel—Poor soul! Unsuspecting their treachery, he goes, and bids adieu to liberty for ever . . . [His wife] leaves her home and walks towards the sea; she sees him embark—her child goes too—the sailors spread the sails—the vessel moves—she shrieks—but there my heart was wrung so keenly, I could go no farther." See *The Inquisitor; or the Invisible Rambler* (Philadelphia: Mathew Carey, 1794), pp. 88–89.

60. Charles Crawford, *Observations on Negro Slavery* (Philadelphia: Eleazer Oswald, 1790), pp. 75–76.

61. See, for example, *The Consumption of Culture*; Neil McKendrick, John Brewer, and J. H. Plumb, *The Birth of a Consumer Society: The Commercialization of Eighteenth-Century England* (Bloomington: Indiana University Press, 1986); *Consumption and the World of Goods*, eds. John Brewer and Roy Porter (London: Routledge, 1993), esp. Porter, "Consumption: Disease of the Consumer Society?"; Paul Langford, *A Polite and Commercial People: England, 1727–83* (Oxford: Clarendon, 1989).

62. Breen's argument describes how colonial nonimportation movements transformed a social mode of symbolism into a political one: "A semiotic order was

changing. Articles that had been bound up with local cultures, with individual decisions within households, were gradually thrust into public discourse, and during the constitutional crisis with Great Britain these 'baubles' were gradually and powerfully incorporated into a general moral critique of colonial society. . . ." See Breen, "Baubles of Britain," p. 88.

63. In literary studies of eighteenth-century British culture, this scholarship on consumption takes up the issue of gender. Recently, for example, Charlotte Sussman has argued that antislavery writing's campaign against consumption of West Indian commodities—particularly sugar—reflected the ideological desire to purify feminized, domestic space. If this antislavery discourse of consumption obsessed on the female body as the site of potential contamination, the antislavery movement just as readily enabled women to theorize the domestic as the political. "Thus, the British antislavery movement of the 1790s, while it struggled to force a social recognition of the humanity of cultural others, also worked to renegotiate British cultural identities and gender roles." See Sussman, *Consuming Anxieties: Consumer Protest, Gender, and British Slavery, 1713–1833* (Stanford: Stanford University Press, 2000), p. 129. My discussion below concerns the effect that changing ideologies about habits of consumption had on the representation of Africans themselves.

64. Anon., "The Negro Trade," *American Museum* (Philadelphia: Carey, 1787), p. 46. Cf. Priestley: "But no less are we guilty ourselves, who, in order to have our sugars, and other West-Indian commodities, a little cheaper (though this will be found to be a mistake) connive at, and encourage, these iniquitous proceedings. It is not therefore the *abuse* of the trade but the *trade itself,* that must be abolished." Priestley, *Sermon,* p. 11.

65. Abbé Raynal summarized the problem: "This punishment [of slavery] in process of time, has been inflicted for the most trivial of offenses. . . . Injustice hath known no bounds or restraints. At a great distance from the coast there are chiefs, who give orders for every thing they meet with in the villages around them to be carried off. The children are throw'n into sacks: the men and women are gagged to stifle the cries." See Raynal, *A Philosophical and Political History of the Settlements,* vol. 5, pp. 221–222.

66. Levi Hart, *Liberty Described and Recommended; in a Sermon Preached to the Corporation of Freemen* (Hartford: Eben Watson, 1775), p. 17. John Newton's antislavery spiritual autobiography noted that slave women and girls "naked, trembling, terrified . . . are often exposed to the wanton rudeness of white savages." See Newton, *Thoughts Upon the Slave Trade* (London: J. Buckland, 1788), p. 105.

67. Samuel Hopkins, *A Dialogue Concerning the Slavery of the Africans; Shewing it to be the Duty and Interest of the American Colonies to Emancipate all their African Slaves* (Norwich: Judah P. Spooner, 1776), pp. 7–8. Scholarship about eighteenth-century evangelicals like the New Divinity minister Hopkins tends to emphasize their denunciations of "luxury" and "wordliness" as simply anticapitalist

expressions of evangelical piety. Hopkins's move to Newport's First Congregational Church in 1770 of course landed him in the throes of a commercial society founded largely on the African slave trade. My argument, however, qualifies the critical opposition between capitalism and evangelical piety and instead emphasizes the one between "virtuous" and "barbaric" forms of commerce. See Joseph Conforti, *Samuel Hopkins and the New Divinity Movement: Calvinism, the Congregational Ministry, and Reform in New England Between the Great Awakenings* (Grand Rapids: Christian University Press, 1981); and James D. Essig, *The Bonds of Wickedness: American Evangelicals Against Slavery, 1770–1808* (Philadelphia: Temple University Press, 1982).

68. Abbé Gregoire, *On the Cultural Achievement of Negroes*, trans. Thomas Cassirer and Jean-Francois Briere (Amherst: University of Massachusetts Press, 1996), p. 115.

69. William Fox, *An Address to the People of Great Britain, on the Propriety of Obtaining from West India Sugar and Rum* (Philadelphia: Daniel Lawrence, 1792), pp. 11, 4.

70. James Beattie, *Elements of Moral Science,* vol. 2 (Edinburgh: T. Caddell and William Creech, 1793), p. 173.

71. Anthony Benezet, "Notes on the Slave Trade" in *The Plainness and Innocent Simplicity of the Christian Religion. With its Salutary Effects, Compared to the Corrupting Nature and Dreadful Effects of War* (Philadelphia: Joseph Crukshank, 1783), p. 7. Cf. Clarkson: "Immortal Alfred! Father of our invaluable constitution! Parent of the civil blessings we enjoy! . . . How much does nature approve thy laws, as consistent with her own feelings, while she absolutely turns pale, trembles, and recoils at the institutions of these *receivers!* Execrable men! Sleep then you *receivers,* if you can, while you scarcely allow these unfortunate people to rest at all!" Clarkson, *Slavery and Commerce,* pp. 154–155.

72. Joanne Melish has argued that in pre-Revolutionary New England, all attempts to regulate the slave trade deferred the issue of a free African American population "safely in the hazy future": "By proposing restrictions on the importation of Africans as a commodity, antislavery protesters tacitly accepted and naturalized their commodity status." See Melish, *Disowning Slavery: Gradual Emancipation and "Race" in New England, 1780–1860* (Ithaca: Cornell University Press, 1998), p. 53.

73. *The Writings of Thomas Paine, vol 1: 1774–1779,* ed. Moncure Conway (New York: Franklin), pp. 4–5.

74. Raynal, *Philosophical History,* vol. 5, p. 226.

75. *American Museum* (Philadelphia: Carey, 1790), pp. 332–333.

76. Montesquieu, *Spirit of the Laws,* p. 345. As James Kloppenberg comments, "Liberals . . . conceived of freedom . . . not as license but as enlightened self-interest . . . Exercising liberal freedom requires the disposition to find one's true good and to choose the proper means to it, which is the meaning of prudence." Kloppenberg, *The Virtues of Liberalism* (New York: Oxford University Press, 1998), p. 5.

77. Ramsay, *Treatment and Conversion*, pp. 64–65.
78. William Bell Crafton, *A Short Sketch of the Evidence Delivered before a Committee of the House of Commons for the Abolition of the Slave Trade* (London: M. Gurney, 1792), p. 18.
79. William Ellford, the chairman of the Plymouth chapter of the English Antislavery Society, produced the initial version of the famous print depicting the cramped conditions of the typical slave vessel. Clarkson, along with the antislavery publisher James Phillips and others, reworked it and applied it to the *Brookes*. For background to its publication, see Ellen Gibson Wilson, *Thomas Clarkson: A Biography* (New York: St. Martin's, 1990), pp. 47–50.
80. Newton, *Thoughts*, p. 110.
81. *American Museum* (Philadelphia: Carey, 1789), p. 429.
82. The Act limited the slaves-per-tonnage ratio, required the presence of surgeons on board slave traders, and even offered financial incentives to ship captains to curtail mortality rates. See Hugh Thomas, *The Slave Trade: The Story of the Atlantic Slave Trade, 1440–1870* (New York: Simon and Schuster, 1997), pp. 508–510.
83. The language of Parliamentary debate during this era resonates in much the same way: "Now if it be considered that the ship Brookes is 320 tons, and that she is allowed to carry by Act of Parliament *four hundred and fifty-four persons*, it is evident that if three more could be wedged among the number represented in the plan, this plan would contain precisely the number which the Act directs; and if it should be further considered that there ought to be in each apartment in the plan one or more tubs, as well as stanchions to support the platforms and decks, for which no deduction has been made, in order to give every possible advantage in stowing, then the above plan may be considered as giving a very favourable representation of the Negroes *even since the late regulating Act*." See *An Abstract of the Evidence Delivered Before a Select Committee of the House of Commons in the Years 1790 and 1791; on the Part of the Petitioners for the Abolition of the Slave-Trade* (London: J. Phillips, 1791), p. 38.
84. As Karen Weyler has argued, early American novelists employed the language of speculation in order "to isolate gambling as a seductive obsession, as a practice separate from virtuous trade." See Weyler, "'A Speculating Spirit': Trade, Speculation, and Gambling in Early American Fiction," *Early American Literature* 31 (1996), p. 217. My argument about gambling provides an earlier historical instance of its use as a cultural metaphor legitimating capitalism, which, as Ann Fabian has so ably argued, characterized nineteenth-century American culture. See Fabian, *Card Sharps and Bucket Shops: Gambling in Nineteenth-Century America* (Ithaca: Cornell University Press, 1990).
85. Langford, *A Polite and Commercial People*, p. 572.
86. Lord Sheffield, *Observations on the Project for Abolishing the Slave Trade, and on the Reasonableness of Attempting Some Practicable Mode of Relieving the Negroes* (London: J. Cooper, 1791), pp. 20–21.
87. Raynal, *Philosophical History*, vol. 8, p. 198.
88. Clarkson, *Impolicy*, p. 26.

89. On the state level it worked politically as well. Responding to the Virginia jurist St. George Tucker's specific queries about the history of slavery and emancipation in Massachusetts, Jeremy Belknap commented rather on Rhode Island's extensive involvement in the slave trade: "A few only of our [Massachusetts] merchants were engaged in this kind of traffick. It required a large capital, and was considered as peculiarly hazardous, though gainful. See Belknap, "Queries Respecting the Slavery and Emancipation of Negroes in Massachusetts, Proposed by the Hon. Judge Tucker of Virginia, and Answered by the Rev. Dr. Belknap," in *Collections of the Massachusetts Historical Society,* vol. 4 (Boston, 1795) p. 197.

90. Mifflin, *A Serious Expostulation, p. 5.*

91. Mary Louise Pratt, *Imperial Eyes: Travel Writing and Transculturation* (London: Routledge, 1992), pp. 69–72. Her discussion focuses in large part on Mungo Park's *Travels in the Interior Districts of Africa* (1799) in which "expansionist commercial aspirations idealize themselves into a drama of reciprocity. Negotiating his way across Africa, Park is the picture of the entrepreneur. Yet the decidedly non-reciprocal momentum of European capitalism can scarcely be discerned in his lone and long-suffering figure, no matter how long you (the reader or the Africans) stare at him. Trade he does, but *never for profit,*" p. 81.

92. James Dana, "The African Slave Trade," in Sandoz, *Political Sermons,* p. 1049.

93. Jedidiah Morse, *A Discourse Delivered at the African Meeting House, in Boston, July 14, 1808, in Grateful Celebration of the Abolition of the African Slave Trade by the Governments of the United States, Great Britain, and Denmark* (Boston: Lincoln and Edmunds, 1808), p. 19.

94. Swan, *Disuasion,* pp. 45–46, 49–50, and 57–60.

95. As Samuel Hopkins imagined the value of black expatriation to Africa to spread the Word, his images of evangelical and commercial empires become entangled: "And such a settlement in Africa, properly conducted and supported, might be greatly beneficial to the commercial interest both of this nation and of those in Africa, and, in the end, produce a temporal good and prosperity, which might, as far as is now practicable, atone for the evils of the slave trade and slavery." See Hopkins, *A Discourse Upon the Slave Trade of the Africans,* in *Timely Articles on Slavery* (Boston: Congregational Board of Publication, 1854), p. 609. Kant's commentary occurs in his geographical writings: "The number of names of countries and towns on the map of Africa is quite considerable. . . . The reason that the interior of Africa is so unknown to us, as if they were countries of the moon, lies far more with us Europeans than with the Africans, in that we have made ourselves suspects through the slave trade. The coast of Africa is, in fact, visited by Europeans; but these journeys are very violent because Europeans carry away each year between 60,000 and 80,000 Negroes to America." *See Race and the Enlightenment,* ed. Emmanuel Chukwudi Eze (Cambridge, Mass.: Blackwell, 1997), p. 59.

96. See *A Collection of Voyages and Travels, Some Now First Printed from Original Manuscripts. Others Translated out of Foreign Languages. . . .* (London: Awnsham and

John Churchill, 1704); and *A New General Collection of Voyages and Travels: Consisting of the Most Esteemed Relations, Which Have Been Hitherto Published in any Language: Comprehending Every Thing Remarkable in its Kind, in Europe, Africa, and America,* 4 vols. (London: Thomas Astley, 1745–1747). These include such writers as Jean Barbot, William Bosman, Adam Brue, Francis Moore, and Thomas Phillips. For their varying accounts of Africa, see P. J. Marshall and Glyndwr Williams, *The Great Map of Mankind: Perceptions of New Worlds in the Age of Enlightenment* (Cambridge, Mass.: Harvard University Press, 1982), pp. 227–257.

97. See Roxann Wheeler, *The Complexion of Race: Categories of Difference in Eighteenth-Century British Culture* (Philadelphia: University of Pennsylvania Press, 2000), pp. 235–237. My argument differs from Wheeler's in that she sees the solidification of racial ideology occurring in the 1770s. The antislavery writings that I cite from the 1780s and 1790s continue to demonstrate significant tensions between race and culture, especially regarding the present state of Africa.

98. Priestley, *Sermon,* p. 26.

99. Clarkson, *Impolicy of the Slave Trade,* p. 115.

2. The Poetics of Antislavery

1. David Humphreys, *A Poem on Industry: Addressed to the Citizens of the United States of America* (Philadelphia: Mathew Carey, 1794), p. 12. The poem appears in various revised versions and is included (in expanded form) in *The Miscellaneous Works of David Humphreys* (1804; Gainesville, Fla.: Scholars' Facsimiles, 1968).

2. My understanding of eighteenth-century antislavery poetry resembles Suvir Kaul's—both of us emphasize the moral and ideological pressures the African slave trade placed on the health of the British empire. Kaul focuses on the primacy of the British nation, partly because he believes "most of the proponents of U.S. independence had no qualms about slaveholding or slavery per se." I offer comparative readings of British and American poets in order to locate transatlantic contexts for the "the world of antislavery poetry." This does not necessarily undermine his argument about "enlightened nationalism," but it does provide a larger lens for thinking about national ideologies. See Kaul, *Poems of Nation, Anthems of Empire: English Verse in the Long Eighteenth Century* (Charlottesville: University Press of Virginia, 2000), pp. 230–268.

3. Humphreys, *A Poem on Industry,* p. 11.

4. "Literature about the black was unabashedly propagandistic, often making effective use of melodrama." Mukhtar Ali Isani, "Far from 'Gambia's Golden Shore': The Black in Late Eighteenth-Century American Imaginative Literature," *William and Mary Quarterly,* 3rd ser. 36 (1979), p. 359. The argument against antislavery solipsism derives largely from Winthrop D. Jordan's *White Over Black: American Attitudes Toward the Negro, 1550–1812* (Chapel Hill: University of North Carolina Press, 1968). The traditional critical assessment of British poetry is quite similar. Long ago, Wylie Sypher dismissed British antislavery

poetry as "false in the worst sense of the word—not alone in its inane phrase-
ology, but in its heedlessness of the truth with which it purported to deal." See
Sypher, *Guinea's Captive Kings: British Anti-Slavery Literature of the Eighteenth Century* (Chapel Hill: University of North Carolina Press, 1942), p. 156. David
Dabydeen has observed that antislavery writers were faced with the problem
of "how to reconcile their belief in the civilizing effects of commerce to the barbaric realities of the slave trade." But he also critiques antislavery literature for
an "evasiveness" that supposedly preserved the sanctity of the British commercial empire. I argue that this literature formulates the very nature of this commercial empire. See Dabydeen, "Eighteenth Century English Literature on
Commerce and Slavery," in *The Black Presence in English Literature,* ed.
Dabydeen (Manchester: Manchester University Press, 1985), p. 32.

5. Markman Ellis, *The Politics of Sensibility: Race, Gender and Commerce in the Sentimental Novel* (Cambridge: Cambridge University Press, 1996), p. 86. See also
pp. 65–66, 126–127.

6. Julie Ellison, *Cato's Tears and the Making of Anglo-American Emotion* (Chicago:
University of Chicago Press, 1999), pp. 97–98. In a similar vein, Alan Richardson comments: "It seems evident that the literary discourses we group together
for convenience under the banner of 'Romanticism,' particularly in their mutually reinforcing naturalizing and nationalizing tendencies and their 'passion
for ethnicity,' helped to precipitate the emergence of modern racism." See
Richardson, "Darkness Visible? Race and Representation in Bristol Abolitionist
Poetry, 1770–1810," in *Romanticism and Colonialism: Writing and Empire 1780–
1830,* eds. Tim Fulford and Peter J. Kitson (Cambridge: Cambridge University
Press, 1998), p. 146.

7. Peter J. Kitson, "Races, Places, People, 1785–1800," in *Romanticism and Colonialism, p. 18.*

8. Abraham Booth, *Commerce in the Human Species, and the Enslaving of Innocent Persons, Inimical to the Laws of Moses, and the Gospel of Christ* (London, 1792), p. 30.

9. For analysis of the amorphous meaning of "race" in the classical and early
modern eras, see Ivan Hannaford, *Race: The History of an Idea in the West* (Baltimore: Johns Hopkins University Press, 1996). He argues, for example, that
"there is very little evidence of a conscious idea of race until after the Reformation," p. 187. As Nicholas Hudson has argued, the semantic transformation
from "nation" to "race" during the eighteenth century entailed the conceptual
distinction between "natural" and "cultural" characteristics that one finds, for
example, in David Hume's "Of National Characters" (1748). See Hudson,
"From 'Nation' to 'Race': The Origins of Racial Classification in Eighteenth-
Century Thought," *Eighteenth-Century Studies* 29 (1996), pp. 247–264. In *The
Complexion of Race: Categories of Difference in Eighteenth-Century British Culture*
(Philadelphia: University of Pennsylvania Press, 2000), Roxann Wheeler offers
a thorough account of the relation between racial and cultural ideologies in
eighteenth-century Britain. She argues that "race" was inseparable from trade,
manners, and Christianity. For European ideological backgrounds to racial the-

ory, see also Londa Schiebinger, "The Anatomy of Difference: Race and Sex in Eighteenth-Century Science," *Eighteenth-Century Studies* 23 (1990), pp. 387–405. For a view of race that differs from the one I offer in this chapter, see Wilfred D. Samuels, "Review Essay: Enlightened Black Voices: Witnesses and Participants," *Eighteenth-Century Studies* 31 (1997–98), pp. 239–246.

10. As Thomas Krise notes, however, the author's racial identity is disputed. See *Caribbeana: An Anthology of English Literature of the West Indies, 1657–1777*, ed. Krise (Chicago: University of Chicago Press, 1999), pp. 104–105.

11. Another instance of this occurs, for example, in Philip Freneau's "Stanzas Written at the Foot of Mount Souffriere, near the Town of Basseterre, Guadeloupe" (1787). In the last stanza Freneau cautiously imagines the region's hopeful future: "Ascending here, may this warm sun / With freedom's beams, divinely clear, / Throughout the world his circuit run / Till these dark scenes shall disappear, / And a new race, not bought or sold, / Springs from the ashes of the old." The poem appeared (untitled) in *Bailey's Pocket Almanack for 1787*.

12. On one side of these debates were "monogenists," who embraced the traditional biblical version of the single creation of mankind, and on the other were "polygenists," including such figures as Thomas Jefferson, Lord Kames, and David Hume, who self-consciously relied on "scientific" evidence supporting the hierarchy of human species. Anthony Barker claims that during the late eighteenth century the polygenist argument was still in such a minority that proslavery writing generally avoided justifying slavery on the basis of racial inferiority. See Barker, *The African Link: British Attitudes to the Negro in the Era of the Atlantic Slave Trade, 1550–1807* (London: Frank Cass, 1978), pp. 41–58, 157–178. It is worth noting as well that even though antislavery polemics emphasized the importance of both universal humanity and environmental causes for racial differences, it, too, assumed its own version of cultural, if not racial, hierarchy based on the historical model of "progress" in which every society passed through the stages of hunting, pastoralism, agriculture, and commerce.

13. See Wheeler, *The Complexion of Race*, pp. 235–260.

14. William Dickson, *Letters on Slavery* (London: J. Phillips, 1789), Letter 8.

15. Jonathan Edwards, Jr., *The Injustice and Impolicy of the Slave Trade, and of the Slavery of the Africans: Illustrated in a Sermon Preached Before the Connecticut Society for the Promotion of Freedom, and for the Relief of Persons Unlawfully Holden in Bondage, at Their Annual Meeting in New Haven, September 15, 1791* (Boston: Lilly and Wells, 1822), p. 4. As Booth put it in 1792, "Nor, other things being equal, is there the least reason for us to imagine, that the white skin of a European would afford any more protection against a violent seizure, than does the black skin of an African," p. 24.

16. Thomas Clarkson, *An Essay on the Slavery and Commerce of the Human Species, Particularly the African* (London: J. Phillips, 1786), pp. 189–190. His argument derives from John Mitchell's *An Essay on the Causes of the Different Colours of People in Different Climates* (London, 1744).

17. James Ramsay, *An Essay on the Treatment and Conversion of African Slaves* (London: James Phillips, 1784), p. 235. As Foucault has argued, "In the seventeenth and eighteenth centuries, the peculiar existence and ancient solidity of language as a thing inscribed in the fabric of the world were dissolved in the functioning of representation: all language had value only as discourse." Michel Foucault, *The Order of Things: An Archeology of the Human Sciences* (New York: Vintage, 1994), p. 43.

18. Paul Gilroy, *The Black Atlantic: Modernity and Double Consciousness* (Cambridge, Mass.: Harvard University Press, 1993), p. 9. More recently, he has argued for a "non-racial" humanism as an ideological alternative to that which developed out of the Enlightenment. See Gilroy, *Against Race: Imagining Political Culture Beyond the Color Line* (Cambridge, Mass.: Harvard University Press, 2001).

19. Lawrence E. Klein, "Politeness for Plebes: Consumption and Social Identity in Early Eighteenth-Century England," in *The Consumption of Culture, 1600–1800: Image, Object, Text,* eds. Ann Bermingham and John Brewer (London: Routledge, 1995), p. 365.

20. Jared Gardner has argued that in post-Revolutionary America the discourse of race helped to anchor (and whiten) an emerging national identity, but I contend that the instability of "race" at times just as easily disrupted it. See Gardner, *Master Plots: Race and the Founding of an American Literature, 1787–1845* (Baltimore: Johns Hopkins University Press, 1998), pp. 1–24.

21. Karen Halttunen, "Humanitarianism and the Pornography of Pain in Anglo-American Culture," *American Historical Review* 101 (1995), p. 309.

22. Joseph Priestley, *A Sermon on the Subject of the Slave Trade* (Birmingham: Pearson and Rollason, 1788), p. 7.

23. Levi Hart, *Liberty Described and Recommended; in a Sermon Preached to the Corporation of Freemen, at Their Meeting on Tuesday, September 20, 1774* (Hartford: Eben, Watson, 1775). It is collected in *American Political Writing During the Revolutionary Era, 1760–1805,* vol. 1, eds. Charles Hyneman and Donald Lutz (Indianapolis: Liberty, 1983), p. 314.

24. Noah Webster, *Effects of Slavery on Morals and Industry* (Hartford: Hudson and Goodwin, 1793), p. 18.

25. John Newton, *Thoughts Upon the African Slave Trade* (London: J. Buckland, 1788), p. 104.

26. William Belsham, *An Essay on the African Slave Trade* (Philadelphia: Daniel Humphreys, 1790), p. 15.

27. Thomas [Robert Treat] Paine, "The Nature and Progress of Liberty," *The American Apollo* 1 (1792), p. 345. The footnote reads "*Vide Revelation,* xviii, 13."

28. Thomas Morris, *Quashy, or The Coal-Black Maid* (Philadelphia: James Humphreys, 1797), ll. 161–168.

29. Edwards denounced slavery but recognized its inevitability. For the colonial and metropolitan phases of Edwards's career, as well as his gradual embrace of West Indian slavery, see David Brion Davis, *The Problem of Slavery in the Age of Revolution, 1770–1823* (Ithaca: Cornell University Press, 1975), pp. 185–190.

30. Bryan Edwards, *Poems Written Chiefly in the West Indies* (Kingston, Jamaica: Alexander Aikman, 1792), p. 47.

31. They produced work that was patronized or heavily influenced by the newly formed English Abolition Society (1787). More was associated with the English evangelicals, under William Wilberforce, known as the Clapham Sect, and the Abolition Society solicited her poem "Slavery" (alternatively titled "The Slave Trade"), as a way of swaying members of Parliament against the trade. When Parliament failed to do so in the early 1790s, Barbauld wrote the "Epistle to William Wilberforce" as an open critique of its moral cowardice.

32. Moira Ferguson has argued that "what was new in both prose and poetry, starting in the late 1670s, and continuing through the eighteenth-century, was colonial slavery as a specific referent applied to the circumstances of contemporary British women." See Ferguson, *Subject to Others: British Women Writers and Colonial Slavery, 1670–1834* (London: Routledge, 1992), p. 23. For her discussion of More, see pp. 146–154.

33. Yearsley's own struggles with poverty intensified her awareness of the severity of modern capitalism. The story of her family's near-starvation before their eventual rescue gave her poetry iconic stature, though she soon publicly rejected her literary patrons, More and Elizabeth Montagu, over financial control of the trust established for her. Critics rightly emphasize this conflict as the register for the "ideological contradictions" between bourgeois and working-class values in her work. See Donna Landry, *The Muses of Resistance: Laboring-Class Women's Poetry in Britain, 1739–96* (New York: Cambridge University Press, 1990). Both Landry and Ferguson read *A Poem on the Inhumanity of the Slave Trade* (1788) as an example of her civic imagination in which Christian benevolence ideally will purify cities like Bristol. See Moira Ferguson, *Eighteenth-Century Women Poets: Nation, Class, Gender* (Albany: State University of New York Press, 1995).

34. For Coleridge in this context, see Joan Baum, *Mind-Forg'd Manacles: Slavery and the English Romantic Poets* (North Haven, Conn.: Archon, 1994), pp. 16–17.

35. Ann Yearsley, *A Poem on the Inhumanity of the Slave Trade. Humbly Inscribed to the Right Honourable and Right Reverend Frederick, Earl of Bristol, Bishop of Derry* (London: G. G. and J. Robinson, 1788), pp. 1–2.

36. Seymour Drescher, *Capitalism and Antislavery: British Mobilization in Comparative Perspective* (New York: Oxford University Press, 1987), pp. 1–24.

37. Until recently, Barbauld's work has been read as sentimentalized. In *A Vindication of the Rights of Woman*, Mary Wollstonecraft, for example, lampooned her as the epitome of female mawkishness. Critics now see Barbauld as a more serious social and religious critic associated with the Warrington Academy, one of the strongholds of English Dissent. See Daniel E. White, "The 'Joineriana': Anna Barbauld, the Aikin Family Circle, and the Dissenting Public Sphere," *Eighteenth-Century Studies* 32 (1999), pp. 511–533, and William Keach, "Barbauld, Romanticism, and the Survival of Dissent," *Essays and Studies* 51 (1998), pp. 44–61.

38. *The Poems of Anna Letitia Barbauld,* eds. William McCarthy and Elizabeth Kraft (Athens: University of Georgia Press, 1994), pp. 114–118, ll. 27, 29. Further citations appear parenthetically in the text.

39. Kaul, *Poems of Nation,* p. 263.

40. Ellison argues that "Barbauld replaces the conventions of sensibility, which rely on vicarious emotion to induce pity, with the threat of contagious corruption. . . . This process of role reversal or poetic justice [where the English become slaves to vice] seems to abandon moral judgment to the impersonal reflexes of economic logic." I contend, rather, that "economic logic" itself is premised on sentimentalized "moral judgment" about the very nature of trade and English manners in the slave-holding West Indies. See *Cato's Tears,* p. 110.

41. See Laura Brown, *The Ends of Empire: Women and Ideology in Early Eighteenth-Century English Literature* (Ithaca: Cornell University Press, 1993) and Deidre Lynch, *The Economy of Character: Novels, Market Culture, and the Business of Inner Meaning* (Chicago: University of Chicago Press, 1998).

42. James Montgomery, *The West Indies,* in *Poems on the Abolition of the Slave Trade* (London: R. Bowyer, 1809), part III, ll. 222–223.

43. Philip Freneau, *Poems Written and Published During the Revolutionary War, and now Republished from the Original Manuscripts,* vol. 2 (Philadelphia: Lydia R. Bailey, 1809), pp. 192–193.

44. Dwight condemns slavery in general but offers a rather attenuating image of it in Connecticut: "He toils, 'tis true; but shares his master's toil; / With him, he feeds the herd, and trims the soil; / Helps to sustain the house, with clothes, and food, / And takes his portion of the common good." See Timothy Dwight, *Greenfield Hill: A Poem in Seven Parts* (New York: Childs and Swaine, 1794), ll. 209–212.

45. Many critics recognize the ambivalence with which writers from Behn onwards viewed the noble African. See, for example, Mary Louise Pratt, "Scratches on the Face of the Country," in *Race, Writing and Difference,* ed. Henry Louis Gates, Jr. (Chicago: University of Chicago Press, 1986), and Richardson, "Darkness Visible?" in *Romanticism and Colonialism,* eds. Fulford and Kitson. Markman Ellis discusses the dramatizations of *Oroonoko* by Thomas Southerne and others, who appropriated the story to fulfill the conventions of "courtly romantic love" to show the "essential humanity in the African slave." The "paradoxical trope of the noble slave" combines egalitarian and hierarchical meanings. See Ellis, *The Politics of Sensibility,* pp. 120–121.

46. Washington Irving praises Roscoe in *The Sketch Book* (1819–20) as the rare example of someone able to maintain an aesthetic sensibility while "going forth into the highways and thoroughfares of life." Recent appraisals of Roscoe's importance focus on his cosmopolitan vision that aimed to disentangle English culture from the influence of the Anglican Church. His embodiment of "high-bourgeois liberalism and low-bourgeois sentimentality" might be applied not only to his famous *Life of Lorenzo de Medici* and *Life and Pontificate of Leo X,* but to his antislavery writing as well. See Nanora Sweet, "'Lorenzo's' Liverpool and

'Corinne's' Coppet: The Italianate Salon and Romantic Education," in *Lessons of Romanticism: A Critical Companion,* eds. Thomas Pfau and Robert F. Gleckner (Durham: Duke University Press, 1998), p. 252.

47. William Roscoe, *A General View of the African Slave Trade, Demonstrating its Injustice and Impolicy: With Hints Towards a Bill for its Abolition* (London: R. Faulder, 1788), p. 20.

48. William Roscoe, *The Wrongs of Africa: a Poem.* Part the First (Philadelphia: Joseph James, 1788), p. iv. Roscoe's collaborator, Dr. James Currie, wrote the preface. See Sypher, *Guinea's Captive Kings,* pp. 181–182. Further citations to the poem appear parenthetically in the text.

49. Shaftesbury theorized manners much in the same way earlier in the century. Compare as well Hannah More's complaint that "It is, perhaps, one of the most alarming symptoms of the degeneracy of morals in the present day, that the distinctions of right and wrong are almost swept away in polite conversation." See A. A. Cooper, Earl of Shaftesbury, *Thoughts on the Importance of the Manners of the Great to General Society,* 12th American ed. (Wilmington, Del.: William Pryce, 1805), p. 54.

50. Cf. Freneau's "The Beauties of Santa Cruz," in which the African slave recalls his homeland: "And view soft seats of ease and fancied rest, / Their native groves new painted on the eye, / Where no proud misers their gay hours molest / No lordly despots pass, unsocial, by." *Early American Poetry,* ed. Jane Donahue Eberwein (Madison: University Of Wisconsin Press, 1978), pp. 206–221, ll. 289–292.

51. David Shields has noted how Singleton provided a "representational program" for later antislavery poets, which humanized the slave by calling for the reader's imaginative projection of his suffering. See Shields, *Oracles of Empire: Poetry, Politics, and Commerce in British America, 1690–1750* (Chicago: University of Chicago Press, 1990), p. 82.

52. John Singleton, *A General Description of the West-Indian Islands, as far as Relates to the British, Dutch, and Danish Governments, from Barbados to Saint Croix* (Barbados: George Esmand and William Walker, 1767), II, ll. 40–52. Further citations appear parenthetically, and by line numbers, in the text.

53. Long ago, Sypher argued that More combined "the enlightened theme of the equality of man with the benevolistic, Hutchesonian theme that all men are equal because *all men feel.*" See Sypher, *Guinea's Captive Kings,* p. 194. Recent readings emphasize More's association of Africa with moral "blackness": "More's verses . . . evoke tendencies within Romantic rhetoric . . . in their intensification of the trope of 'African savagery' and their insistent connection between 'darkness' or blackness and 'rude,' 'luxuriant,' African 'energy,' the 'wild vigour of a savage root.'" Richardson, "Darkness Visible?," p. 138.

54. Hannah More, *Slavery, a Poem* (London: T. Caddell, 1788), ll. 117–118. Further citations appear parenthetically in the text.

55. Elizabeth Kowaleski-Wallace has noted that the poem initially associates "Mad Liberty" with "an inhuman savagery that must become subject to human con-

trol and domination." See Kowaleski-Wallace, *Their Father's Daughters: Hannah More, Maria Edgeworth, and Patriarchal Complicity* (New York: Oxford University Press, 1991), p. 36. See also Davis, *Problem of Slavery in the Age of Revolution,* pp. 246–248.

56. As one recent critic of this period's language of race has put it, "there is room, I think, to speak of the Enlightenment as a historical period that provided for its various writers identifiable scientific and philosophical vocabulary: 'race,' 'progress,' 'civilization,' 'savagery' . . . This vocabulary belongs to, and reveals, a larger world of analytical categories that exists as a universe of discourse, an intellectual worldview." See the Introduction to *Race and the Enlightenment: A Reader,* ed. Emmanuel Chukwudi Eze (London: Blackwell, 1997), p. 7.

57. Recall that Malachy Postlethwayt and others argued that "ancient Britons" differed little from black Africans, or that Noah Webster, to take another example, claimed that the ancient Romans were no more "barbarous" than white slave masters: "But were the Romans more cruel by nature than modern nations? Were they more savage in their tempers than the lordly despots of the present age, who are accustomed to tyrannize over slaves?" See Webster, *Effects of Slavery on Morals and Industry,* p. 19.

58. Abdul JanMohamed, for example, has argued for the "manichean allegory" of "moral and even metaphysical difference" that juxtaposes "white and black, good and evil, superiority and inferiority, civilization and savagery, intelligence and emotion, rationality and sensuality, self and Other, subject and object." See JanMohamed, "The Economy of Manichean Allegory: The Function of Racial Difference in Colonialist Literature," in *Race, Writing and Difference,* ed. Gates, Jr., p. 82. To JanMohamed, colonialist texts are characterized by "imaginary" and "symbolic" forms: "This adamant refusal to admit the possibility of syncretism, of a rapproachement between self and Other, is the most important factor distinguishing the 'imaginary' from the 'symbolic' colonialist text. The 'symbolic' text's openness toward the Other is based on a greater awareness of *potential* identity . . . between self and Other," pp. 92–93.

59. The argument about American Revolutionary racial identification derives largely from Bernard Bailyn, who, in the 1960s, argued for the "paradox" of the American Revolution: "The identification between the cause of the colonies and the cause of the Negroes bound in chattel slavery—an identification built into the very language of politics—became inescapable." See *The Ideological Origins of the American Revolution* (Cambridge, Mass.: Harvard University Press, 1968), p. 235. For a revision of this argument, see A. Nwabueze Okoye, "Chattel Slavery as the Nightmare of the American Revolutionaries," *William and Mary Quarterly,* 3rd ser. 37 (1980), pp. 5–28. Recent commentators have argued that the "metaphorization of slavery in Revolutionary discourse" paradoxically trivialized slavery while heightening whites' sympathetic identification with blacks. See Jay Fliegelman, *Declaring Independence: Jefferson, Natural Language and the Culture of Performance* (Stanford: Stanford University Press, 1993), pp. 141–142. I recognize that the paradox of American republicanism

and African slavery was a major motif of American antislavery writing—David Cooper's *A Serious Address to the Rulers of America* (1783) is a good example of it—but argue below that Anglo-American ideas about the slave trade form another context for reading the language of antislavery poetry. For a psychosexual narrative of Revolutionary racism, see John Saillant, "The Black Body Erotic and the Republican Body Politic, 1790–1820," *Journal of the History of Sexuality* 5 (1995).

60. Cowper's letters consistently show his aesthetic preoccupation with slavery, "a theme so important at the present juncture, and at the same time so susceptible of poetical management." Critics note his private ambivalence over the aesthetic potential of antislavery, since Cowper later commented on the slave trade "as a subject for Song [that] did not strike me much." And "a theme which never pleased me, but which in the hope of doing [the "tortured Negroes] some little service, I was not unwilling to handle." See *The Letters and Prose Writings of William Cowper,* vol. 3, eds. James King and Charles Ryskamp (Oxford: Clarendon, 1982), pp. 103, 137–138, and Davis, *Problem of Slavery in the Age of Revolution,* p. 369.

61. See Cowper, *Letters and Prose Writings,* p. 103.

62. *Cowper: Verse and Letters,* ed. Brian Spiller (Cambridge, Mass.: Harvard University Press, 1968), pp. 281, 283.

63. Davis reads this poem as part of antislavery's "ambiguous attitudes toward liberty and authority," a reading that relies on the African as the projected site of Europeans' "primitivistic fantasies" about natural liberty. See Davis, *The Problem of Slavery in the Age of Revolution,* pp. 370, 372.

64. See Henry Louis Gates, Jr., *Figures in Black: Words, Signs, and the "Racial" Self* (New York: Oxford University Press, 1986), pp. 61–79. Traditional critics cite Wheatley's racial self-abnegation and literary indebtedness to English neoclassical poets like Pope and Dryden. Recent scholars, however, see her simultaneously inside and outside white cultural and literary forms, working subversively within them to critique the subjects of race and slavery. Rafia Zafar, for example, has argued that the poem is representative not only of the complexity of Wheatley's language but of the changing critical disposition towards her work. Borrowing from Mae Henderson's sense that African American maintain multiple subject positions simultaneously, Zafar's belief in Wheatley's "literary masking," "rhetorical subterfuge," and "multivalence" is in keeping with the recent movement in Wheatley criticism to acknowledge her work's radical potential. See Zafar, *We Wear the Mask: African Americans write American Literature, 1760–1870* (New York: Columbia University Press, 1997), pp. 16–17. For Wheatley's manipulation of biblical rhetoric see Landry, *The Muses of Resistance,* Sondra O'Neale, "A Slave's Subtle War: Phillis Wheatley's Use of Biblical Myth and Symbol," *Early American Literature* 21 (1986), pp. 144–165, and James Levernier, "Phillis Wheatley and the New England Clergy," *Early American Literature* 26 (1991), pp. 21–38. For her handling of neoclassical conventions to produce a syncretically African and American identity, see Paula Bennet,

"Phillis Wheatley's Vocation and the Paradox of the 'Afric Muse,'" *PMLA* 113 (1998), pp. 64–76.

65. See Philip Richards, "Phillis Wheatley and Literary Americanization," *American Quarterly* 44 (1992), pp. 163–91, and Betsy Erkkila, "Phillis Wheatley and the Black American Revolution," in *A Mixed Race: Ethnicity in Early America,* ed. Frank Shuffelton (New York: Oxford University Press, 1993). As Helen Burke has put it, Wheatley's work shows "her remarkable degree of success . . . in establishing herself as a subject in American cultural discourse." See Burke, "The Rhetoric and Politics of Marginality: The Subject of Phillis Wheatley," *Tulsa Studies in Women's Literature* 10 (1991), p. 33.

66. For Wheatley's ambivalence to antislavery culture in general, see David Grimsted, "Anglo-American Racism and Phillis Wheatley's 'Sable Veil,' 'Length'ned Chain,' and 'Knitted Heart,'" in *Women in the Age of the American Revolution,* eds. Ronald Hoffman, Peter Albert, and Linda Kerber (Charlottesville: University Press of Virginia, 1989), pp. 338–444.

67. Jupiter Hammon, "An Address to Miss Phillis Wheatly [sic], Ethiopian Poetess, in Boston, who came from Africa at eight years of age, and soon became acquainted with the gospel of Jesus Christ," ll. 41–44.

68. James Levernier, "Wheatley's 'On Being Brought from Africa to America,'" *Explicator* 40 (1981): pp. 25–26. As Zafar notes, the "punning use of 'refin'd' here has a salutary effect on criticism that seems to flatten poems like [this one] to one-dimensional status." See Zafar, *We Wear the Mask,* p. 195.

69. For example, consider Joshua Atherton's "Speech in the New Hampshire Ratifying Convention, ca. February 13, 1788": "Let us figure to ourselves a company of these manstealers, well equipped for the enterprise, landing on our coast. They seize or carry off the whole or part of the town of Exeter [New Hampshire]. Parents are taken and children left, or possibly they may be so fortunate as to have a whole family taken and carried off together by these relentless robbers. What must be their feelings in the hands of their new and arbitrary masters! Dragged at once from every thing they held dear to them, stripped of every comfort of life, like beasts of prey, they are hurried on a loathsome and distressing voyage to the coast of Africa . . . and here if anything can be added to their miseries comes on the heart-breaking scene—a parent sold to one, a son to another, and a daughter to a third. . . . The scene is too affecting; I have not fortitude to pursue the subject." See Atherton, in *A Necessary Evil? Slavery and the Debate Over the Constitution,* ed. John P. Kaminsky (Madison: Madison House, 1995), pp. 99–100.

70. For Lott, minstrelsy reveals the psychological complexity of fear, fascination and desires for control over black masculinity, particularly black sexuality. "The black mask offered a way to play with collective fears of a degraded and threatening—and male—Other while at the same time maintaining some symbolic control over them. Yet the intensified American fears of succumbing to a racialized image of Otherness were everywhere operative in minstrelsy, continually exceeding the controls and accounting, paradoxically, for the minstrel

show's power, insofar as its 'blackness' was unceasingly fascinating to audiences and performers alike." See Eric Lott, *Love and Theft: Blackface Minstrelsy and the American Working Class* (New York: Oxford University Press, 1995), p. 25. For "whiteness" studies, see Alexander Saxton, *The Rise and Fall of the White Republic: Class Politics and Mass Culture in Nineteenth-Century America* (London: Verso, 1990), and David Roediger, *The Wages of Whiteness: Race and the Making of an American Working Class* (London: Verso, 1991).

71. The problem with historically expansive models of "race" is that they universalize the very categories they aim to contest. Consider, for example, Leonard Cassuto's argument about the "grotesque": "Every culture has its grotesque. As cultures differ across time and place, so does the grotesque. (This variability is one reason the term is so difficult to define.) For the American Puritans, the Indians were grotesque. For nineteenth-century Americans, the objectified African slave and his descendants came to occupy a similar shifting space in the system of meaning and value. Neither the Indian nor the slave was seen consistently as a person in the Western worldview, but on the other hand . . . neither could be seen consistently as a thing, either. Each occupied a liminal state between human and thing. . . . In both cases, the grotesque emerges from this conflict on the edges of the category system." This fails to account for changes in the "category system" of humanity. See Cassuto, *The Inhuman Race: The Racial Grotesque in American Literature and Culture* (New York: Columbia University Press, 1997), p. 7.

72. Jedidiah Morse, *The American Geography; or View of the Present Situation of the United States of America* (Elizabethtown, N.J.: Shepard Kollock, 1789), p. 65.

73. Taking the environmentalist position, Beattie cited the example of a slave girl "who had been six years in England, and . . . spoke with the articulation and accent of an [English] native. . . . See James Beattie, *Elements of Moral Science* (Edinburgh: T. Caddell and William Creech, 1793), pp. 202–203.

74. Ramsay, *Treatment and Conversion*, p. 248.

75. Ibid., pp. 252–253.

76. *The Works in Verse and Prose of William Shenstone, Esq.,* vol. 1 (London: J. Dodsley, 1773), p. 83.

77. Ibid., pp. 84–85.

78. Hannah More, "The Sorrows of Yamba; or the Negro Woman's Lamentation" (Boston: Lincoln and Edmonds, 1819), p. 2. For the possibility that More coauthored the poem, see *Slavery, Abolition, and Emancipation.* Vol. 4, ed. Alan Richardson (London: Pickering and Chatto, 1999), p. 224.

79. Ibid., p. 5.

80. Ibid., p. 7.

81. Poetic versions of feeling in the African family recall James Clifford's summation of the problem of accounting for difference in western ethnography: "Strange behavior is portrayed as meaningful within a common network of symbols—a common ground of understandable activity valid for both observer and observed, and by implication for all human groups. Thus ethnography's

narrative of specific differences presupposes, and always refers to, an abstract plan of similarity." See "On Ethnographic Allegory," in *Writing Culture: The Poetics and Politics of Ethnography,* eds. Clifford and George E. Marcus (Berkeley: University of California Press, 1986), p. 101.

82. Some American versions of Cowper selectively edited out the most radical portions of the "African"'s critique of white avarice. See, for example, the version published in *The American Moral and Sentimental Magazine* (1797), pp. 381–382. Other magazines published antislavery poems using African speakers under the title of "The Negro's Complaint," which was likely due to Cowper's popularity. See *The American Magazine* (1788), p. 751. Another poem of Cowper's, "Charity," was excerpted in America in *The Christian's, Scholar's, and Farmer's Magazine* (1789), p. 120.

83. "The Negro's Complaint," *The Poems of William Cowper, vol. 3: 1785–1800,* eds. John D. Baird and Charles Ryskamp (Oxford: Clarenden, 1995), pp. 95–97, ll. 15–16.

84. Samuel Jackson Pratt, *Humanity; or, the Rights of Nature: A Poem in Two Books* (London: T. Cadell, 1788).

85. Cf. Shields: "The wish of many Europeans to be the other—not only for the refreshment of a strange point of view or the opportunity to occupy a different perspective from which to judge the European self (the task of *The Persian Letters* and *The Citizen of the World*) but to assert the power of the European psyche to subsume and encompass all other subjectivities—was the Enlightenment's particular addition to imperialism." Shields, *Oracles of Empire,* p. 184.

86. Dwight's poem appeared as well in the *New-Haven Gazette and Connecticut Magazine* in February 1788, and was collected in *American Poems,* ed. Elihu Hubbard Smith (Litchfield, Conn.: Collier and Buel, 1793), pp. 217–219.

87. Theodore Dwight, "Picture of African Distress," *American Museum* (October 1789), p. 328.

88. This motif occurs in many of the antislavery poems and prose sketches in American periodicals of this era. See, for example, "The Slave," *The Columbian Magazine, or Monthly Miscellany* (1789), pp. 293–295; "The Slave," *Massachusetts Magazine* 1 (1789), p. 387, and "The Faithful Negro," *Boston Magazine* 3 (1786), pp. 78–80. For the abundance of antislavery poetry in New York magazines in particular, see David N. Gellman, "Race, the Public Sphere, and Abolition in Late Eighteenth-Century New York," *Journal of the Early Republic* 20 (2000), pp. 607–636, though the essay fails to recognize the reprinting of texts like Cowper's "The Negro's Complaint" as part of "American" debates over black humanity and citizenship.

89. Bicknell likely sent Day an early version of the poem, which Day then edited and significantly expanded. See Sypher, *Guinea's Captive Kings,* pp. 177–180. See also George Warren Gignilliat, Jr., *The Author of Sanford and Merton: A Life of Thomas Day* (New York: Columbia University Press, 1932), pp. 102–110.

90. Thomas Day and John Bicknell, *The Dying Negro* (London: W. Flexney, 1773).

91. See, for example, *A New General Collection of Voyages and Travels: Consisting of the*

Most Esteemed Relations, which Have Been Hitherto Published in Any Language: Comprehending Every Thing Remarkable in its Kind, in Europe, Asia, Africa, and America. 4 vols. (London: Thomas Astley, 1745–47) and Awnsham Churchill, *A Collection of Voyages and Travels: Some now First Printed from Original Manuscripts, Others now First Published in English,* 6 vols. (London: Churchill, 1744–46).

92. For Day's republication in American magazines, see Isani, "'Gambia's Golden Shore,'" p. 370.

93. Cf. *A Poetical Epistle to the Enslaved Africans, in the Character of an Ancient Negro, Born a Slave in Pennsylvania* (Philadelphia: Jospeh Crukshank, 1790), which was reprinted in the *Universal Asylum and Columbian Magazine* (December 1790). Here the slave speaker is the mouthpiece not only of Christian forbearance but also of the association of modern commercial society with the moral depravity of slavery: "Shun Cities then, unwieldy haunts of Trade, / Industry beckons to the rural shade: / There honest Labour earns two-fold reward, / First health, then plenty from the well-turn'd sward" (p. 21).

94. Krise, *Caribbeana,* p. 143. As Krise notes, the epithet "Negro" describes dark skin rather than African heritage. For its literary genealogy see Sypher, *Guinea's Captive Kings,* 122–37. For the mutability of Yarico's "racial" identity see Nandini Bhattacharya, "Family Jewels: George Colman's *Inkle and Yarico* and Connoisseurship," *Eighteenth-Century Studies* 34 (2001), pp. 207–226.

95. *Cowper: Verse and Letters,* p. 284.

96. *Poems of Cowper,* vol. 3, pp. 26–27, l.6.

97. Robert Ferguson, "The American Enlightenment, 1750–1820," in *The Cambridge History of American Literature, Volume One: 1590–1820,* ed. Sacvan Bercovitch (New York: Cambridge University Press, 1994), pp. 401, 415.

98. Elhanan Winchester, *The Reigning Abominations, Especially the Slave Trade. Considered as Causes of Lamentation; Being the Substance of a Discourse Delivered at Fairfax County, Virginia, December 30, 1774* (London: H. Trapp, 1788), pp. 18, 28.

99. John McWilliams argues that the poem displaces "God's grace" with "human reason." See McWilliams, *The American Epic: Transforming a Genre, 1770–1860* (New York: Cambridge University Press, 1990), p. 54. See also Emory Elliott, *Revolutionary Writers: Literature and Authority in the New Republic, 1725–1810* (New York: Oxford University Press, 1982), p. 117. In *Poetry and Ideology in Revolutionary Connecticut* (Athens: University of Georgia Press, 1990), William Dowling reads liberal capitalism backwards onto a late eighteenth-century figure like Barlow, arguing speciously that the poem's final optimism depends upon its "apotheosis of commerce," and hence makes it "nothing more than an elaborate and unwitting apologia for the dynamics of Western capitalism," p. 123.

100. *The Columbiad* in *The Works of Joel Barlow, vol. 2,* (Gainesville, Fla.: Scholars Facsimiles, 1970), p. 122, ll. 150–152. Further citations occur by book and line number, parenthetically in the text.

101. Elliott argues that Barlow's revisions to *The Vision of Columbus* recast the problem of "slavery" in just those terms: "Slavery remained for Barlow the worst example of the pattern of the strong's exploitation of the weak. . . . Barlow be-

lieved that the system of slavery resided behind the same veil that masked an array of other evils: land speculation, corrupt politics, the sustained ignorance of the many, the religious hypocrisy of social climbers and clergy, the flabby doctrines of benevolence, and the emptiness of all the language supporting the crimes against mankind, which the Revolution was to have eliminated." See Elliot, *Revolutionary Writers*, p. 121. What he casually calls "the flabby doctrines of benevolence," however, actually generates the poem's larger articulation of the problem of slavery to Americans.

102. Clarkson, *An Essay on the Slavery and Commerce of the Human Species*, p. 155.
103. William Bell Crafton, *A Short Sketch of the Evidence Delivered before a Committee of the House of Commons for the Abolition of the Slave Trade* (London: M. Gurney, 1792), p. 19.
104. Ibid.
105. James Montgomery, *The West Indies, and Other Poems* (London: Longman, Hurst, Rees, and Orme, 1810), pp. i–ii.
106. Winchester, *Reigning Abominations*, pp. 19–20.
107. *The Selected Writings of Benjamin Rush*, ed. Dagobert D. Runes (New York: Philosphical Library, 1947), p. 15.

3. American Slaves in North Africa

1. As Paul Baepler has noted, this word derived from the Greek "barbaros," uncivilized outsiders or strangers. The word also has Arabic derivation ("berbera") that suggested the inability to communicate clearly. Hence "Barbary" contained "not only pejorative connotations but a sense of commercial and cultural resistance." See Baepler, Introduction to *White Slaves, African Masters: An Anthology of American Barbary Captivity Narratives* (Chicago: University of Chicago Press, 1999), pp. 2–3. Throughout, I use the term "Barbary" to enforce the argument that this genre of captivity literature was structured ideologically by the opposition between civilization and barbarity rather than race per se.
2. See David Brion Davis, *The Problem of Slavery in the Age of Revolution, 1770–1823* (Ithaca: Cornell University Press, 1975), p. 308.
3. Baepler, "Introduction" to *White Slaves, African Masters*, p. 19. Cathy Davidson similarly observes that in *The Algerine Captive* "Algiers . . . becomes the mirror version that especially shows up American distortions." See Davidson, *Revolution and the Word: The Rise of the Novel in America* (New York: Oxford University Press, 1986), p. 209. "How could Americans condemn Algiers," Robert J. Allison asks, "for enslaving Americans when Americans themselves were busily enslaving Africans?" See Allison, *The Crescent Obscured: The United States and the Muslim World, 1776–1815* (New York: Oxford University Press, 1995), p. 87.
4. "Adelos" authored this piece in the *Northampton Hampshire Gazette*, February 6, 1788, and it is reprinted in *A Necessary Evil?: Slavery and the Debate Over the Constitution*, ed. John P. Kaminski (Madison: Madison House, 1995), p. 96.
5. Samuel Hopkins, *A Dialogue Concerning the Slavery of the Africans* (Norwich: Ju-

dah Spooner, 1776), p. 11. Hopkins also asked, "If many thousands of our children were slaves in *Algiers,* or any part of the *Turkish* dominions, and there were but few families in the *American* colonies that had not some child, or near relation in that sad state, without any hope of freedom to them, or their children, unless there were some extraordinary exertion of the colonies to effect it; how would the attention of all the country be turned to it! . . . And why are we not as much affected with the slavery of the many thousands of blacks among ourselves, whose miserable state is before our eyes?" See pp. 33–34.

6. Warner Mifflin, *A Serious Expostulation with the Members of the House of Representatives of the United States* (Philadelphia, 1793), p. 14.

7. Benilde Montgomery has argued that this literature comprises "a forgotten aspect of the abolition movement in late eighteenth-century America": "Like some Oriental tales, these 'Algerian' plays imitate the plot of the captivity narrative and use the experience of white American sailors enslaved in Algiers as a mask behind which their abolitionist authors could criticize moral abuses in the political establishment at home." See Montgomery, "White Captives, African Slaves: A Drama of Abolition," *Eighteenth-Century Studies* 27 (1994), p. 617.

8. See Joanne Melish, *Disowning Slavery: Gradual Emancipation and "Race" in New England, 1780–1860* (Ithaca: Cornell University Press, 1998), pp. 155, 160–1.

9. Malini Johar Schueller, *U.S. Orientalisms: Race, Nation, and Gender in Literature, 1790–1890* (Ann Arbor: University of Michigan Press, 1998), p. 45.

10. Jared Gardner, *Master Plots: Race and the Founding of an American Literature, 1787–1845* (Baltimore: Johns Hopkins University Press, 1998), p. 51.

11. Raymond Williams, *Marxism and Literature* (New York: Oxford University Press, 1977), p. 14.

12. John Brewer, "'The Most Polite Age and the Most Vicious': Attitudes Towards Culture as a Commodity, 1660–1800," in *The Consumption of Culture, 1600–1800: Image, Object, Text,* eds. Ann Bermingham and Brewer (London: Routledge, 1995), pp. 341–359.

13. For historical backgrounds, see Reginald Horsman, *The Diplomacy of the New Republic, 1776–1815* (Arlington Heights, Ill.: Harlan Davidson, 1985), Gary Wilson, "American Hostages in Moslem Nations, 1784–1796: The Public Response" *Journal of the Early Republic* 2 (1982), pp. 123–141; Michael Kitzen, "Money Bags or Cannon Balls: The Origins of the Tripolitan War, 1795–1801," *Journal of the Early Republic* 16 (1996), pp. 601–624.

14. For discussion of the treaty, see Stanley Elkins and Eric McKitrick, *The Age of Federalism: The Early American Republic, 1788–1800* (New York: Oxford University Press, 1993), pp. 375–449, and Todd Estes, "Shaping the Politics of Public Opinion," *Journal of the Early Republic* 20 (2000), pp. 393–427.

15. Elkins and McKitrick, *The Age of Federalism,* pp. 376, 384.

16. *The American Remembrancer; or an Impartial Collection of Essays, Resolves, Speeches, &c. Relative, or Having Affinity, to the Treaty with Great Britain,* vol. 1, ed. Mathew Carey (Philadelphia: Mathew Carey, 1795).

17. *An Address from Robert Goodloe Harper of South Carolina to his Constituents, Con-*

taining his Reasons for Approving of the Treaty of Amity, Commerce and Navigation, with Great-Britain (Philadelphia: Ormrod and Conrad, 1795), p. 12.

18. Article II, for example, allowed English citizens to remain as such within the United States. Article III proclaimed that both English and Americans were "freely to pass and repass by land or in land navigation, into the respective territories and countries of the two parties, on the continent of America . . . and to navigate all the lakes, rivers, and waters thereof, and freely to carry on trade and commerce with each other." See *The Treaties Between the United States and Great Britain* (Boston: E. G. House, 1815), pp. 7–8, 14.

19. *Boston Gazette and Weekly Republican Journal,* 19 May 1794, (Boston: Benjamin Edes and Son, 1794), n.p.

20. *The Speech of Mr. Ames in the House of Representatives of the United States, When in Committee of the Whole, on Thursday, April 28, 1796* (Philadelphia: John Fenno, 1796), pp. 26–27.

21. *American Remembrancer,* vol. 2, p. 214.

22. *Newport Mercury,* Tuesday, August 4, 1795, n.p.

23. See Anonymous, *An Emetic for Aristocrats! Or, a Chapter, Respecting Governor Jay, and His Treaty: Also, a History of the Life and Death of Independence; To Which is added, A Poem on the Treaty* (Boston, 1795), p. 19.

24. This question derives from the Revolutionary jeremiad, which often insisted that the British were merely agents of divine retribution. See Perry Miller's essay, "From the Covenant to the Revival," in his *Nature's Nation* (Cambridge, Mass.: Harvard University Press, 1967), and Nathan Hatch, *The Sacred Cause of Liberty: Republican Thought and the Millennium in Revolutionary New England* (New Haven: Yale University Press, 1977).

25. James Wilson Stevens, *An Historical and Geographical Account of Algiers; Comprehending a Novel and Interesting Detail of Events Relative to the American Captives* (Philadelphia: Hogan and M'Elroy, 1797), p. 67.

26. St. George Tucker, *Remarks on the Treaty of Amity, Navigation and Commerce, Concluded Between Lord Grenville and Mr. Jay, on the Part of Great Britain and the United States, Respectively* (Philadelphia: Henry Tuckniss, 1796), p. 31.

27. Mathew Carey, *A Short Account of Algiers, and of Its Several Wars Against Spain, France, England, Holland, Venice and Other Powers of Europe, From the Usurpations of Barbarossa and the Invasion of Emperor Charles V, to the Present Time* (Philadelphia: Mathew Carey, 1794), p. 36. For other accounts of British culpability in precipitating the Algerian conflict, see *The Boston Gazette and Weekly Republican Journal* for 20 January, 1794; the address by "Caius" in *The American Remembrancer,* vol. 1, that critiqued "the true policy of Great-Britain; namely, to countenance and encourage Algerine depredations on the American trade," p. 107; and *Debates in the House of Representatives of the United States During the First Session of the Fourth Congress, Upon Questions Involved in the British Treaty of 1794,* vol. 2 (Philadelphia: William Duane, 1808), pp. 281–282.

28. Anonymous, *Humanity in Algiers: or, the Story of Azem* (Troy: R. Moffitt, 1801). p. 3.

29. Carey, *Short Account,* p. 5.

30. William Ray, *Poems on Various Subjects* (New York, 1826), p. 84.

31. Critics of Britain extended this strategy to include Native Americans as well. As the epigraph to this chapter shows, anti-Federalist sentiment could take this rhetorical form. The "Political Alphabet; or Touch of the Times" reads: "*E* notes our enemies—Savage, Briton, and Algier, / Who plunder our shipping, or scalp on the frontier, / A triple Alliance, congenial in warfare," *Boston Gazette and Weekly Republican Journal* (Boston: Benjamin Edes and Son, 1794). The poem appears on 20 January, 1794, n.p.

32. Kenneth Silverman, *A Cultural History of the American Revolution* (New York: T. Y. Crowell, 1976), pp. 82–87; Jay Fliegelman, *Prodigals and Pilgrims: The American Revolution Against Patriarchal Authority, 1750–1800* (Cambridge: Cambridge University Press, 1982;, and Julie Ellison, *Cato's Tears and the Making of Anglo-American Emotion* (Chicago: University of Chicago Press, 1999).

33. "Are the officers and crews of his Britannic majesty's ships of war and privateers so remarkably observant of the rights of neutral nations, and the laws of courtesy, that we should trust them more than any others?" See Tucker, *Remarks on the Treaty of Amity*, pp. 14–15, 24.

34. Notwithstanding its immediate political goal, this argument derived from the British and American antislavery critique of slave trading as a barbaric form of "piracy." Thomas Clarkson noted that in "the more uncivilized ages of the world" piracy had the reputation of adventure and honor: "But as the notions of men in the less barbarous ages, which followed, became more corrected and refined, the practice of piracy began gradually to disappear." See Clarkson, *An Essay on the Slavery and Commerce of the Human Species* (London: James Phillips, 1786), p. 15.

35. Carey, *Short Account*, p. 16.

36. *Boston Gazette and Weekly Republican Journal* (February 16, 1795), n.p.

37. Anonymous, *The American in Algiers, or the Patriot of Seventy-Six in Captivity: a Poem in Two Cantos* (New York: J. Buel, 1797), pp. 6–7, 12–14. Further citations appear parenthetically in the text.

38. Cathcart commented "that we had not been used worse than many of our fellow citizens had been during the Revolutionary war in the different British prisons." See "The Captives, Eleven Years a Prisoner in Algiers," in Baepler, ed., *White Captives*, p. 111.

39. William Ray, *Horrors of Slavery, or, the American Tars of Tripoli* (Troy: Oliver Lyon, 1808), p. 18.

40. Ibid., p. 20.

41. Ibid., p. 25.

42. Stevens, *Historical*, p. 234.

43. Ibid., pp. 234–235.

44. See Elkins and McKitrick, *The Age of Federalism*, p. 413.

45. Earlier readings recognize Rowson's importance to the development of the early American theatre and emphasize the play's nationalist language. See, for example, Walter J. Meserve, *An Emerging Entertainment: The Drama of the Ameri-*

can People to 1828 (Bloomington: University of Indiana Press, 1977), pp. 117–119. This argument ironically echoes William Cobbett's acerbic review of the play, which challenged the sincerity of Rowson's sudden patriotism. His unfair review took her as a test case of the emptiness of American cultural politics: "Notwithstanding all this, there are (and I am sorry to say it), some people, who doubt of her sincerity, and who pretend that her sudden conversion to republicanism, ought to make us look upon all her praises as ironical. But these uncandid people do not, or rather will not, recollect, what the miraculous air of America is capable of. . . . Is not the sound of *Liberty,* glorious *Liberty!* heard to ring from one end of the continent to the other?" See "A Kick for a Bite; or Review Upon Review; with a Critical Essay on the Works of Mrs. S. Rowson; in a Letter to the Editor, or Editors, of the *American Monthly Review,*" in *Peter Porcupine in America,* ed. David A. Wilson (Ithaca: Cornell University Press, 1994), p. 133.

46. See Davidson's Introduction to Rowson, *Charlotte Temple* (New York: Oxford University Press, 1986), p. xxv, and Mary Anne Schofield, "The Happy Revolution: Colonial Women and the Eighteenth-Century Theater," in *Modern American Drama: The Female Canon,* ed. June Schlueter (Rutheford, Penn.: Farleigh Dickinson University Press, 1990), p. 34. See also Patricia Parker, *Susanna Rowson* (Boston: Twayne, 1986), p. 68, Dorothy Weil, *In Defense of Women: Susanna Rowson* (University Park: Pennsylvania State University Press, 1976), p. 39, and Amelia Howe Kritzer, "Playing with Republican Motherhood: Self-Representation in Plays by Susanna Rowson and Judith Sargent Murray," *Early American Literature* 31 (1996), pp. 150–166. See also Allison, *The Crescent Obscured,* pp. 74–76.

47. My reading below of Rowson emphasizes the complexity of her national and imperial subject positions. Edward Watts has argued that all post-Revolutionary Americans maintained the hybrid posture of colonizer and colonized that is characteristic of "Second World" societies. He argues that "Revolutionary Second World settlers like Franklin and Jefferson testify to the internal paradoxes of this dual inscription and eventually sought to win 'national identity' as a way of escaping the margin of the British Empire," p. 9. Rowson, however, entirely recasts the cultural relation between the metropole and colony/nation. See Watts, *Writing and Postcolonialism in the Early Republic* (Charlottesville: University of Virginia Press, 1998), pp. 1–26, p. 9 for quotation.

48. Amelia Howe Kritzer, Introduction to *Plays by Early American Women, 1775–1850* (Ann Arbor: University of Michigan Press, 1995), p. 9.

49. See Kritzer, ed., *Plays by Early American Women,* p. 91. All further citations are noted parenthetically in the chapter.

50. "Tell me, ye tender mothers, what must have been the feelings . . . of Jochebed at this awful crisis; to leave this goodly, beautiful child thus exposed!" See Isaac Story, *A Discourse Delivered February 15, 1795, at the Request of the Proprietors' Committee; as Preparatory to the Collection, on the National Thanksgiving, the Thursday Following, for the Benefit of Our American Brethren at Algiers* (Salem: Thomas C.

Cushing, 1795), p. 11. See also *A Sermon Preached February 19, 1795, Being the Federal Thanksgiving, Appointed by Our Beloved President, the Illustrious George Washington, Esq.* (Salem: T. Cushing, 1795.)

51. See Leonard Tennenhouse, "The Americanization of Clarissa," *The Yale Journal of Criticism* 11 (1998), pp. 190, 192.

52. In this light Constant symbolizes the norms of benevolence and gratitude, which, as Gordon S. Wood has argued, provided the new means for social cohesion and social authority in the transition from monarchical to republican society. See Wood, *The Radicalism of the American Revolution* (New York: Random House, 1992).

53. Compare more conventionally nationalist treatments of Barbary captivity, such as *The American in Algiers:*

> Thy long triumphant flag once more unfurl,
> And on piratic fleets thy thunders hurl;
> Then steer the hostile prow to Bar'ry's shores,
> Release thy sons, and humble Afric's pow'rs.
> Secure old Janus' doors with double bars,
> And free the world from massacres and wars.
> If thou, my country, deign'st to hear my prayer,
> I live to breathe thy vivifying air. (p. 16)

54. The motif of the moral and cultural conversion of "good" North Africans characterizes this kind of antislavery literature. For comparison with Rowson, see James Ellison's *The American Captive* (1812), where the restored Tripolitan bashaw benevolently liberates his slaves, or Isaac Bickerstaffe's more comic *The Sultan* (1810), in which the English protagonist Roxalana refines Muslim manners. As the reformed sultan finally declares to his new English wife, "The illiberal mind, by no distinction bound, / Thro' Nature's glass, looks all the world around; / Would all that's beautiful together join, / And find perfection in a mind like thine." See Bickerstaffe, *The Sultan, or, a Peep into the Seraglio* (Washington, D.C.: William Rind, 1810), p. 34.

55. The critique Schueller offers is that the play's "emancipatory feminist discourse" is "hierarchically raced," a feature that belies "Rowson's split position as woman and imperial subject." See Schueller, *US Orientalisms*, pp. 61, 67.

56. For the politics of the faculties particularly during the 1790s, see Chris Jones, *Radical Sensibility: Lectures and Ideas of the 1790s* (New York: Routledge, 1993).

57. For this convention in Barbary slavery poetry, see, for example, "The Tripoline Captive" in the *Boston Weekly Magazine* (Boston: Gilbert and Dean, 1805), p. 96. Rowson contributed and may have edited the periodical. The convention usually highlights the failure of American benevolence and the consequential death of the captive: "Ah! Why then this cruel delay, / While your children in slav'ry you see! / Where's the *gold that you lavish away?* / Where's the valour that once made you FREE?"

58. The poem was published in 1786 in London and later included in *The Miscellaneous Works of Colonel Humphreys* (New York: Hodge, Allen, and Campbell,

1790). As Humphreys noted in a later edition of his works, published in 1804, the poem initially went through ten editions. The 1804 edition significantly truncates the original version, and makes that excluded material "A Poem on the Future Glory of the United States of America."

59. See William Dowling, *Poetry and Ideology in Revolutionary Connecticut* (Athens: University of Georgia Press, 1990), pp. 16, 23, 38, and *passim.*

60. Humphreys, *A Poem on the Happiness of America, Addressed to the Citizens of the United States* (Portsmouth, N.H.: George Jerry Osborne, 1790), ll. 793–796, 809–818. See Carey, *Short Account,* p. 47.

61. Humphreys, *A Poem,* ll. 551–52, 556–66.

62. Davidson, for example, argues that Tyler is suspicious of British-derived aristocracy in America as it was expressed through the politics of New England Federalism. Instead, Tyler offers an "open-minded, pluralistic, democratic [nationalism] utterly opposed to oligarchy or autocracy, to one people dominating over another." See Davidson, *Revolution and the Word,* p. 209. In light of Tyler's close personal and literary relationship with the conservative Joseph Dennie (with whom he collaborated as "Colon and Spondee"), as well as his participation in putting down Shays Rebellion in 1787, such an assessment of his politics is probably overstated. Watts reads *The Algerine Captive* as an anti-British invective: "By focussing exclusively on the Algerian slavery, Updike remains a colonial, unable to see beyond of [*sic*] the hierarchy of civilization implicit to imperial thought; by creating Updike as conflicted in these ways, however, Tyler engages in the work of decolonization." See Watts, *Writing and Postcolonialism,* p. 92.

63. *The Algerine Captive, or, the Life and Adventures of Doctor Updike Underhill: Six Years a Prisoner Among the Algerines,* ed. Don L. Cook (College and University Press Services, 1970), p. 28. The novel was first published in 1797 in Walpole, New Hampshire. Further citations appear parenthetically in the text.

64. Mitchel Breitwieser understands this in postmodern terms: "It should be no surprise that in our fin-de-siecle the intellectual interest of many should travel back to the age of Jefferson, not because our time is revolutionary, but because circumstances push upon us an awareness of improvisation or poiesis as foundation." See Breitwieser, "Commentary: Afterthought," *ALH* 5 (1993), p. 591.

65. For discussion of this see Chapter 1. Lawrence Klein takes up this issue in *Shaftesbury and the Culture of Politeness* (Cambridge: Cambridge University Press, 1994).

66. Tyler certainly appreciates the benefits of cultural refinement in such early writings as "Vauxhall Gardens," a poem that appeared as part of the "Colon and Spondee" series in *The Farmer's Weekly Museum.* It addresses Boston's new Public Gardens with light-hearted humor, and its title suggests that American cultural refinement is necessarily modeled on British examples. Yet the poem consistently shows that the "heat" of the day—in political animosity and professional anxiety—can be assuaged "beneath the evening star" in such a civilized and refined setting: "While groups of social life shall there / Quaff that

cool draught of evening air, / Which bounteous Nature gives away, / To the cool sultry heat of day / Whilst music joys the raptur'd air, / And CHASTEN'D PLEASURES foots it there!" See *The Verse of Royall Tyler,* ed. Marius B. Peladeau (Charlottesville: University Press of Virginia, 1968), pp. 77–78.

67. For commentary on this critical debate about the relation between the novel's two parts, see Gardner, *Master Plots,* pp. 37–38. In *Royall Tyler* (Cambridge: Harvard University Press, 1967), G. Thomas Tanselle argues against unifying the two. For readings of the novel's ironic ending, see John Engell, "Narrative Irony and National Character in Royall Tyler's *The Algerine Captive,*" *Studies in American Fiction* 17 (1989), pp. 19–32.

68. See Allison, *The Crescent Obscured,* p. 94, Davidson, *Revolution,* pp. 206–207, and Gardner, *Master Plots,* p. 48.

69. *The Algerine Spy in Pennsylvania: or, Letters Written by a Native of Algiers on the Affairs of the United States of America, From the Close of the Year 1783 to the Meeting of the Convention* (Philadelphia: Prichard and Hall, 1787), p. 72. Influenced by works like Montesquieu's *Persian Letters* and Goldsmith's *The Citizen of the World,* Markoe's is a thinly veiled cultural critique of the Confederation-era republic. On Markoe himself, see Mary Diebels, *Peter Markoe: A Philadelphia Writer* (Washington, D.C.: Catholic University Press, 1944).

70. See David Porter, "A Peculiar but Uninteresting Nation: China and the Discourse of Commerce in Eighteenth-Century England," *Eighteenth-Century Studies* 33 (1999–00), p. 185.

71. William Hedges, *Washington Irving: An American Study, 1802–1832* (Baltimore: Johns Hopkins University Press, 1965), p. 58. I concentrate on Irving's specific contributions to *Salmagundi,* though I realize its collaborative effort and haphazard revisions complicate the issue of authorship. For attribution of authorship to individual pieces, see the editorial apparatus in *The Complete Works of Washington Irving,* vol. 6, eds. Bruce I. Granger and Martha Hartzog (Boston: Twayne, 1977), pp. 327–336.

72. Jeffrey Rubin-Dorsky, *Adrift in the Old World: The Psychological Pilgrimage of Washington Irving* (Chicago: University of Chicago Press, 1988).

73. Hedges subtitles his landmark study of Irving "an American Study." Rubin-Dorsky recuperates Irving's reputation as "a truly representative American author," who remained, even while living abroad, "first and foremost a son of the Republic," and who "filtered everything through an American consciousness." See Rubin-Dorsky, *Adrift in the Old World,* pp. xv, 30–31. Christopher Looby similarly sees the importance of Mustapha in light of the anxiety Irving and others felt over "the unprecedented verbal violence of the nation." See Looby, *Voicing America: Language, Literary Form, and the Origins of the United States* (Chicago: University of Chicago Press, 1996), p. 82.

For a prescient critique of this developmental model of American culture, consider Laura J. Murray's comment, "I would claim that both the idea of the nation as anxious individual and the idea of the nation as decentered subject promote an exclusive or engulfing conception of American culture, always thought of as singular and continuous even if troubled within itself." Murray's understanding of Irving's "aesthetic of dispossession" resists this model by breaking down the binary between the colonizer and the colonized. The post-Revolutionary United States was simultaneously a colonial and imperial nation. While my argument similarly rejects what she calls the cultural "narrative of maturation," its transatlantic reading of Irving focuses less on America's imperial position—its status as a colonizer—and more on its cultural position as a colonial nation, specifically its ambivalent attitudes towards the persistence of British cultural affiliations. See Murray, "The Aesthetic of Dispossession: Washington Irving and Ideologies of (De)Colonization in the Early Republic," *ALH* 8 (1996), p. 208.

74. *The Citizen of the World and the Bee*, ed. Richard Church (London: J. M. Dent & Sons, 1934), p. 54.

75. *Complete Works of Washington Irving*, vol. 6, p. 194. Further citations appear parenthetically in the text.

76. *The Complete Works of Washington Irving*, vol. 23, eds. Ralph Aderman, Herbert L. Kleinfield, and Jennifer S. Banks (Boston: Twayne, 1978), p. 80.

77. As Charlotte Sussman recently has shown, this was a prevailing motif in British antislavery literature, which tried to purify domestic—feminized—space from corrupted forms of consumption associated directly with slavery. See Sussman, *Consuming Anxieties: Consumer Protest, Gender, and British Slavery, 1713–1833* (Stanford: Stanford University Press, 2000).

78. See Brissot de Warville, *An Oration, Delivered at Paris, on the 19th of February, 1788. Before a Select Society; Convened at the Request of the Committee of London. In Which is Pointed Out the Necessity of Forming a Society at Paris to Cooperate with Those of America and London, in Procuring the Abolition of the Traffic and the Slavery of the Negroes* (Philadelphia: Francis Bailey, 1789), p. 142.

79. This passage is cited in Anthony Benezet, *Some Historical Account of Guinea* (London: J. Phillips, 1788), p. 62.

80. Humphreys, *A Poem on the Happiness of America*, ll. 417–430.

4. Liberty, Slavery, and Black Atlantic Autobiography

1. Paul Gilroy, *The Black Atlantic: Modernity and Double Consciousness* (Cambridge, Mass.: Harvard University Press, 1993).

2. "Benjamin Banneker's Revision of Thomas Jefferson: Conscience vs. Science in the Early American Antislavery Debate," in *Genius in Bondage: The Literature of the Early Black Atlantic*, eds. Vincent Carretta and Philip Gould (Lexington: University of Kentucky Press, 2001), pp. 218–241.

3. See *Unchained Voices: An Anthology of Black Authors in the English-Speaking World of the 18th Century*, ed. Vincent Carretta (Lexington: University of Kentucky Press, 1997), p. 319.

4. Ibid., pp. 320–321.

5. Gilroy, *Black Atlantic*, p. 220.

6. Ibid., p. 38.
7. Saidiya Hartman, *Scenes of Subjection: Terror, Slavery, and Self-Making in Nineteenth-Century America* (New York: Oxford University Press, 1997), p. 122. The distrust of liberal ideology is fairly widespread in the field. See, for example, Valerie Smith's skeptical view of Frederick Douglass's liberal masculinity in *Self-Discovery and Authority in Afro-American Narrative* (Cambridge, Mass.: Harvard University Press, 1987). My argument is in keeping with J. Martin Favor's objection to the critical privileging of "authentic" or "folk" blackness against the cultural infiltration of white liberalism. See Favor, *Authentic Blackness: The Folk in the New Negro Renaissance* (Durham: Duke University Press, 1999). For discussion of the limitations of liberal rights ideology for African Americans, see John Saillant, "The American Enlightenment in Africa: Jefferson's Colonizationism and Black Virginians' Migration to Liberia, 1776–1840," *Eighteenth-Century Studies* 31 (1998), pp. 261–282.
8. Ira Berlin, *Many Thousands Gone: The First Two Centuries of Slavery in North America* (Cambridge, Mass.: Harvard University Press, 1999), p. 225.
9. Joanne Pope Melish, *Disowning Slavery: Gradual Emancipation and "Race" in New England, 1780–1860* (Ithaca: Cornell University Press, 1998), p. 113. Compare Berlin: "Slavery's slow demise had powerful consequences for African-American life in the North, handicapping the efforts of black people to secure households of their own, to find independent employment, and to establish their own institutions. It encouraged the notion that black free people were no more than slaves without masters, thus hardening racial stereotypes, giving former slave owners the time to construct new forms of subordination, and preventing the integration of black people into free society as equals." Berlin, *Many Thousands Gone*, p. 239.
10. As Samira Kawash has argued, "The stubborn persistence of the color line in representation and experience is not a problem of false consciousness or anachronistic thinking; rather it indicates the power and continuity of the cognitive, discursive, and institutional workings of the color line as simultaneously the limit and constitutive condition for cultural and social life." See Kawash, *Dislocating the Color Line: Identity, Hybridity, and Singularity in African-American Narrative* (Stanford: Stanford University Press, 1997), p. 6.
11. In his seminal study of early African-American autobiography, for example, William L. Andrews emphasizes the problems of "repression" and "restriction" by white amanuenses with editorial power. He argues that "the very language of much early Afro-American autobiography is of indeterminate origin." See Andrews, *To Tell a Free Story: The First Century of Afro-American Autobiography, 1760–1865* (Urbana: University of Illinois Press, 1986), pp. 35–36. John Sekora goes even further in theorizing that the genre of black autobiography always presents the problem of the "black message" that is contained by the "white envelope." See "Black Message/White Envelope: Genre, Authenticity and Authority in the Antebellum Slave Narrative," *Callaloo* 10 (1987), pp. 482–515.
12. Robert Desrochers, "'Not Fade Away': The *Narrative* of Venture Smith, an Afri-

can American in the Early Republic," *Journal of American History* 84 (1997), p. 43. Rafia Zafar similarly claims that "domination by the white editor, no matter how significant, can never be complete." Zafar, *We Wear the Mask: African Americans write American Literature, 1760–1870* (New York: Columbia University Press, 1997), p. 54.

13. Theoretical approaches to collaborative autobiography confront, for example, Philippe Lejeune's belief that nonwriting authors inevitably become "models" or "sources" that fulfill "the public's demand." See Lejeune, "The Autobiography of Those Who Do Not Write," in *On Autobiography,* ed. Paul John Eakin (Minneapolis: University of Minnesota Press, 1989), pp. 185–215. Anne E. Goldman has argued that this position "reproduce[s] the coercive context in which such writing is produced" and permits us "to forget that the 'other' may exercise the ability (even if it must be carried out in an oblique fashion) to speak against editorial appropriation." See "Is That What She Said? The Politics of Collaborative Autobiography," *Cultural Critique* 25 (1993), p. 183. In "Theorizing the Collaborative Self: The Dynamics of Contour and Content in the Dictated Autobiography," *New Literary History* 25 (1994), pp. 445–458, Mark Sanders argues that dictator and writer control their respective realms of content and form. My reading of Black Atlantic autobiography similarly views collaboration as a complex rhetorical negotiation, though it blurs the autonomous realms of form and content.

14. Gordon Wood, *The Radicalism of the American Revolution* (New York: Vintage, 1993), p. 145. For critiques of this argument, see "How Revolutionary was the Revolution: A Discussion of Gordon S. Wood's *The Radicalism of the American Revolution,*" *William and Mary Quarterly,* 3rd ser. 51 (1994), pp. 677–716.

15. Cathy Matson, "Capitalizing Home: Economic Thought and the Early National 'Economy,'" in *The Wages of Independence: Capitalism in the Early American Republic,* ed. Paul Gilje (Madison: Madison House, 1997), p. 119. For a discussion of the development of modern society and economics in early America, see Winifred Barr Rothen, *From Market-Place to Market Economy: The Transformation of Rural Massachusetts, 1750–1850* (Chicago: University of Chicago Press, 1992), and Daniel Vickers, "'Competency and Competition: Economic Culture in Early America," *William and Mary Quarterly* 3rd ser. 47 (1990), pp. 3–29.

16. David Brion Davis, *The Problem of Slavery in the Age of Revolution, 1770–1823* (Ithaca: Cornell University Press, 1975), p. 82.

17. Ibid., p. 350.

18. See Thomas Clarkson, *An Essay on the Impolicy of the African Slave Trade* (Philadelphia: Francis Bailey, 1789), p. 5.

19. Anthony Benezet, *Some Historical Account of Guinea, its Situation, Produce, and the General Disposition of its Inhabitants* (London: James Phillips, 1788), p. 120. This explains as well fears of immediate emancipation. As the British antislavery writer William Dickson declared, there was never "so mischievous a project" as immediate emancipation, for it would only create "idleness and debauchery" for West Indian blacks who were "totally ignorant of Christianity." "To the

Free Negroes and Mulattoes, and to the More Enlightened and Regular Slaves in the Island of Barbadoes," in Dickson, *Letters on Slavery* (London: James Phillips, 1789), pp. 172–173.

20. Granville Sharp to Anthony Benezet, 21 August 1772, in *Am I not a Man and a Brother: The Antislavery Crusade of Revolutionary America, 1688–1788*, ed. Roger Bruns (New York: Chelsea House, 1977), p. 199.

21. James Ramsay, *An Essay on the Treatment and Conversion of the African Slaves in the British Sugar Colonies* (London: James Phillips, 1784), pp. 3, 8.

22. Joseph Priestley, *A Sermon on the Subject of the Slave Trade; Delivered to the Society of Protestant Dissenters, at the New Meeting in Birmingham.* (Birmingham: Pearson and Rollason, 1788), p. vii.

23. Jedidiah Morse, *A Discourse Delivered at the African Meeting House, in Boston, July 14, 1808, in Grateful Celebration of the Abolition of the African Slave Trade by the Governments of the United States, Great Britain, and Denmark* (Boston: Lincoln and Edmands, 1808), p. 6.

24. Ibid., p. 18.

25. Cf. Granville Sharp: "Other Negroes that are not capable of managing and shifting for themselves, nor are fit to be trusted, all at once, with liberty, might be delivered over to the care and protection of a county committee, in order to avoid the baneful effects *of private property in men.*" See Sharp, *The Just Limitation of Slavery in the Laws of God, Compared with the Unbounded Claims of the African Traders and British American Slaveholders* (London: B. White, 1776), p. 59. This approach characterizes the emancipation plans of such diverse figures as Noah Webster and St. George Tucker.

26. George Lawrence, *An Oration on the Abolition of the Slave Trade, Delivered on the First Day of January, 1813, in the African Methodist Episcopal Church* (New York: Hardcastle and Van Pelt, 1813), p. 14.

27. Peter Williams, *A Discourse, Delivered on the Death of Capt. Paul Cuffe, before the New-York African Institution, in the African Methodist Episcopal Zion Church* (New York: B. Young, 1817), pp. 4, 6.

28. Ibid., p. 4.

29. Ibid., p. 8.

30. Carretta suggests that in South Carolina Marrant owned a slave. *The Black Loyalist Directory* lists "Mellia Marrant, 30, squat wench, B, ([Thomas Grigg]). Formerly the property of John Marrant, near Santee, Carolina; left him at the siege of Charleston." John and Mellia Marrant's relations are shrouded in ambiguity; theirs may have been a sexual relationship, a master-slave one, or one based on indentured servitude—all of which turn on the rhetorical ambiguity of the word "master." See *The Black Loyalist Directory*, ed. Graham Russell Hodges (New York: Garland, 1996), pp. 56–57.

31. See Carretta, *Unchained Voices*, p. 110. All further references are from this edition and are noted parenthetically in the text.

32. Benilde Montgomery, "Recapturing John Marrant," in *A Mixed Race: Ethnicity in Early America*, ed. Frank Shuffelton (New York: Oxford University Press, 1993),

p. 108. Henry Louis Gates, Jr. has argued that the *Narrative* avoids the issue of chattel slavery and does not directly "speak to the perilous condition of black bondsmen or even the marginally free." Gates, *The Signifying Monkey: A Theory of Afro-American Literary Criticism* (New York: Oxford University Press, 1988), p. 145.

33. Nancy Ruttenberg, *Democratic Personality: Popular Voice and the Trial of American Authorship* (Stanford: Stanford University Press, 1998), p. 118. Ruttenberg recognizes Whitefield's inability "to contemplate the uncontainable enlargement of black Christians" (p. 117). For a reading of eighteenth-century Black Atlantic writing in context of the convergence of dissenting Protestantism, the rise of Romanticism, and the hybrid potential of the African diaspora, see Helen Thomas, *Romanticism and Slave Narratives: Transatlantic Testimonies* (Cambridge: Cambridge University Press, 2000).

34. For a discussion of the severity of indentured labor, see, for example, Richard Hofstadter, *America at 1750: A Social Portrait* (New York: Alfred Knopf, 1971).

35. As historians of the eighteenth-century West Indies have noted, "In the slave islands, planters had consistently feared black music for it represented an independent realm of slave life over which whites had no control." See Paul Edwards and James Walvin, *Black Personalities in the Era of the Slave Trade* (Baton Rouge: Louisiana State University Press, 1983), p. 28.

36. Joyce Appleby, *Liberalism and Republicanism in the Historical Imagination* (Cambridge, Mass.: Harvard University Press, 1992), pp. 143–144.

37. See, for example, Timothy Hall, *Contested Boundaries: Itinerancy and the Reshaping of the Colonial American Religious World* (Durham: Duke University Press, 1994), and Frank Lambert, *"Pedlar in Divinity": George Whitefield and the Transatlantic Revivals, 1737–1770* (Princeton: Princeton University Press, 1994).

38. Appleby, *Liberalism and Republicanism*, p. 182.

39. See, for example, Houston A. Baker, Jr., *Blues, Ideology and Afro-American Literature: A Vernacular Theory* (Chicago: University of Chicago Press, 1984). Baker argues that the *Interesting Narrative* "can be ideologically considered as a work whose protagonist masters the rudiments of economics that condition his very life" (p. 33). Having been reduced to property, the autobiographical subject decides that "neither sentiment nor spiritual sympathies can earn his liberation. He realizes, in effect, that only the acquisition of property will enable him to alter his designated status *as property*" (p. 35). Joseph Fichtelberg has taken a more skeptical reading of Equiano's authorial agency: "To assess Equiano's *Narrative* from [the Jamesonian] standpoint involves not simply the governing statement to which the text reacted but the discourses it engaged, and that in turn deformed it. For Equiano, these discourses were both revolutionary and punitive—a mixture of Evangelicalism, liberalism, and popular anthropology occurring at the precise moment when England was consolidating its position as the world's preeminent power—and it was all but impossible to avert one set of constraints without inviting others." See Fichtelberg, "Word Between Worlds: The Economy of Equiano's *Narrative*," *ALH* 5 (1993), p. 462. Despite

their obvious differences, both Baker and Fichtelberg understand the major cultural context for Equiano's commercial self-representation as a form of "liberalism" that is separate from sentimental culture. A similar approach, which argues for Equiano's sense of "a racial-national limit of mercantile capitalism and its promise of formal, abstract equality," is in David Kazanjian's "Race, Nation, Equality: Olaudah Equiano's *Interesting Narrative* and a Genealogy of U.S. Mercantilism," in *Post-Nationalist American Studies,* ed. John Carlos Rowe (Berkeley: University of California Press, 2000), 129–165, quotation p. 132. For another view of Equiano and capitalism, see Elizabeth Hinds, "The Spirit of Trade: Olaudah Equiano's Conversion, Legalism, and Merchant's Life," *African-American Review* 32 (1998), pp. 635–697.

40. *The Interesting Narrative of Olaudah Equiano, or Gustavus Vassa, the African. Written by Himself,* ed. Werner Sollors (New York: Norton, 2001), p. 7. All further citations will appear parenthetically in the text.

41. See Angelo Costanzo, *Suprising Narrative: Olaudah Equiano and the Beginnings of Black Autobiography* (New York: Greenwood, 1987), p. 43.

42. For the possibility that Equiano was not from West Africa, see Vincent Carretta, "Olaudah Equiano or Gustavus Vassa?" *Slavery and Abolition* 21 (1999), pp. 96–105.

43. Hall, *Contested Boundaries,* p. 56.

44. Sandra M. Gustafson, *Eloquence Is Power: Oratory and Performance in Early America* (Chapel Hill: University of North Carolina Press, 2000), pp. 102–110. Comparing Marrant to the Native American minister Samson Occom, Gustafson emphasizes the rhetorical power of the "savage speaker," which derives, in Marrant's case, from the creative encounter of Christian, African American and Native American cultural languages.

45. Caesar Sarter's "Essay on Slavery" first appeared in the *Essex Journal and Merimack Packet,* Salem, Massachusetts, August 17, 1774. The piece is signed.

46. As he puts it, "Reacting to the questionable allegations made against their capacity to be original, black writers have often assumed a position of extreme negation, in which they claim for themselves no black literary antecedents whatsoever, or claim for themselves an anonymity of origins. . . ." See Gates, *The Signifying Monkey,* p. 114.

47. *Race and the Enlightenment: A Reader,* ed. Emmanuel Chukwudi Eze (Cambridge: Blackwell, 1997), p. 33.

48. Eric Cheyfitz, *The Poetics of Imperialism: Translation and Colonization from the Tempest to Tarzan* (Philadelphia: University of Pennsylvania Press, 1997), p. 50.

49. Samuel Sherwood, *Scriptural Instructions to Civil Rulers,* in *Political Sermons of the American Founding Era, 1730–1805,* ed. Ellis Sandoz (Indianapolis: Liberty Press, 1991), p. 398.

50. Winthrop Jordan, *White Over Black: American Attitudes Toward the Negro, 1550–1812* (Chapel Hill: University of North Carolina Press, 1968), p. 351.

51. Anthony Benezet, *A Short Account of That Part of Africa, Inhabited by Negroes* (Philadelphia, 1762; London: W. Baker and J. W. Galabin, 1768), p. 30. Cf. The

Presbyterian minister Samuel Miller's attack on the proslavery defense of property rights: "The right which every man has to *himself* infinitely transcends all other human tenures." See Miller, *A Discourse Delivered April 12, 1797, at the Request of and before the New-York Society for Promoting the Manumission of Slaves* (New York: T. and J. Swords, 1797), p. 15.

52. David Rice, *Slavery Inconsistent with Justice and Good Policy,* in *American Political Writing During the Founding Era, 1760–1805,* vol. 2, eds. Charles Hyneman and Donald S. Lutz (Indianapolis: Liberty Press, 1983), pp. 870–871.

53. Richard Nisbet, *Slavery not Forbidden by Scripture. Or a Defense of the West-India Planters, from the Aspersions Thrown out Against Them, by the Author of the Pamphlet, Entitled, "An Address to the Inhabitants of the British Settlements in America Upon Slave-Keeping"* (Philadelphia: John Sparhawk, 1773), p. 10. Lest one imagine that racial stereotyping was a proslavery possession, consider Noah Webster's commentary: "But I cannot believe that *all* the slaves in this country are so dull that motives of interest will make no impression on their minds, or that they are so unprincipled and ungrateful, that if set at liberty, they would turn their hands against their masters." See Webster, *Effects of Slavery on Morals and Industry* (Hartford: Hudson and Goodwin, 1793), p. 38.

54. Daniel Coker, *A Dialogue Between a Virginian and an African Minister* (Baltimore: Benjamin Edes, 1810), p. 6.

55. See, for example, Desrochers, "Not Fade Away," Melish, *Disowning Slavery,* and Gary Nash, *Race and Revolution* (Madison: Madison House, 1990) for this view. For an alternative perspective, see Zafar, *We Wear the Mask,* who objects to this masculine norm because of its gendered exclusions. "By combining the myth of the self-made man with the slave narrative, 'Franklinian' Douglass created an individual African American life story out of prefabricated elements. . . . [H]is New World African had been anticipated by Venture Smith and Olaudah Equiano. And as in the narratives of [Henry] Bibb and [William Wells] Brown, his masculine strategies for self-revelation remind us of the dearth of antebellum black women's divergent and parallel stories of freedom and success" (187).

56. *A Narrative of the Life and Adventures of Venture, a Native of Africa: But Resident Above Sixty Years in the United States of America. Related by Himself,* in Carretta, *Unchained Voices,* p. 369. All further citations are noted parenthetically in the text.

57. See James Olney, *Metaphors of Self: The Meaning of Autobiography* (Princeton: Princeton University Press, 1972). As Paul John Eakin has noted, Olney actually anticipated the de Manian deconstruction of the referentiality and ontology of autobiography by arguing that its meanings were representational. In invoking this influential paradigm for autobiographical writing, I am less invested than Olney in arguing for the transcendental powers of the individual consciousness to re-create meaning in the world (a meaning that de Man of course sees as illusory) and more interested in understanding the autobiographical act, mediated through cultural context. See Paul de Man, "Autobiography as De-facement," *MLN* 94 (1979), and Eakin, *Fictions in Autobiography:*

Studies in the Art of Self-Invention (Princeton: Princeton University Press, 1985), pp. 184–191.

58. Orlando Patterson, *Slavery and Social Death: A Comparative Study* (Cambridge, Mass.: Harvard University Press, 1982), p. 55.

59. Desrochers, "'Not Fade Away'," argues convincingly that Smith does not necessarily abandon his African origins: "Smith represented *one*, rather than *the*, black voice of early republican America. And if anecdotal themes of rugged, self-sufficient individualism have made Smith seem at first glance much like his white neighbors, close reading reveals the complex story of a man with intertwining African and Yankee sensibilities" (p. 45).

60. For a discussion of this, see Robert J. C. Young, *Colonial Desire: Hybridity in Theory, Culture and Race* (London: Routledge, 1995), pp. 20–24.

61. Shane White, *Somewhat More Independent: The End of Slavery in New York City, 1770–1810* (Athens: University of Georgia Press, 1991), p. 152.

62. Robert Ferguson, "The Literature of Enlightenment," in *The Cambridge History of American Literature*, vol. 1 (New York: Cambridge University Press, 1994), p. 521.

63. Richard Wright, *White Man, Listen!* (New York: Doubleday, 1957; Westport: Greenwood, 1978), p. 115.

64. See, for example, Andrews, *To Tell a Free Story;* Baker, *Blues, Ideology;* Desrochers, "'Not Fade Away'"; Fichtelberg, "Word Between Worlds"; Gates, *Signifying Monkey;* and Zafar, *We Wear the Mask.*

5. Yellow Fever and the Black Market

1. John Trenchard and Thomas Gordon, *Cato's Letters, or Essays on Liberty, Civil and Religious, and Other Important Subjects,* vol. 1, ed. Ronald Hamowy (Indianapolis: Liberty Press, 1995), p. 40.

2. For these epithets see Samuel Taylor Coleridge's antislavery ode, l. 72, in Anthea Morrison, "Samuel Taylor Coleridge's Greek Prize Ode on the Slave Trade," in *An Intimate Complexity: Essays in Romanticism,* ed. J. R. Watson (Edinburgh: Edinburgh University Press, 1983), pp. 145–160; James Grahame, *Africa Delivered,* in *Poems on the Abolition of the Slave Trade* (London: R. Bowyer, 1809), III, l. 94; William Roscoe's *The Wrongs of Africa* (Philadelphia: Joseph James, 1788), pp. 15, 18; and Anna Barbauld, "Epistle to William Wilberforce, Esq. On the Rejection of the Bill for Abolishing the Slave Trade," in *The Poems of Anna Letitia Barbauld,* eds. William McCarthy and Elizabeth Kraft (Athens: University of Georgia Press, 1994), p. 117.

3. Thomas Branagan, *The Penitential Tyrant: a Juvenile Poem in Two Cantos* (Philadelphia: Printed for the Author, 1805), p. 1.

4. Grahame, *Africa Delivered,* ll.23–24.

5. Ibid., III, ll. 90–105.

6. Ibid., III, ll. 205–218.

7. Critics of the epidemic often tend to think about this in political rather than

commercial terms. See, for example, Martin S. Pernick, "Politics, Parties, and Pestilence: Epidemic Yellow Fever in Philadelphia and the Rise of the First Party System," *William and Mary Quarterly* 3rd ser. 29 (1972), pp. 559–586, and Shirley Samuels, *Romances of the Republic: Women, the Family, and Violence in the Literature of the Early American Nation* (New York: Oxford University Press, 1996).

8. For historical background see J. H. Powell, *Bring Out Your Dead: The Great Plague of Yellow Fever in Philadelphia in 1793* (Philadelphia: University of Pennsylvania Press, 1949); J. Worth Estes, "Introduction: The Yellow Fever Syndrome and its Treatment in Philadelphia, 1793," in *A Melancholy Scene of Devastation: The Public Response to the 1793 Philadelphia Yellow Fever Epidemic,* eds. Estes and Billy G. Smith (Canton, Mass.: Science History Publications, 1997); Eve Kornfield, "Crisis in the Capital: The Cultural Significance of Philadelphia's Great Yellow Fever Epidemic," *Pennsylvania History* 51 (1984), pp. 189–205; and Mark Workman, "Medical Practice in Philadelphia at the Time of the Yellow Fever Epidemic, 1793," *Pennsylvania Folklife* 27 (1978), pp. 33–39.

9. *Dunlap's Daily American Advertiser,* 2 September 1793, n.p.

10. *Manuscript Correspondence of Benjamin Rush,* Historical Society of Pennsylvania, vol. 12, pp. 32–33.

11. Sally F. Griffith, "'A Total Dissolution in the Bonds of Society': Community Death and Regeneration in Mathew Carey's *Short Account of the Yellow Fever,*" in Estes and Smith, *A Melancholy Scene,* p. 55.

12. Powell, *Bring Out Your Dead,* p. xix.

13. Gary B. Nash, *Forging Freedom: The Formation of Philadelphia's Black Community, 1720–1840* (Cambridge, Mass.: Harvard University Press, 1988), p. 123. Similarly, Jacqueline Bacon calls the episode part of "the transformation in African American identity" where black leaders were forced to reconcile individual and communal goals and identities. See Bacon, "Rhetoric and Identity in Absalom Jones and Richard Allen's *Narrative of the Proceedings of the Black People, During the Late Awful Calamity in Philadelphia,*" *Pennsylvania Magazine of History and Biography* 125 (2001), pp. 61–90.

14. Julia A. Stern, *The Plight of Feeling: Sympathy and Dissent in the Early American Novel* (Chicago: University of Chicago Press, 1997), pp. 219, 221.

15. Recent discussions of Charles Brockden Brown's novel about the city's yellow fever epidemic, *Arthur Merwyn* (1798–1800), have pointed out the connections Brown draws between yellow fever and slave trading, and the moral and cultural ambiguities he exposes in this capitalist and "diseased" urban society. See Teresa A. Goddu, *Gothic America: Narrative, History, and Nation* (New York: Columbia University Press, 1997), pp. 31–51, and Carroll Smith-Rosenberg, "Black Gothic: The Shadowy Origins of the American Bourgeoisie," in *Possible Pasts: Becoming Colonial in Early America,* ed. Robert Blair St. George (Philadelphia: University of Pennsylvania Press, 2001), pp. 243–269. Both discuss the importance of Brown's gothic literary effects in representing a modern commercial world associated with West Indian slave capitalism and equally repres-

sive forms of black labor in Philadelphia itself. While Goddu points out Brown's skepticism about the "civilizing influence of commerce" (p. 32), Smith-Rosenberg emphasizes the racial ambiguities that arise from "the novel's deep-seated fears about the dangers commercial and fiscal capitalism poses to civic virtue" (p. 258). Both arguments are premised on the historical conflict between republicanism and liberal individualism.

16. See, for example, Henry May, *The Enlightenment in America* (New York: Oxford University Press, 1976), pp. 197–222.

17. Elizabeth Fox-Genovese and Eugene Genovese, "Physiocracy and Propertied Individualism: The Unfolding Challenge of Bourgeois Property to Unfree Labor Systems," in Fox-Genovese and Genovese, *Fruits of Market Capital: Slavery and Bourgeois Property in the Rise and Expansion of Capitalism* (New York: Oxford University Press, 1983), p. 287.

18. Ashworth asks rhetorically, "Why should self-interested individuals not seek to buy the law? Why should they not sell out the nation for gain? Why should they not rob, kill, or maim their competitors? It might well be in their interest to put an end to the system by which everyone else's interest can be pursued." His argument thus explains antislavery humanitarianism as a cultural form of compensation for capitalist ideology. See John Ashworth, "The Relationship Between Capitalism and Humanitarianism," in *The Antislavery Debate: Capitalism and Abolitionism as a Problem of Historical Interpretation,* ed. Thomas Bender (Berkeley: University of California Press, 1992), p. 192.

19. For discussion of the importance of this concept in early American political economy, see Janet Riesman, "Money, Credit, and Federalist Political Economy," in *Beyond Confederation: Origins of the Constitution and American National Identity,* eds. Richard Beeman, Stephen Botein, and Edward C. Carter III (Chapel Hill: University of North Carolina Press, 1987), pp. 128–161. As Riesman argues, the "quantity theory" of currency, which posited "a delicate balance between goods at market and money in circulation" (p. 132), contended with the "intrinsic value" of currency.

20. Thomas Condie, "A History of Yellow Fever," *The Philadelphia Monthly Magazine, or Universal Repository of Knowledge and Entertainment* (Philadelphia: Thomas Condie, 1798), p. 71.

21. See David Brion Davis, *The Problem of Slavery in the Age of Revolution, 1770–1823* (Ithaca: Cornell University Press, 1975), p. 307.

22. Samuel Stearns, *An Account of the Terrible Effects of the Pestilential Infection in the City of Philadelphia* (Providence: William Child, 1793), p. 1.

23. J. Henry Helmuth, *A Short Account of the Yellow Fever in Philadelphia, for the Reflecting Christians,* trans. Charles Erdmann (Philadelphia: Jones, Hoff, and Derrick, 1794), p. 13.

24. Daniel Defoe, *A Journal of the Plague Year, Being Observations or Memorials of the Most Remarkable Occurrences, as Well as Public as Private, Which Happened in London During the Last Great Visitation in 1665. Written by a Citizen who Continued all the While in London. Never Made Public Before,* ed. Anthony Burgess (London: Pen-

guin, 1986), pp. 37–38. For an analysis of the combination of historical fact and fiction in the *Journal*, see Robert Mayer, "The Reception of *A Journal of the Plague Year* and the Nexus of Fiction and History in the Novel," *ELH* 57 (1990), pp. 529–556.

25. Defoe, *Journal of the Plague Year*, p. 110.

26. William Currie, *Memoirs of the Yellow Fever, Which Prevailed in Philadelphia, and Other Parts of the United States of America, in the Summer and Autumn of the Present Year, 1798* (Philadelphia: John Bioren, 1798), p. 31.

27. David Waldstreicher, *In the Midst of Perpetual Fetes: The Making of American Nationalism, 1776–1820* (Chapel Hill: University of North Carolina Press, 1997).

28. Anon., "A Dialogue Between a Citizen of Philadelphia, and a Jersey Farmer," *National Gazette*, ed. Philip Freneau, vol. 11 (September 28, 1793), p. 384.

29. Ibid.

30. Roxann Wheeler, *The Complexion of Race: Categories of Difference in Eighteenth-Century Britain* (Philadelphia: University of Pennsylvania Press, 2001), pp. 22–28.

31. See Estes, "Introduction" to *A Melancholy Scene*, p. 9. For the gendered ramifications of solidist theories of the flow of bodily fluids, see Susan M. Stabile, "A 'Doctrine of Signatures': The Epistolary Physicks of Esther Burr's Journal," in *A Centre of Wonders: The Body in Early America*, eds. Janet Moore Lindman and Michele Lise Tarter (Ithaca: Cornell University Press, 2001), pp. 109–126.

32. Joseph Lew, "'That Abominable Traffic': *Mansfield Park* and the Dynamics of Slavery," in *History, Gender and Eighteenth-Century Literature*, ed. Beth Fowkes Tobin (Athens: University of Georgia Press, 1994), pp. 288–289. For discussion of the power of the metaphor of circulation for "free" trade policy, see David Porter, "A Peculiar but Uninteresting Nation: China and the Discourse of Commerce in Eighteenth-Century England," *Eighteenth-Century Studies* 33 (1999–2000), pp. 181–199. As Porter notes, "Prior to the first translation of William Harvey's treatise on circulation of blood in 1653, according to the *OED*, the verb 'to circulate' referred primarily to the processes of rotation and distillation. The expanded sense of circular movement through a complex system was invoked increasingly with reference to both blood and money in the following decades" (p. 198).

33. Roy Porter, "Consumption: Disease of the Consumer Society?," *Consumption and the World of Goods*, eds. John Brewer and Porter (London: Routledge, 1993), p. 60.

34. This is an American edition, revised and tailored for a national audience by Samuel Griffitts, a leading Quaker physician in Philadelphia and a colleague of Rush's. See *Domestic Medicine; or a Treatise on the Prevention and Cure of Diseases, by Regimen and Simple Medicines. Revised by Samuel Griffitts* (Philadelphia: Thomas Dobson, 1797), p. 219.

35. Jean Deveze, *An Enquiry into, and Observations Upon the Causes and effects of the Epidemic Disease, Which Raged in Philadelphia from the Month of August till Towards the Middle of December, 1793* (Philadelphia: Parent, 1794), p. 142.

36. Washington Irving notably satirized this position in *Salmagundi* when he likens the "dancing mania" in New York to an epidemic: "The doctors immediately, as is their usual way, instead of devising a remedy, fell together by the ears, to decide whether it was native or imported, and the sticklers for the latter opinion traced it to a cargo of trumpery from France, as they had before hunted down the yellow-fever to a bag of coffee from the West-Indies." See *The Complete Works of Washington Irving*, ed. Bruce Granger and Martha Hartzog (Boston: Twayne, 1977), p. 292.

37. *The Medical Works of Richard Mead* (Edinburgh: Alexander Donaldson and Charles Eliot, 1775), p. 180.

38. Mead, *Medical Works*, p. 195. Mead's treatise on the plague was an influential source for Defoe's *Journal of the Plague Year:* "The manner of [the disease's] coming first to London proves this also, viz., by goods brought over from Holland, and brought thither from the Levant." Defoe's narrator later complains about the Dutch exploitation of the crisis in English trade during the plague: "for if it was true that our manufactures as well as our people were infected, and that it was dangerous to touch or to open and receive the smell of them, then those people ran the hazard by that clandestine trade not only of carrying the contagion into their own country, but also of infecting the nations to whom they traded with those goods" (pp. 206, 226).

39. Currie and many others read Dr. John Lining's account of the 1748 epidemic in Charleston, South Carolina: "[W]henever the disease appeared here, it was easily traced to some person who had lately arrived from some of the West Indian islands, where it was epidemical." See Lining, *A Description of the American Yellow Fever, Which Prevailed at Charleston in 1748* (Philadelphia: Thomas Dobson, 1799), p. 284. Lining's influential argument that "the constitution of the Negroes" made them naturally immune to yellow fever was first published in 1753.

40. Powell, *Bring Out Your Dead*, p. 14. Cf. Thomas Jefferson's letter in 1804 to the Governor of the New Orleans Territory: "There is also no spot where yellow fever is so much to be apprehended. . . . But under the cloudless skies of America where there is so constant an accumulation of heat, men cannot be piled on one another with impunity. Accordingly, we find this disease confined to the solid-built parts of our towns and the parts of the waterside where there is most matter for putrefaction, rarely extending into the thinner built parts of the town, and never known in the country. . . . Is not this a strong indication that we ought not to contend with the laws of nature, but decide at once that our cities should be thin-built? You will perhaps remember that in 1793 yourself, the present governor Harrison . . . dining with me in Philadelphia, the then late yellow fever being the subject of our conversation, I observed that in building cities in the U.S. we should take a chequer board for our plan, leaving the white squares open and unbuilt for ever, and planted with trees." *The Portable Thomas Jefferson*, ed. Merrill D. Peterson (New York: Penguin, 1975), pp. 499–500.

41. Benjamin Rush, *A Vindication of the Address to the Inhabitants of the British Settle-ments, on the Slavery of Negroes in America* (1773). The piece is collected in *Am I Not a Man and a Brother: The Antislavery Crusade of Revolutionary America, 1688–1788*, ed. Roger Bruns (New York: Chelsea House, 1977), p. 241, emphasis added.

42. See Chapter 1 as well as Paul Langford, *A Polite and Commercial People: England, 1727–1783* (Oxford: Clarendon, 1989); T. H. Breen, "'Baubles of Britain': The American and Consumer Revolutions of the Eighteenth Century," *Past and Present* 119 (1988), pp. 73–104 and Breen, "Narrative of Commercial Life: Con-sumption, Ideology, and Community on the Eve of the American Revolution," *William and Mary Quarterly* 3rd ser. 50 (1993), pp. 471–501; and Brewer and Porter, *Consumption and the World of Goods.*

43. College of Physicians, *Facts and Observations Relative to the Nature and Origin of the Pestilential Fever, Which Prevailed in the City of Philadelphia in 1793, 1797, and 1798* (London: James Phillips and Sons, 1799), p. 6.

44. William Currie, *A Sketch of the Rise and Progress of the Yellow Fever, and of the Pro-ceedings of the Board of Health in Philadelphia, in the Year 1799* (Philadelphia: Budd and Bartram, 1800), p. 61.

45. Ibid., p. 76.

46. "Review," *The Massachusetts Magazine, or Monthly Museum,* vol. 5 (Boston: I. Thomas and E. T. Andrews, 1793), p. 751.

47. "For these reasons the slave trade may be considered, like the fabulous hydra, to have a hundred heads, every one of which it was necessary to cut off before it could be subdued. And as none but Hercules was fitted to conquer the one, so nothing less than extraordinary prudence, courage, labor, and patience, could overcome the other." Thomas Clarkson, *The History of the Rise, Progress, and Accomplishment of the Abolition of the African Slave-Trade, by the British Parlia-ment* (1808; New York: John S. Taylor, 1836), pp. 26–27.

48. I would argue that the *Short Account* reveals the same understanding of a healthy economy as do writings against the slave trade (Carey, by the way, publicly criticized the trade). See, for example, Carey's "African Colonization," *The Daily Chronicle* (1 September 1829 and 4 September 1829), published under the name of Hamilton. He makes the rather predictably Anglophobic argument that Britain was largely responsible for the "accursed slave trade, on of the greatest stains that ever sullied the human character" (p. 1).

49. Mathew Carey, *A Short Account of the Malignant Fever, Lately Prevalent in Philadel-phia: with a Statement of the Proceedings That Took Place on the Subject in Different Parts of the United States, 2nd ed.* (Philadelphia: Carey, 1793), p. viii. All further citations (unless otherwise noted) come from this edition and are placed par-enthetically in the text. As I discuss below, the *Short Account* went through four major editions in 1793–94. Generally, Carey expanded his materials, adding chapter divisions, and sometimes in this process reorganized his work. The lat-ter editions include more detailed accounts of mortality; the fourth edition of 1794 includes appendices on the London plague of 1665 and the Marseilles

plague of 1720. I have used the second edition to show his work before Jones and Allen responded to him. When discussing his commentaries on African Americans, however, I consider the changes he made both before and after their response as a way of tracing his attitude towards the city's blacks and their leaders.

50. Indeed, the biography of Carey fits the Franklinian mold: "Mathew Carey landed in Philadelphia on November 1, 1784 with about a dozen guineas in his purse—less than he had embarked with because of the ministrations of card sharps aboard ship." See James N. Green, *Mathew Carey: Publisher and Patriot* (Philadelphia: The Library Company of Philadelphia, 1985), p. 5.

51. For Carey's publishing innovations and entrepreneurial spirit, see Green, *Mathew Carey,* and Cathy N. Davidson, *Revolution and the Word: The Rise of the Novel in America* (New York: Oxford University Press, 1986).

52. Mathew Carey, "An Address to the Public Respecting the Conduct of the Coloured People During the Late Fever in Philadelphia, April 4, 1794," in *Pamphlets and Papers* (Philadelphia: Joseph R. A. Skerrett, 1826), p. 3.

53. Green, *Carey,* p. 8.

54. Quoted in Griffith, "'Total Dissolution,'" p. 53.

55. Mathew Carey, *A Desultory Account of the Yellow Fever, Prevailing in Philadelphia, and the Present State of the City* (Philadelphia, 1793), p. 5.

56. This passage is part of the additions Carey made to the revised third and fourth editions. See *A Short Account,* 4th ed. (1794), pp. 12–13.

57. Ibid., p. 36.

58. Deveze similarly argued that this "man blessed with an affluent fortune, regardless of the injury he must sustain by abandoning his house of commerce, gave way only to the generous dictates of humanity. . . . [He showed] that philanthropy that proceeds from the heart alone . . . forgetting himself to think only of the sufferings of his fellow-creatures." See Deveze, *Enquiry,* pp. 24, 26.

59. Carey, *Desultory Account,* p. 5, italics added.

60. Richard Teichgraeber III, *"Free Trade" and Moral Philosophy: Rethinking the Sources of Adam Smith's Wealth of Nations* (Durham: Duke University Press, 1986), p. 9.

61. As published by Carey, James McHenry's letter about Banneker includes the important final paragraph usually not included in modern reprintings: "I consider this negro as a fresh proof that the powers of the mind are disconnected with the colour of the skin, or, in other words, a striking contradiction to Mr. Hume's doctrine, that, 'the negroes are naturally inferior to the whites. . . .' In every civilized country, we shall find thousands of whites, liberally educated, and who have enjoyed greater opportunities of instruction than this negro, his inferiors in those intellectual acquirements and capacities that form the most characteristic features in the human race." See *The American Museum* (September, 1792), pp. 185–187.

62. Carey's inability to think of the city's blacks as part of the benevolent republic may be immediately glossed by his later advocacy of African colonization. Not unlike *Notes on the State of Virginia* (1785), in which Jefferson expressed pessimism about black assimilation into American society, Carey's *Letters of the Colo-*

nization Society (1832) cited the "inexorable force of public prejudice" as the rationale for colonization: "I waive all inquiry whether this be right or wrong. I speak of things as they are—not as they might or ought to be. They are cut off from the most remote chance of amalgamation with the white population by feelings of prejudices, call them what you will, that are ineradicable." See Carey, *Letters on the Colonization Society; and on its Probable Results* (Philadelphia: Carey, 1832), p. 27.

63. Richard Allen and Absalom Jones, *A Narrative of the Proceedings of the Black People, During the Late Awful Calamity in Philadelphia, in the Year, 1793: and a Refutation of Some Censures, Thrown Upon Them in Some Late Publications* (Philadelphia, 1794; London: Darton and Harvey, 1794), pp. 21, 23. All further citations appear parenthetically in the text.

64. See Matthew L. Davis, *A Brief Account of the Epidemical Fever which Lately Prevailed in the City of New York* (New York: Matthew L. Davis, 1795), p. 5.

65. As a Quaker writes in a letter to his brother, "Scarsely [sic] anybody to be seen in many parts of the town, and those who are seen are principally French, and Negroes, amongst whom it dose [sic] not seem to be so prevalent, especially among the negroes. Indeed I don't know what the people would do, if it was not for the Negroes, as they are the Principal nurses." See Edwin B. Bronner, "Letter from a Yellow Fever Victim, Philadelphia, 1793," *Pennsylvania Magazine of History and Biography* 86 (1962), p. 205.

66. Unsigned poem in *The Massachusetts Magazine, or Monthly Museum* (Boston: I. Thomas and E. T. Andrews, 1793), p. 756.

67. The advertisement appeared in the *National Gazette* on 11 September 1793, p. 363.

68. Ira Berlin, *Many Thousands Gone: The First Two Centuries of Slavery in North America* (Cambridge, Mass.: Harvard University Press, 1998), p. 254.

69. Phillip Lapsansky, "'Abigail, a Negress': The Role and Legacy of African Americans in the Yellow Fever Epidemic, in Estes and Smith, *A Melancholy Scene,* p. 64.

70. Ibid., p. 65.

71. Carey, "Address to the Public," p. 5.

72. Carey, *Short Account,* 4th ed., p. 63.

73. Carey, *Short Account,* 3rd ed., p. 79.

74. Carey, "Address to the Public," p. 3.

75. Ibid., pp. 3–4.

76. See Michael Warner, *The Letters of the Republic: Print, Publication and the Public Sphere in Eighteenth-Century America* (Cambridge, Mass.: Harvard University Press, 1990), and Grantland Rice, *The Transformation of Authorship in Early America* (Chicago: University of Chicago Press, 1997).

Epilogue

1. Anonymous, *Right and Wrong in Boston: Report of the Boston Female Anti-Slavery Society* (Boston: Isaac Knapp, 1836), p. 101.

2. Samuel May, *A Discourse on the Slavery in the United States* (Boston: Garrison and Knapp, 1832), pp. 7–8.

3. David Lee Child, *The Despotism of Freedom; or the Tyranny and Cruelty of American Republican Slave-Masters, Shown to be the Worst in the World* (Boston: Young Men's Antislavery Association, 1834), p. 16.

4. Lydia Child, *An Appeal in Favor of that Class of Americans Called Africans*, ed. Carolyn L. Karcher (Amherst: University of Massachusetts Press, 1996), p. 18.

5. "Speech on the Kansas-Nebraska Act at Peoria, Illinois, October 16, 1854," in *The Portable Abraham Lincoln*, ed. Andrew Delbanco (New York: Penguin, 1992), p. 61. Compare, again, Lincoln's letter of 1855 to his friend from Kentucky, Joshua Speed: "The slave-breeders and slave-traders, are a small, odious, and detested class among you; and yet in politics, they dictate the course of all of you, and are as completely your masters, as you are the masters of your own negroes" (p. 87).

6. Child, *Appeal*, p. 161.

7. Ralph Waldo Emerson, "Anniversary of West Indian Emancipation" (1 August 1845), in *Emerson's Antislavery Writings*, eds. Len Gougeon and Joel Myerson (New Haven: Yale University Press, 1995), p. 38.

8. Emerson, "Letter to the Kidnapping Committee" (23 September 1846), in *Emerson's Antislavery Writings*, p. 45.

Index